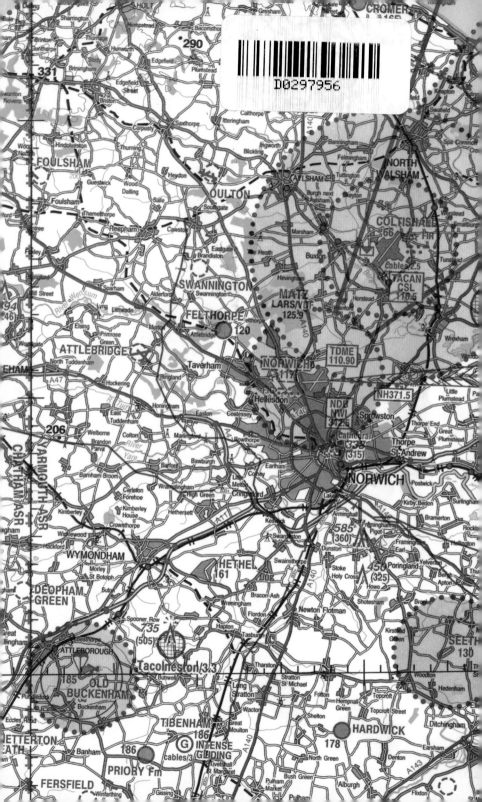
D0297956

PROPELLERHEAD

PROPELLERHEAD

Antony Woodward

HarperCollins*Publishers*

HarperCollins*Publishers*
77-85 Fulham Palace Road
Hammersmith, London W6 8JB

www.**fire**and**water**.com

Published by HarperCollins 2001

1 3 5 7 9 8 6 4 2

Copyright © Antony Woodward 2001

Antony Woodward asserts the moral right
to be identified as the author of this work.
Illustrations by Mike Kirby and Lorna Maxwell (p. 257).

ISBN 0 00 710728 5

Set in Adobe Caslon

Printed and bound in Great Britain by
Omnia Books Limited, Glasgow

All rights reserved. No part of this publication may be
reproduced, stored in a retrieval system, or transmitted
in any form or by any means, electronic, mechanical,
photocopying, recording, or otherwise, without the prior
permission of the publishers.

This book is sold subject to the condition that it shall not,
by way of trade or otherwise, be lent, re-sold, hired out or
otherwise circulated without the publisher's prior consent
in any form of binding or cover other than that in which it
is published and without a similar condition including this
condition being imposed on the subsequent purchaser.

To my mother and my father

Contents

AUTHOR'S NOTE

Although this is a true story and the characters described are real, most names have been changed to protect privacy and—chiefly— pilots' licences. All the events took place but details of chronology, in the interests of narrative continuity, have been shifted. Likewise, all dialogue was spoken, though not always at exactly the moments indicated. Anyone determined enough to work out where Barsham Green or Marston Mallet are will find circumstances at both places so altered as to be unrecognisable.

Flying without feathers is not easy.
Plautus, 254-184 BC

'Remember, gentleman, you cannot fuck and fly.'
Lord Trenchard, 1873-1956, First Marshal of the RAF

The Selection and Maintenance of a Flying Machine

It had all the flying characteristics of a handful of mortar.
Journalist on the Langley Aerodrome, *1903*

Pointing at the joystick, Miles, my instructor (known as 'Air' Miles), said: 'That's the houses lever. Push it forward and the houses get bigger; pull it back and they get smaller.'
Letter to The Times, *week ending 14th March 1998*

My career as an aviator began on a soggy Saturday in March somewhere off the A303.

I was not remotely interested in flying. Flying was, quite simply, not my thing. My first word wasn't 'plane'. If, when I was little, I ran round with my arms out making NNEEEEEOOOOOWWW noises, I certainly didn't do it any more than other children. I never made Airfix models or paper darts. When people at school got those little single-cylinder model plane engines and spent interminable periods flicking the plastic propeller round with their forefinger to coax them into a few seconds of ear-splitting and fuel-spitting life, I thought—well, I didn't think anything. I didn't cut the RAF ads out of the Sunday magazines (the ones which always turned out to be for navigators). I didn't look up if a plane went over. I never asked to be taken to an air show. As an adult airline passenger, I always listened to the safety lectures a good deal more carefully than I pretended; I noted the positions of the emergency exits (or, preferably, sat next to one—alleging that this was for leg-room reasons) and I heaved an inner sigh of relief the moment we touched down. Apart from that, the full and total extent of everything I knew about flying, until the age of twenty-five, came from reading *Jonathan Livingston Seagull* when I was nine. Planes and flying did not feature.

Until Richard came back from Africa with his pilot's licence. That was when it started.

Before he went away, we had been equals: a couple of twenty-four-year-old mates from college sharing a flat in London. Now, somehow, all that had changed. Big (rarely less than fourteen stone), bluff, blunt, tactless, impatient, bone-idle Richard, with the rounded, ergonomic physique from which shirts naturally untucked themselves and trousers sagged (collecting in little wrinkles of material above his shoes), had suddenly acquired a sophisticated worldly aura. His couch potato existence in front of the television resumed, but now it seemed window-dressing for a person of deeper substance; someone with proven capabilities unusual in a twenty-five-year-old—tinged with a romantic whiff of intelligence, wealth and daring. Or so girls plainly seemed to think.

What made Richard's new sex appeal—and irksome gravitas—particularly objectionable was that, before he went away it was I, arguably, who had the edge. I worked in advertising as a copywriter. I could arrive at work after ten in the morning, wearing what I liked. I could name-drop famous photographers and directors. I could talk of casting sessions with supermodels, location shoots, special effects, celebrities I was working with. I could look at my watch after a weekday lunch and say, almost plausibly, 'Shit. Gotta go. Pre-prod with Ridley'. I could justify carrying pretentious broadsheet magazines like *The Manipulator* and talk about films like *Repo Man*. Occasionally I could point out my creations in papers, magazines and the cinema, on posters, radio or the television.

Richard was a bank manager. Correction—a *trainee* bank manager. For Barclays.

It seems hard to believe, knowing what I do now, that Richard's new qualification could really have had as dramatic an effect as it seemed at the time. But *Out of Africa* had come out three years earlier, and had recently made it onto television, and the mere juxtaposition of the words 'flying' and 'Africa' seemed to induce a sort of swooning, goggle-eyed, hypnotic state in twentysomething girls inconceivable today without the assistance of amphetamine-based pharmaceuticals.

The dominant (in fact, only) motive force in my life at this time—apart from trying to get my career in advertising off the ground and stop my overdraft getting any larger—was to maintain a sufficiently buoyant social life to supply me with girls to pursue. Potential subjects were selected more according to how they would reflect on me than any intrinsic compatibility—not that this greatly affected the outcome, which was long periods of unrelieved celibacy, interspersed with sporadic, lucky spells of action. These either came to nothing or led to short-lived, vaguely unsatisfying relationships where, from the moment of consummation, I always seemed to be interested in someone else. As a lifestyle, though, it felt exciting and kept me busy. I had even persuaded myself that I was quite good at it, until I found myself losing ground. To a bank manager.

The more I saw how other people—male and female—reacted to the new Richard, the more it became evident that here was an effective and workable system of sexual procurement. I was going to have to learn to fly. As Richard (if he wanted to hang onto his hard-won image) needed to maintain a regular number of flying hours each year, it suited him to have a companion. And as neither of us could afford to fly 'real' planes, we decided on a fact-finding mission to discover what the new craze of microlighting was about. Popham Airfield in Hampshire was the nearest place to London that this could be done.

Hence the A303.

Our trial flight was booked for twelve. It was now a quarter past, and we were lost in narrow country lanes on a third attempt to locate the entrance to the airfield we had tantalisingly glimpsed three times from the opposite side of the dual carriageway. The journey had not gone well. Starting late, after a late night, we had become seized in weekend traffic before we had even reached the Cromwell Road. Over the next two hours, the tracing paper sky had grown heavier and heavier: by the time we reached the M3 it was spitting—enough for every lorry we passed to spray us with a slimy film, but just insufficient to stop the wipers squeaking. Thereafter the intensity had increased steadily until now it seemed inconceivable that there was a chance of getting airborne.

Richard had said nothing for twenty minutes, registering his emotional state by accelerating through the spray to six inches from the bumper of cars in front. Since leaving the dual carriageway, this had switched to exhorting loud screams from the gearbox and tyres of his company Rover, as the minutes ticked by and one signpost after another, failed to deliver either Popham village or Popham Airfield.

My own thoughts were more concerned with what was in store if we did *not* miss our trial flight. What were microlights like? How basic were they? What kind of people did this sort of thing? The only image I could summon was a sort of morph of the autogyro pilot from *Mad Max 2*, Terry Thomas in *Those Magnificent Men in Their Flying Machines* (representative of Dangerous Sports Club types in general) and the bearded students from Bristol University whom I had seen hang-gliding off the Mendip Hills in Somerset where I grew up. Apart from these, my references were limited to newspaper reports of the 'Plane Takes off Without Pilot', 'Man Lands on Motorway', 'Microlighter Caught in Tree', variety. Would I get vertigo? Would I be sick? If so, what sort of provision would be made? Were I to freak out, what would be the consequences? I could be reasonably sure that Richard would not freak out; *ergo* could he be trusted if I did? Not necessarily, was the answer.

There was also the question as to my suitability for pilot training. My spatial awareness and hand-eye co-ordination is such that the first time I tried to light a cigarette with a car-lighter, I succeeded in branding the end of my nose (the agonising coil-shaped scar lasted for weeks). I took three attempts to pass my driving test. I have yet to catch a set of car keys, can't do maths, and loathe and detest anything technical or mechanical. I even had empirical evidence for my lack of aptitude: having joined Richard to go travelling at the end of his posting (which, it is worth recording, was a place called Big Bend, Swaziland) to find him delayed, I had filled the time by taking some flying lessons myself. After five days of mind-numbing theory, and fourteen claustrophobic sessions in the cockpit of a Cessna*, Lindsay, his instructor, had taken me aside. In twenty-two years of teaching, she had said solemnly, she had never come across anyone with quite so little natural feel for flying. I had not passed this information on to Richard, but nor had I forgotten it.

Finally, an unsigned cinder track from an unsigned lane turned out to be the entrance to the unsigned airfield. The dashboard clock read ten to one. As we locked the car, there was a croak of thunder. I felt a rising wave of irritation, frustration, impatience, nervous trepidation, doubt and excitement. I did not realise that, before I had even set eyes on a microlight, my induction into the delights of shoe-string aviation had begun.

The landing strip was nowhere near flat. It had a pronounced concave bow, numerous bumps and several patches of mud amongst the tussocks of grass. Down one side, beneath stretched grey-green covers, shiny and dripping, was a row of esoterically-shaped bundles with propellers sticking out of one end and tail-planes the other. There was only one building in the field; a Portakabin wedged against the hedge halfway down. The door was framed by a lavatory bowl containing bedding plants (my first taste of microlighting humour), and half a

---

* Common make of basic training aeroplane in conventional private flying.

rusty oil drum, containing a sludge of charcoal embers, filling with water.

As I opened the door, there was a wild rustling and flapping of paper from hundreds of notices pinned on every inch of wall space, and a gas heater fluttered and roared. 'Shut that door,' said a big man nearest to me, who was alternately rubbing his hands and holding them in front of the heater. He was wearing greasy padded overalls, undone far enough for the sleeves to be tied round his waist. Richard shut the door and the heater returned to an even hiss. The fug inside was tinged with the smell of frying beefburgers from a Calor gas stove in one corner, and the reek of damp clothing. The misted windows streamed moisture. It was hard to tell who was in charge. On one side a man sat behind a counter next to a radio set. Periodically this burst into life with a loud blast of static and a stream of incomprehensible pilot-speak: '*Sierra zulu downwind zero eight.*' Mainly this was ignored, but sometimes the man would pick up the mouthpiece, press a button, and say crisply something like, '*Sierra zulu wind one two zero fifteen repeat one two zero fifteen QFE one zero one two report finals.*' I faintly wished that I understood what he meant.

There were several tables. At one, two men pored over an air chart surrounded by books, rulers, protractors and marker pens, periodically pushing buttons on a calculator and filling in boxes on a printed form. At others, people drank cups of tea or coffee, chatted or read magazines. Under the glass counter where the man with the radio sat were text books, manuals, cassettes, log books, woven cap badges, rulers and objects which looked like circular slide rules for sale.

I asked the man by the radio who we should talk to about trial flights.

'Three-axis or weightshift?' he said. I wondered if I had misheard him, and was about to repeat the question when something in my expression must have struck him. He turned in his seat, rubbed the condensation on the window with his sleeve and pointed at a machine beginning its take-off run.

'See that?' Two figures, swathed in peppermint and purple

neoprene, wearing crash helmets, were squeezed one behind the other in a torpedo-shaped pod on three wheels with an engine in the back and what looked like a hang-glider attached above. 'Flexwing,' he said.

'Flexwing?'

'Also called a "weightshift", because you manoeuvre it in the air by shifting your weight about, see?'

'Ah.'

He swivelled through 90°, to where two figures in old cords and jackets were stepping awkwardly over wing wires and tubing struts to install themselves side-by-side in a more robust-looking machine. This bore at least a passing resemblance to an aeroplane; it looked as if it could have appeared on the first page of the *Ladybird Book of Flight*, or as a prop in *Those Magnificent Men in Their Flying Machines*. It had a recognisable wing over the cockpit, a curved windscreen, and a long fuselage sloping back to a tail-plane resting on a little wheel behind.

'Fixed-wing. So called because the wing is fixed and doesn't move. Also known as "three axis", because it has control in all three axes: pitch—' He held his hand out, fingers together, palm down, and nodded it up and down. 'Yaw—' He wagged it from side to side. 'And roll—' He tilted it from side to side.

'Which is better?'

'Depends what you want, mate.'

'Which do you fly?'

'I fly both.'

'Who do we ask for a go in the weightshift?'

He called across the room to the man by the heater. 'Bloke wants a go in a trike, Jim. Will you take him?' The man looked out of the window and sniffed.

'Getting a bit breezy. Why doesn't he go in the Thruster?'

My man turned back to me. 'I'd go in the Thruster mate.' The Thruster, it transpired, was the machine resembling a plane. We were told that if we each wrote a cheque for £12, and gave it to the woman behind the counter, we could go out and take a trip with 'Geoff' when he landed.

We sat down to wait. I looked at the notices on the boards. 'Think Noise Abatement', said one. 'Think Hedgerow, not Heathrow,' said another. 'Beware Spinning Propellers' (here a Ralph Steadman drawing of someone having their head sawn off by a propeller). There were abstruse-looking meteorological charts, weather reports and maps of the local area with shadings and markings all over them, and similar-looking charts for the whole of the south of England. There were line-drawn maps on architects' paper with shading all over them marked 'Airspace Classifications' and identical maps with different shading marked 'Areas of Intense Aerial Activity'. There were pictures of microlights with headlines saying 'The Safest Way to Make the Earth Move'. And, more exotically, a poster: 'Imported by Plane? Drugs Kill' and 'Coast Watch: Have You Seen Anything Suspicious?' There was an advertisement board with photographs of various planes for sale, and other notices: 'Alençon Trip', 'Le Touquet trip', 'Sherborne Farm Fly-in and BBQ'.

After ten minutes the man by the radio told us Geoff had returned and to go outside. The microlight taxied up, and with no reduction in speed swept round ready to take-off again. The engine was throttled back from a mad scream to a rough popping and, from the left-hand seat, a figure levered himself out and walked stiffly over. He was flushed and could not stop grinning. He started trying to take off his flying suit, but was soon hopping about like a morris dancer as three of the four zips had jammed in separate places. Finally, he handed me the clammy bundle and started tugging at his helmet strap. I managed to break the fourth zip as I forced my foot into the leg aperture. The helmet was too small but I wedged it as far over my head as I could. As I shuffled over to the machine I was surprised by the strength (and iciness) of the blast from the propeller stream. Ducking under the wing I looked into the cockpit. The left-hand seat was empty. From the right, a grizzled ginger beard and a pair of sharp little eyes stared impatiently out from the helmet.

'The lead,' he bellowed through the din.

I looked blank.

'The lead. *The lead.*'

I stared at him. Eventually he leant over and grabbed a short length of flex that I had not noticed was attached to my helmet. There was the click in my ear of an audio connection being made followed by the noisy crackle and hiss of static.

'Don't put your feet on the floor. You'll go through. Place one foot on the metal bar, there. Then hold the strut and swing yourself in.' He did not ask my name.

When I was in, he leant over me, and started fiddling around with my outer thigh. After rummaging for a moment he extricated a strap I was sitting on, found another the other side which linked up with two belts which ran over my shoulders, all buckling into the clip on the waist straps. He tightened the waist strap until I was pinned in. Then he inserted a finger between my chin and the chinstrap of the helmet.

'Tighter.'

He thrust a pair of skiing mitts into my hand. Our seating position must have been no more than six or eight inches off the ground. We were protected from the drizzle by the wing above and an enclosing fibreglass pod; our forward view was framed through a curved, scratched, murky cowling and windshield. At our sides, where the doors would have been—had there been doors—was nothing. Above and in front of us was a tiny engine, about the size of two shoe boxes placed on top of each other.

I looked round the breezy cockpit, Geoff's left thigh pressed up against mine. There appeared to be a singular lack of dials or instrumentation compared to the cockpit of any other plane I had ever seen: four gauges, in fact; compass, altimeter, airspeed indicator and engine rev counter. With satisfaction, I realised that I could identify all four. Between (and slightly in front) of us was a stick.

'Keep clear of this ...' Geoff wagged the stick from side to side to side to indicate its range of travel.

'And the throttle.' He indicated a lever down on my left which moved in tandem with a lever his side.

'... and the rudders.' He paddled two stirrups at my feet, which I hadn't noticed. The engine screamed, we flicked round in a sharp U-turn and we were off.

Now that the moment had come, I found I was not really nervous at all. I knew that, statistically, there could not be much real danger. The machine—judging by its worn appearance—had flown safely many times before. Geoff was evidently pretty confident about things. I relapsed into a happy state of abandoned mental neutrality, the kind which accompanies devolved responsibility and the need for no understanding. As we surged across the grass (with surprising momentum) I felt disconcertingly low: so low that I could almost, had I not been pinned into my seat, have run my fingers through the wet tussocks. I did not notice when we left the ground. Suddenly the ride seemed to have become smoother, the grass was falling away and we were climbing over the hedge and a clump of scrubby trees in the corner of the field, then crossing the A303 and a patch of woodland.

The view was extraordinary. The open sides and huge windscreen meant unimpeded visibility to the front and sides. As we rose towards the low cloud, the ground began to become obscured by murky grey-white wisps of water vapour.

The intercom hissed and crackled.

'Done any flying before?'

'A few hours in a Cessna.'

'Heh-heh-heh. No, then.'

'You think this is better?'

'This is flying.'

'What's wrong with Cessnas?'

'What's wrong with Ford Mondeos?'

'So why is this so much better? What can she do?'

'Put your hand here.' He placed my hand round the rubber grip on top of the stick. 'Now put your feet on the rudder pedals. Now, basically …' He pulled the stick sharply back. The seat beneath me suddenly hardened and pressed up against me. The g-force felt enormous and a charge ran through my loins as I found myself looking vertically up into the murk.

'Up.'

We hung there for a moment, then he pushed the stick hard forward. It was like going over Nemesis at Alton Towers. Except that rather than a childish 90° dive, we went through 180°. The nose pitched forward as if we were going to turn a complete somersault, until the view ahead through the windscreen was the ground directly beneath. The canopy of a large old oak loomed in front of me as a wood pigeon flapped languidly out. My stomach reversed up my oesophagus like a bubble in a spirit level, and I felt that not unpleasant shivering loin-ache of going over a humpback bridge fast.

'Down.'

He levelled us, and I began to take stock of my condition; I had no idea that sensational feelings like this—which I had presumed were the prerogative of Tornado or Space Shuttle pilots alone—would be available in a toy plane like this. Geoff, however, was not finished. He brought the stick sharply over to the right, its full range of travel, until it pressed up against his thigh. The horizon spun round to vertical and my helmet crashed against his with an undignified clunk as I was thrown against him. I found myself staring across his body at the ground again. This time I studied the furrows of the ploughed field.

'Right.'

Now he brought the stick hard over in the opposite direction against my right thigh. The horizon spun again as the little machine rolled crazily over the other way. There was a creak as the harness took my twelve-and-a-half stone, suspending me over the void beneath. There was nothing now between me and the plough. I imagined myself dropping into it with a muddy squelch.

'And left. Got it? Your turn.' As he rolled us back to level, the little craft bucking and swivelling like a settling gyro, I wondered if I detected, through the static, a slightly defiant note in his voice. As if to say 'That's what she can do, Cessna man'. I sensed that this was a practised routine for scaring 'trial flighters', and that usually he had his victims screaming for mercy by this stage.

Gingerly I dabbed the stick this way, then that. Not much seemed to happen. When it did it felt very imprecise: as if we were perpetually skidding or slipping. Also, without any reference points for speed and direction, it was hard to tell how fast (or slowly) we were going.

'You're climbing. Watch the nose.'

The nose seemed to me to be exactly where it had been when he was flying, but to pacify Geoff I eased the stick slightly forward.

'Now, you're descending. Pull the stick back. No, not that much. Just keep her straight and level.'

'Does the engine ever fail?'

'Oh yes.' I waited for further information, but none was forthcoming. In the interval I became more aware of the engine roaring and vibrating away up in front of us, and how far away the ground looked.

'Often?'

'Not often enough.'

I was beginning to get a fix on Geoff.

'What happens then?' As the question came out, I realised what a moronic invitation it was to someone like him. But before I had a chance to rephrase it, he had cut the engine.

'Like this, you mean? Let's see, shall we?'

In fact he didn't stop it completely. But he reduced it to such a lazy idling tick-over that it felt as if he had. Compared to the racket of a second before, it seemed like silence.

'See? She glides just fine. All you do is pick yourself a field and down you go.' We were losing height rapidly. 'People with Cessnas ...' —he had a way of saying the word which made it sound like having lice—'People with Cessnas can fly their whole life without ever having an engine failure.' It sounded like an indictment against the Board and Directors of the Cessna company. 'Trouble is, when they do ...'

He opened up the throttle and we began to climb again.

'These days aircraft engines run forever,' he went on. 'Makes you take them for granted. Makes you lazy. Makes you assume it'll never happen. But this—' Here a tone of warm affection re-entered his voice. 'This doesn't have an aircraft engine. This has a two-stroke designed for a Snowmobile, not made to strain away at high revs all the time. You're bound to get a failure now and again. Part of the fun. That's what makes you a real pilot. Engine failures keep you on your toes. Never get them and you never expect them.'

'Do people often get hurt?'

'Only if they deserve it.'

'What about the other kind of microlight? The flexwing kind?'

'A trike?' (How many names did these machines have, I wondered.) 'All right. If you like that kind of thing. Easy to fly. Bit boring. Most people prefer it.'

'You think this is better?'

'This needs something you don't need to fly a trike. Or a Cessna.'

'What's that?'

'Skill.'

'Ah. Ha-ha-ha.'

'It's true. The Thruster is a tail-wheel aeroplane, like all the great planes. That means it's much more difficult to land. Lot of people find it impossible. Don't get it just right, and she'll bounce. Anyone can pancake a plane with a trike undercarriage onto the ground, but only a few can learn to land a tail-dragger. If in doubt, I'd go for a trike.'

We were descending again. The A303 re-appeared beneath us and there, alongside it, was the airfield. With a hiss, a film of drizzle covered the windshield. As we came in to land, I grasped the stout tube of the A-frame on my side of the cockpit with my left hand; it felt as if we were going to fly straight into the ground. As the moment of impact approached, I braced myself for the bump, but it never came. By the time I realised we had landed, we were bowling along the grass towards the clubhouse where Richard was waiting.

As I sat in the clubhouse, sipping a cup of coffee, my cheeks were burning. I could only have been up for fifteen minutes, but my hangover had disappeared. And one thing was in no doubt: there had been more flying sensations in fifteen minutes than in all my lessons in Africa. I wandered a little way up the field, kicking clouds of moisture from the sodden clumps of grass. (I wondered how hard 'difficult to land' could be.) If we ever got a microlight, I had already decided there was no way it was going to be a flexwing. I wondered how Richard was getting on, in particular how he would receive the information that flying a Cessna was like driving a Mondeo. I could rely on the fact that he would have told Geoff he had his pilot's licence.

'Did you find that man as irritating as I did?' asked Richard cheerfully as we made our way back to the car. He still had flattened hair, red ears and white pressure marks from the ill-fitting crash helmet; his face was pink, his eyes were bright and his nose was running. As we headed into London, the weather began to clear—a routine development, I would learn, at the end of a flying day.

'… Yes, not bad, not bad. Very different to a Cessna, of course. But not bad at all,' said Richard. 'What was it called again?'

'A Thruster.'

'Yes, at least it's like a proper aircraft. Stick and rudder. Did you see those other things? They looked like kites.'

'What about the landing? How difficult do you think that can be?'

'Landing?' said Richard. 'Why should there be any problem with landing? Look at the people who do it.' Richard's spirits were completely restored and I noticed that I was in a better mood than I had been in for months. It only struck me much later that Geoff was an excellent salesman.

Normal for Norwich

95% of the people who own light planes today can't
afford to own them.

A Gift of Wings, Richard Bach

A new Thruster cost £12,000. A private pilot's licence to fly it
required a minimum of twenty-five hours flying time (though we had
been warned to allow a great deal more on account of the British
weather) of which a large proportion might be 'dual' or with an
instructor, charged at around £75 per hour. My bank balance stood at
£542.62 overdrawn.

Microlighting, it transpired, fell into that select category of sports
—alongside base-jumping, wing-walking, sky-diving, motorcycle
racing, hang-gliding, free-climbing, sky-boarding—where insurance
companies were not tempted by your business, even at a 99 per cent
premium. If you had life policies, health insurance or endowment
mortgages, all were invalid the moment you set foot in a microlight, or
at least until you emerged unscathed. A consequence of this was that,
because microlights could not be insured, they could not be hired. You
could not, therefore, have a few lessons, acquire a licence, then rent a
machine when you felt like flying (as with a Cessna). If you wished to
maintain a licence, there was no alternative but to buy a machine.
There was the option of buying second-hand, but as Richard said, with
an activity of this kind it seemed to make sense to buy new. Thereafter,
from the moment it arrived, it was racking up expense in running,

maintenance and monthly hangarage charges at whichever airfield we ended up keeping it.

Richard—the bank manager—did the sums. Although we differed in the extent of instruction we required (Richard, having a PPL, only had to apply to the Civil Aviation Authority to adapt his licence), the dismal conclusion was the same. We needed £6,000 each now, plus, for me, another £2,000 for instruction and other expenses, spread over however long it took.

Despite what I might intimate to people unfamiliar with the advertising industry, I was still a junior copywriter. I worked for a tiny advertising 'boutique'—one of the rash of 1980s start-ups—located above a Chinese restaurant in Chinatown. Richard earned slightly more but was only in the black himself because it was a condition of his employment. We were in no position to buy an aircraft. 'Saying you haven't got the money, is not a reason,' said Richard. 'It's an excuse. It comes as no surprise to hear you're trying to back out.'

Richard examined my bank statements and declared that, if I followed his instructions, I should be able to raise a £4,000 loan. He could raise about the same. It was not enough.

We asked one or two friends if they would care to come in on our project, but they had read about microlights in the same newspaper reports that I had and, with gracious thanks, the offer was declined. For a time it looked as if the whole scheme would have to be shelved but then it occurred to me that there must be some central organising body for microlighters, and it must have a newsletter. Why not place an ad there? I rang the BMAA—the British Microlight Aircraft Association—and they told me that their quarterly newsletter, *Flightline*, could indeed carry an ad if I joined (£12 per year adult member, £18 family), but they were going to press next day. I dictated: Thruster Syndicate. Third or quarter share to buy new plane. 01-381-8533.'

A week or two later, the magazine arrived. It was an engagingly homespun publication full of pictures of offbeat flying machines and advertisements for engines and propellers. I could understand hardly a word. I flicked through to the small ads. On the last page, in the Miscellaneous section, amid advertisements for windsocks ('8 ft dayglo orange ripstop nylon, ideal for field and private airstrip use'), microlight holidays in the Lake District ('100 hours minimum flying experience'), Mercury flying suits ('smart gear at a smart price'), Skymaster recovery parachute ('full instructions included'), there it was.

There were no responses.

Towards the end of April, letting myself into the flat, I just caught the phone. 'Hullo. Hullo. The name's Watson. Lester Watson.' It was an educated male voice, my parents' age, disengaged but authoritative. Assuming it was a wrong number, I did not pay much attention. 'I'm calling about the advertisement. Yers.' He had a most characteristic way of speaking, as if he were talking mainly to himself. 'Yers, we were wondering about a Thruster, too. Have you got one yet? How do you find it?' He spoke in distinct phrases, like a toy operated by pulling the string. By the time I had realised what he was talking about and mumbled that, as it happened, we had not yet done anything about it, he had moved on. 'Come and stay and we can discuss it. We live in Norfolk. There's an instructor nearby. We can talk to him. Dan, my son, is also interested. Salsingham is the address; Salsingham Hall. We'll see you Friday evening then.' I was too confused to think of a reason why I could not manage the weekend, and by the time I had thought of something, I found I was speaking to a dialling tone.

So on Friday evening, Richard and myself found ourselves back in Richard's bottle-green Rover, in a traffic jam in the Forest Road in north-east London. To my surprise, Richard had been enthusiastic about the trip when I told him about Mr Watson. The truth was that as the novelty of returning from Africa had begun to wane and, as neither of us had girlfriends, any potential new distraction was welcome.

After forty minutes, during which we moved no more than a hundred yards, he swung suddenly into a side street, accelerated down it, turned left at the end, accelerated down the next street, decisively turned left at the end of that, accelerated again, until he was forced to brake sharply at a row of concrete bollards which separated us from the road we required. 'Well?' he said impatiently. 'Which way?'

The only navigational aid was an ancient black-and-white paperback *London A-Z*. The corners were so turned back on each other and overlapping the pages either side that it was a job to open it. When I did, the pages covering Central London, fell out—not that this mattered, as we were far outside this zone, adrift in a no-man's labyrinth of minute print and unrecognisable roads. I had found where we were, cross-referenced it with where we needed to go, and was about to give him instructions when Richard set off again. Moments later we were at another dead end. 'Urgh,' he sighed, clicking his tongue. 'I forgot you can't read maps.'

Richard and I were used to each other's company despite being friends by accident. We had met in the early 1980s when we occupied rooms across a corridor in a faceless brick and concrete block of student accommodation, allowing us to observe minutely—and listen to— each other's habits and lifestyles sufficiently to nurse a mutual but confident dislike for each other. He read maths and *The Daily Telegraph*, played rugby and liked student politics; he was someone I knew could not be my friend. Our natural instinct was to disagree on all things. However, as I had a refrigerator and he had a toasted sandwich-maker; and he had a car, and I had a girlfriend he fancied like mad, we ended up seeing more of each other than we would have chosen. She moved on. We were left as friends.

I had never been to Norfolk. All I knew was that it was flat, intensively farmed, on the way to nowhere and that doctors marked the medical records of patients who had survived accidents but been left slightly subnormal 'NFN'—Normal for Norwich. It was also, at the end of the 1980s, the county that transport policy forgot. It was getting dark as the A11 carried us through the Thetford Forest to wide, open fields with huge metal irrigation booms. And it was after 11pm by the time we turned in through a pair of brick lodge gates and up a long drive to what was evidently a vast country house. All was in darkness except for a single downstairs window. When we switched the engine off, the sound of organ music wafted out into the cool spring night air.

We pushed on the bell of the grand main portico. There was no sound from within to indicate that it was working. After a few moments of alternate ringing and knocking, we tried the door. It had appeared to be locked, but when Richard gave it a harder shove it opened, and we found ourselves standing in a huge entrance hall, enveloped by resounding organ music. There was a yellow glow from behind an organ case at the top of the big double staircase. 'Hello?' I called. 'Hello!' The organ music continued.

'*Hello! HELLO!*' shouted Richard.

The music stopped. A male voice echoed back.

'Hello? Is someone there?' It was the voice on the phone.

'Hello!' we shouted back.

A short, wiry figure came down the stairs. He looked at us a little doubtfully, as if unsure what we wanted.

Then he spotted our cases. His face cleared.

'Just off?' He extended a cordial hand. 'Excellent. Very nice to see you again. You've signed the book? Good, good.' He gently ushered us back out through the door. 'Do come again. Bye.' The door shut with a click.

There didn't seem any alternative but to go back in. The room was now in darkness, but we were in time to see our man disappear down an unlit passage which led into a square, high-ceilinged kitchen. When we got there he had disappeared. Or rather, he had metamorphosed into a tall, good-looking and rather formidable woman, standing by an ancient Aga. She had a pen on a string round her neck which, as she looked up, she clicked menacingly.

'Who are you?' she said sharply. I smiled, apologised if we were late, and explained that we had come about the microlight. 'First I've heard of it.' At that moment her husband re-emerged by another door.

'Lester, some people are here. Something to do with lights or lighting or something. Is this something you've arranged?' She looked mildly irritated.

'Lights?'

I attempted to explain again. Lester showed polite interest but no recognition. 'Are you friends of Dan?' he suggested helpfully. This seemed to crystallise something in the woman.

'What sort of time do you call this? We might easily have gone to bed. If you want to stay in this house in future, perhaps you'd care to make your arrangements with the manager, not the lift boy.' Mr Watson had left the room again. I was beginning to feel slightly seasick, and almost wondered if I had imagined my telephone conversation with him. But Mrs Watson had moved on. 'I suppose you want feeding. Do you think these raspberries are defrosted?'

There were no further enquiries about the microlight. In fact no one seemed to mind in the least why we were there. I made one more attempt on Mr Watson when he wandered into the library where I had been sent with instructions to get a drink. 'A Thruster? Yes, from what I can gather they're very good machines. Very good. We've been thinking about getting one ourselves,' he said. 'There's an instructor near here. We could go over tomorrow, if you liked.'

Later Mrs Watson led us up a bare wooden back staircase to the third floor and along a wide passageway. It was lined with bookcases, old magazines, stacked mattresses, ancient convector heaters, old telephones, broken toys and three-legged stools with birdcages perched on top of them. The linoleum had worn through in patches, revealing undulating floorboards beneath which squawked and groaned as we crossed them. Opening doors more or less at random, she settled on a room containing two beds and a mountain of furniture stacked under dust sheets. There was a musty smell, which turned into a heavy scent of musk and vanilla near the window. As she pulled the curtains on their noisy metal runners I glimpsed a branch of wisteria, laden with flowers, which had grown through the open top sash of one of the windows. The branch was at least three inches thick.

'I don't think anyone's slept in here recently,' she said. Her tone implied that this was to our advantage. Tugging on the frayed plaited cord of an ancient electric fire, she retrieved a brown Bakelite round-pinned plug, which she plugged in and flicked the toggle. Sparks fizzed from the middle section, where one of the ceramic bars had at some stage been knocked, though the wire remained intact. 'Make sure you switch it off,' she said sternly. 'The last person left it on for three months.'

As she removed the bed covers, the bars set up a whining, moaning resonance and the tarnished reflection plate began to tick as it heated up. In the bathroom across the corridor she twisted the newest (and only chrome-coloured) tap of some four different sets of plumbing which converged upon the bathtub, crossing and weaving round each other as they led off via a maze of pipes. It emitted a groan of air. 'You'll have to wait until the morning for hot water,' she said, adding, with a momentary return to her earlier asperity, 'if we'd known you were coming, we could have switched it on.' With that she said good night.

We had finished breakfast before Dan Watson appeared in the kitchen. Lean and high-cheekboned, radiating unhurried calm, he swept his brown hair away from his eyes but didn't remove his sunglasses as he held out a friendly hand. He had been at a party, he explained, until five. His movements were apparently choreographed always to finish in an elegant position. He sniffed the coffee in the cafetière doubtfully, inspected the sausages and bacon that Mrs Watson had told us in a note were in a roasting tin in the oven, then set about assembling his own breakfast. He ignored most of the fare on offer, set a battered espresso machine to brew on the Aga, scrambled some eggs and added some chopped parsley. He set some butter to melt in a pan, added a big field mushroom which he said he had found the day before. Only when he had assembled everything to his liking, ground salt and pepper coarsely over it, and his coffee was ready, did he start to eat.

Mr Watson we had already seen. He seemed to know all about us now. He had pottered in and out of the kitchen several times, carrying files, or music, or pairs of pliers. Despite being dressed in a grubby fawn nylon jerkin, which made him look like a cross between a grip, a conjuror and a big game hunter, there was something curiously intimidating about him. 'Do you play the piano?' his disconcerting opening remark had been. 'What, *neither* of you? Tst.' Followed by a muttered, 'No-one seems able to do *anything* nowadays.' He was plainly a man of parts. The downstairs loo was festooned with a mass of framed photographs and faded newspaper cuttings of a younger Mr Watson—at Cambridge; in Africa; winning a by-election; as an MP at Westminster.

Nor, it turned out, was Mr Watson a novice when it came to flying. He had flown in Africa, where he had set up an engineering business after the war. His first plane, he told us, he bought for £400 and flew between Khartoum and Nairobi 'until it succumbed. It was made of wood, you see.' Returning to Britain at the end of the Fifties, someone told him about Salsingham Hall—the seat of an Earl complete with wings, lake and landscaped park—that was under threat of demolition. In a servantless post-war Britain of supertax, punishing death duties and agricultural prices which had fallen through the floor, there seemed no future for such white elephants, he explained; aristocratic families, in panic and desperation, were giving away their homes to anyone who would take them. Lester Watson flew up to look at it from the air, fell in love, and bought it for a song—then married Rhona and for their honeymoon took her on an air rally round Sicily.

'Tell them about the Med, Dad,' said Dan.

'I was flying the Auster back to sell it,' he said. 'I'd paid £700 and I knew I could sell it here for more than £2,000. We set out from Marsa Matrûh in Egypt, heading for Crete. Well, we were given the wrong wind forecast. We were told it was ten knots from the west when in fact it was from the east. After two hours, there was no sign of land anywhere. Not surprising. We were sixty miles west of Crete—and we were running low on fuel. There were no direction finder beacons in those days. We had no radio. So we decided to fly on until we found a ship or a fishing vessel which could rescue us. Well, there wasn't a ship anywhere. We had just minutes of fuel left when we saw a German tanker. I told Ron, who was with me, to write a note, telling them we were going to ditch and to rescue us. He put it in his shoe, then I flew low over the bridge and we dropped the shoe onto the deck. It was a German crew, but luckily one of them understood English. Then we ditched. Fortunately, just the week before, my brother-in-law, who's in the Fleet Air Arm, had told me about ditching. He said the crucial thing is to land *crosswind*, so the waves don't tip you up. Approach into wind'—he motioned with his hand, a chopping movement—'then at the last minute'—he turned his hand through 90°—'kick her round crosswind so you land *with* the swell. Stall her just above the water's surface and drop her in. So that's what I did. It was the most brilliant landing. Brilliant.'

We were agog.

He showed us his battered log book, dug out for the microlight instructor. The covers were frayed and sun-baked and the binding loose and worn. The pages recorded hundreds of journeys: 'V. Falls to Bulawayo'; 'Mbeya to Kasama'; 'Nairobi to Mombasa'; 'Panshangar to Lympne (REMARKS: Honeymoon trip)'; 'Lympne to Nice (en route for Giro di Sicilia International Air Race)'; page after page, denoting thousands of hours of flying, with numerous names under AIRCRAFT TYPE: Tiger Moth, Auster, Tripacer, Gemini, Proctor, Rallye. The last entry was in 1964.

'I haven't flown for a bit, but, you know, it never leaves you once you've learnt. This Sean seems a good fellow. I hope he'll let me update my licence without too much fuss.'

'Did you have any other narrow escapes?' I asked.

'Well, once on the way from Jubâ to Malak—'

'Where's Jubâ?'

'You don't know where Jubâ is?' He looked astonished. 'Southern Sudan. We'd left Jubâ, headed for Khartoum, and the cloud got lower and lower. Eventually it was down to 200 feet above the ground. We were going at about 140 mph. Anyway, we eventually hit the Nile, so we knew then that if we followed it at least we'd eventually come to Malakal. We just had to hope the cloud didn't get any lower. We did 180 miles at 150 feet. Don't know what people on the ground thought.' Mr Watson looked quite pleased to have such an enthusiastic audience. 'Then there was the time we were flying down to Skojpe from St Etienne. Well, you know what Skojpe is like: we were surrounded by the military with guns ...'

There seemed to be hardly a part of Africa, the Mediterranean or Northern Europe he had not visited. He told us about stalling an engine on landing at Croydon, a near-miss with a DC6 at Forneby in Oslo. 'Coming out of Jakawalpa we got engine icing at 500 feet. Imagine that. We were literally off the end of the runway when the engine started spluttering.'

'Did you ever make a safe flight?' said Richard.

'Dad, we should be going,' said Dan, looking at his watch. He wore it with the face on the front of his wrist rather than the back.

Sean, the instructor, was based at RAF Barsham Green, ten miles away. The journey took longer than expected. The narrow, frequently fenceless lanes serpentined lazily through the Norfolk fields, and Mr Watson, who was driving, seemed in no hurry. He and Dan became progressively less certain about the way and, once again, locating the entrance of a rural airfield added considerably to the time we had allowed for the journey.

The approaches were misleadingly shipshape. At the main gate we were told to pull over, alongside the scale model Spitfire on its concrete pedestal by the entrance, while the car was searched. It was my first experience of a military airfield, and the guard house, security cameras, razor wire, safety barricades and mirrors on broom-handles for examining underneath the car all seemed very official and impressive until I later learned that, fifty yards up the road, the fence petered out into brambles and the place was open to ramblers. There was an elaborate signing-in procedure including lengthy questions from the duty officer before we were issued with a windscreen sticker and allowed to proceed.

The Norwich and East of England Aero Club, despite its grandiose name, seemed to have facilities remarkably similar to those at Popham: two Portakabins in a state of semi-collapse, propped on breeze blocks.* Sean, the instructor we had come to see, was a year or two older than Richard and me. He had sandy hair, freckles and a bounce in his step. His room in the Portakabin complex was meticulously organised: papers neatly squared and piled in order of size, lined up in rows, pens laid across the top at right angles. 'Yes, hello, yes, come in. I see, quite a few of you. Lester, Richard, Dan and Antony. And you're interested in a Thrasher? No problem.' (Sean, I would learn, always referred to a Thruster as a 'Thrasher'.) 'Yes, it's a good little plane, the Thrasher. You'll have some fun with that.'

There was a pause. Oddly, having got there, there didn't seem to be much to say.

'What's the insurance position?' said Richard.

'How do you mean?' said Sean.

'Well, if something goes wrong, or there is an accident, are you properly insured? Or is the manufacturer of the machine liable?'

'Are you sure you should be doing this?' said Sean.

'Is there any kind of brochure we can look at?' I asked Sean.

'No. No brochures. Don't worry, I'll tell you what you need.'

---

* Where other expensive activities—sailing, golf, polo—tend to have lavish clubhouses set in fastidiously tended grounds, a smart flying club is one not constructed of chip-board or on wheels; perhaps a reflection of the more practically-orientated mindsets of those involved. Two years after this, in a heavy storm, the clubhouse of the 'Norwich and Eastern' was, literally, blown away. There was nothing left at all, except for eight breeze blocks and a patch of bare grass.

There was a pause. No one seemed to know what to say.

'Right,' said Richard, getting out his cheque book, and reaching for a biro. 'Let's get on then.'

Richard was like that. He just decided things. The Watsons seemed happy. Sean produced a photocopied order form and we each wrote out a cheque for £3,000. It was the largest cheque I had ever written.

I felt taken unaware. I had not bargained on any cheque-writing until much further down the line. I was used to a great deal more procrastination before committing myself to things. I felt I lacked the mental preparation—not to mention the funds—to be doing it so soon. Richard told me afterwards that people like me always lacked the mental preparation for doing anything.

No sooner had my cheque for £3,000 been filed away than Sean said

'Right. Helmets and headsets. I recommend the standard SXP helmet with a Narcan 5000 intercom. It's a bit more expensive, but they are better.'

There was silence, except for the scratching of Biros while we each wrote another cheque, this time for £120 each. These were filed away in a separate neat pile.

'Do you want a radio?'

'A radio?' said Dan thoughtfully. 'How much is that?'

'A basic transceiver starts at about £400. I can get you a discount.' We all looked at each other.

'Maybe leave the radio 'til later,' said Sean. 'But you'd better order your ozee suits, if they're to be here by the time the plane arrives. I can probably get a deal if you all order together.' An ozee suit turned out to be a blue Thinsulate-lined zip-up flying overall.

'Do we really need an ozee suit?' I asked. 'Can't we just wrap up well?'

'Oh you must have an ozee suit.'

The cheque was for £80.

'You'll need to arrange third party insurance, as we're flying from Ministry of Defence land,' Sean said, handing out four more photocopied forms. 'I'll leave you to do that yourselves.' The form contained a number of boxes. Alongside the lowest box, containing the highest premium (£80), was a rough cross in blue biro. 'Of course it's up to you whether you decide to insure the hull or not. That can get expensive. Right. Now for the loose ends.'

The loose ends consisted of another £72-worth of equipment: two flying charts—a 1:250,000 scale map of East Anglia and a 1:500,000 scale map of the south of England; a perspex ruler graduated in nautical miles in both these scales; a frightening, but impressive-looking gadget like a circular slide rule called a flight course and distance calculator; a log book (which seemed premature, as we did not yet have an aircraft); a blue plastic ring binder entitled *CAP 85: A Guide to Aviation Law, Flight Rules and Procedures for Applicants for the Private Pilot's Licence*; and, finally, a slim paperback entitled *The Microlight Pilot's Handbook*. This was slimmer and—judging by the ratio of pictures of clouds to diagrams with arrows—considerably simpler than the thick, densely-written text books to which I had been introduced in Africa. The pages started falling out the moment I broke the spine—which somehow seemed to reflect microlighting's marginalised role in the world of aviation. As the objects mounted, it felt a bit like the first day at school. Except, at £72, rather more expensive.

'You'll need to buy a couple of jerry cans each and paint your names on the side. Now, hangarage. I'll give you a deal for the first six months if you're happy for me to take people up for trial flights. Shall we say £50 a month? Oh, and finally, you'll have to join the flying club, of course.'

'How much is that?'

'£15. But make the cheque out to the flying club, not to me.'

Enough was enough.

'It's all right,' I said. 'I won't join for the moment.'

'You have to. Or no flying. It costs the same whether you join now or later.'

Resignedly I reached for my cheque book again. The pain was softened, however, when a few minutes later I was handed a blue credit-card-sized membership card. I slipped it into my wallet. Pleasingly visible for all to read alongside the club name and its winged crest were the words 'FULL FLYING MEMBER'.

In the car on the way back to London on Sunday afternoon, I examined my jeans and shoes. The new 501s were almost black from a combination of mud, oil and green tree mould. My Chelsea boots were so caked that it was impossible to tell that they had once been suede. Both were ruined.

Mr Watson had arrived in our room at eight, as we slept off mild hangovers from staying up talking to Dan, his sister Seph, who had arrived that day and a couple of friends of his who had come for dinner. 'Hullo, hullo. Are you up? D'you mind? There's a fallen tree we need to shift. Shouldn't take long but needs a couple of pairs of hands. Wonder if you'd like to help? And if you see Dan, tell him. Can't think where he's got to—he knew I wanted help. Shall we meet downstairs in fifteen minutes?' And so, after a hasty piece of toast, we found ourselves, on a cool May morning, in charge of a chain-saw, bill hook, and tractor and trailer. At 10.30 am Lester had left to play the organ in the local church.

We left promptly after lunch. Over the not-quite-defrosted summer pudding, Mr Watson had mentioned some mattresses and a piano that needed shifting. There had been no further talk about arrangements for sharing the Thruster when it arrived: how we would avoid clashing, who would fly it when, how we would pay for it if it got damaged. Mr Watson had issued an open invitation and given us the run of a top-floor flat, if we wanted a summer holiday. Somehow any more formal discussion seemed inappropriate. 'Nevertheless, I shall draw up an agreement,' said Richard.

I was still reeling from the decisive turn my life had taken. We had ordered an aeroplane. There was no backing out: it was done. We seemed to have acquired some new friends, albeit of an eccentric and extraordinary kind. It was plain that Mrs Watson ran things, and Dan was friendly and easy-going. But, most of all, it was Mr Watson who had left an impression. He was unlike anyone we had met before. He made doing what you liked look so easy and obvious. He loved Africa, so he had started a business there. He wanted to fly, so he bought a plane. He liked the look of a mansion which everyone else saw as a liability. So he ignored them, and bought it. He answered to nobody except himself, and seemed to have complete control over his life. It was independence of mind of a fierceness that neither of us had encountered.

That evening Richard, as syndicate administrator, drew up a 'Contract of Agreement for the Salsingham Syndicate'. It ran to seven pages, and outlined terms of reference, terms of ownership, booking procedures, damage liability, shared expenses, individual expenses, conditions of leaving, priority of use on weekends and holidays, and other areas. 'Isn't it a bit formal? Doesn't it imply we don't trust each other?'

'It's not a matter of trust,' said Richard. 'It's a matter of procedure.' As *Prime Suspect* began on the television, I opened a cold Beck's and settled down with *The Microlight Pilot's Handbook*: 'The advent of the microlight aeroplane has brought flying within the reach of many …'

Full Flying Member

Most of the time, the aeroplane flies not because of the
pilot's activity on the controls, but despite it.

Wolfgang Langewiesche, *Stick and Rudder*, 1944.

We had booked two weeks holiday in July for some intensive
instruction and were installed in the top floor flat at Salsingham. Now
that the idea had sunk in (the commitment of a bank loan had the effect
of focussing my mind further), and weekends and holidays were now
sorted for the foreseeable future, I was keen to get on and learn to fly as
fast as possible. I had tried to book our holiday from the day the
Thruster was delivered, but Sean said he needed a few days to assemble
the plane, test fly it and generally tighten up any cords and cables which,
because it was new, he said, tended to stretch or slacken in the first few
hours of use.

It was now quarter to ten on Saturday morning. (I had been ready
to start at eight or even seven—I wanted to be sure of getting my licence
by the end of the fortnight—but Sean had told me to be patient. 'Calm
down. You'll get plenty of flying.') There was just the hint of a breeze,
enough to feel the hairs on the back of my hands and arms as we
followed Sean over to the huge black hangar.

The hangar was still shut and no one else was about. Sean picked up
a metal crank leaning against the side and slotted it into a socket in the
vast door. Each of the eight sliding doors, he said, was filled with
sand—a wartime precaution to shield the hangar's fragile contents

from bomb blast—and weighed ten tons. He braced his weight against the crank and heaved, grunting and flushing with the strain until the door gathered momentum, the crank began to twist with a vigorous torque of its own, and the noise of metal wheels grating on gritty runners became drowned by an echoing bass rumble.

The widening strip of sunlight cut a sharp rectangle through the gloom of the interior. Through particles of dust turning in the rays was a jumble of fins and elevators, wings and wires, rotors and aerials. The space was dominated by a giant military jet that looked like a Vulcan nuclear bomber, but which Sean said was a Canberra, a 1950s reconnaissance plane, now used, he said, by RAF technical staff to practise X-ray detecting for metal fatigue. Ranged beneath its wings was a tightly-packed assortment of helicopters, bi-planes, Cessnas, flexwing microlights (most of Sean's teaching was on flexwings) and, amongst all these fins and wings and rotor blades, apologetic and minute in one corner, was the Thruster.

Sean dodged nimbly in amongst the machines—it struck me how awkward and fragile aircraft were in an enclosed space, with all their gawky projections and wires and sharp edges and delicate surfaces— and began to loosen the mesh. He pushed a plane back a few inches, pulled another up (by its prop) to fill the gap, nudged a tail-plane round, turned a propeller a few degrees to clear a wing. In this way he cleared enough of a passageway that, by raising and lowering the tail to clear a tail-fin or a bracing wire, he could just extricate the Thruster without any part of it quite touching another machine. Finally it was clear enough for him to put the tail down and trundle it onto the sunshine of the concrete fairing in front of the hangar. For the first time we had the chance to examine our new purchase properly.

The overall effect was of a large toy aeroplane with a cheeky expression. The rounded nose of the fibreglass pod in which the pilot and passenger were enclosed, and which protected them from the weather and the airstream, gave it the smug, perky expression of a Pekinese—cute or irritating, according to taste. The wings were blue and red, the fibreglass pod was white and the tail blue. It struck me that we could have given more thought to the colour scheme. Large white capitals spelt out her registration letters—Golf Mike Victor Oscar Yankee, or G-MVOY—on the underside of the wings and on the tail. The spotless new tyres and glinting windshield added to an overall effect of pristine prissiness which had been absent from the streaked wings, faded fabric and worn-in, workaday appearance of the machine at Popham. As the progeny of more than three quarters of a century of aeronautical research and development, it was hard not to think that something was missing. The engine had a pull-start like a lawn mower. The seats were the moulded plastic, school stacking variety (minus the metal legs). The tail-wheel was off a supermarket trolley. One of the flight controls looked uncannily like—and, on closer inspection, was—a nylon cord with a bathroom light switch on the end. The impression was simply of a machine unfinished. Her wings, however, were at least a version of traditional doped canvas (if a modern, Dacron-Terylene one) and she had a wooden propeller. 'Right,' said Sean. 'Let's get Thrashing.'

I went up first, leaving Richard reading the paper in the car. Once Sean had me strapped in to the left-hand seat, he told me to hold the throttle lever (car hand-brake position, down on my left) with my left hand, take the stick in my right hand, and steer with my feet on the rudder pedals. Gingerly I opened the throttle from its tick-over rate of 3,000 rpm. We didn't move at all until the revs had reached at least 5,000 rpm, when we sprang forward across the fairing. 'Steady,' said Sean, promptly reducing the power with the dual lever his side.

It all felt most bizarre. Although pressing the left pedal turned the plane left, and vice versa, there was a slight delay in the reaction (and it worked much less effectively at low speed). This made it tempting to over-react, and our path towards the airfield commenced in an undignified zig-zag. When we got to the end of the runway, Sean stopped us on a slight upslope into wind and showed me the checks I had to do. These were mercifully few, boiling down to giving the stick a good stir to see that the controls were 'full and free', checking our seat-belts and helmet chin-straps were done up, that the few instruments were reading within their limits, and that there was sufficient fuel in the tank. Then he instructed me to taxi round in a circle (to check for any 'traffic' in the circuit) and line up. 'Off you go then. What are you waiting for?' he said, when I had done so.

I briskly opened the throttle and immediately incurred criticism.

'*Gently*—everything you do in flying should be gentle. But positive. And open it fully: that's only three quarters.' We began to move forward along the grass, picking up speed. 'Right, stick forward to raise the tail.' As the tail came up, the ride stopped feeling rough and bumpy, and she moved much more easily. 'See? Feel how much better she runs. Right, keep her straight with the rudder pedals. Now. Once you can feel that the tail's up, just gently let the stick back to where it naturally goes, in the centre. *Gently*. That's right. That's all you have to do. Let the speed pick up now, and ... there you are.' Suddenly the ride felt smoother still, and I realised that the grass underneath the wheels was sinking away from us. 'See? Simple as that.' And it really was. The plane took off by itself.

I knew what to do now, from my Cessna lessons, and began to pull the stick back to make us climb. Sean briskly shoved it forward again. 'Don't pull the stick back yet: you're not flying well enough: you'll stall and crash. Just let the speed build up 'til she's flying nicely. OK, now ... just ease the stick back.' A big flock of starlings fluttered into the air and wheeled away from us ahead and to the left.

In front of us, as we climbed, I could see a town. 'Dereham,' said Sean, pointing out the characteristic water tower, a big, ugly, conical edifice, as if a giant, round, plastic funnel had been jabbed into the ground as a mould and filled with concrete. (I did not realise then how much I would grow to love that water tower.) I could see cars moving along the A47 to Norwich. South of the airfield (though at the time I had no idea of my bearings) was the village of Barsham Green, with its church tower. There was another church, of worn and weathered brick and flint and a round tower on the north side of the airfield, and, to the east, a winding river meandered through lakes and gravel pits. A distinctive enough setting, perhaps, for an airfield, but the moment I looked away it disappeared and I was lost over an infinite patchwork mat of countryside.

That is pretty much all I took out of that first lesson. No doubt we practised a few turns and manoeuvres, but in no time we seemed to be back over the airfield and Sean was telling me to reduce the throttle to 5,000 rpm for my descent. *'Gently. Christ,'* he said, as I inadvertently overdid it and we started to plummet. The approach to land was by far the hardest part. To judge, in three dimensions, an even descent from where I was in the air, to a specified point on the ground—let alone carry it out by co-ordinated manipulation of stick and throttle—was a task beyond impossible. 'Right. I have control,' said Sean, as I nearly hit a hedge a field short of the Barsham runway. He gave a burst of throttle which carried us neatly to the airfield.

After the confinement and intensity of the cockpit, it was good to stretch, peel off my flying suit and feel the warm air playing around my arms and ankles. The temperature had been about right at 1,000 feet with my ozee suit on. Back on the ground it was uncomfortably warm. As I slumped onto the grass, Coke in hand, and Richard strapped himself in, Sean shouted. 'Get on with your ground school, Ants,' (he had taken to calling me 'Ants'). 'Don't just laze in the sun.' Circumstances, however, were not conducive. The sun blazed from a spotless blue sky, with the breath of a breeze, just enough occasionally to twitch the big windsock on the west of the airfield.

For lunch Sean took us to the Barsham canteen. 'We could go into Drear-am,' he said doubtfully (Sean called East Dereham 'Drear-am'). 'But it's hardly worth it.' He referred, I knew, to Barsham's labyrinthine one-way system with its platoons of sleeping policemen and 6 mph speed limit, enforced by the military police with the true viciousness of total boredom. The canteen would today win awards for its authentic war-time-rationing experience. From its bare, wiped-down counters all that was available were triangular meat paste sandwiches on curling Homepride (and maybe an apple or two) and Nice, Rich Tea or Digestive biscuits. The one concession to indulgence were some 'Club' biscuits, which turned out to be cracked and pale with age beneath the silver paper. A woman in a nylon apron served cups of stewed tea from a battered aluminium teapot.

After lunch, Sean showed us how to mix fuel for the Thruster. He added 200 mls of blue Duckhams motorbike oil to a 20-litre jerry can of petrol to make up the 'two-stroke mixture', then he swung the heavy can vigorously this way and that, twisting it as he did so to mix it. 'Always make sure you're putting in two-stroke mixture, not just petrol,' he said, inserting a funnel with a stocking over the top into the Thruster's tank. 'You can tell by the colour. Petrol is straw-coloured. Two-stroke mixture, if you use Duckhams, has a blue tinge.' He held the jerry can with the spout uppermost until it was half-empty, then turned it so that it emptied without surging and gulping. 'Never fill up in the hangar, and never over grass. You'll spill it and we get bare patches.'

My afternoon lesson felt a little better. The controls were not quite so strange, though I would not always have guessed it from Sean's noisy imprecations. The taxiing and taking off now seemed straight-forward, though Sean grabbed the throttle lever a couple of times while I was taxiing out and consistently told me to slow down. I had observed that while he made me bump and trundle along at a snail's pace, when he taxied he opened the throttle, raised the tail and scorched along at about 30 mph.

Once off the ground, however, he couldn't stop fussing about the air speed.

'Always keep an eye on the air speed indicator. Your cruising speed should be 50-55 knots. *Never* let the air speed drop below 40 knots. What will happen if you do?'

'We'll stall.'*

* Not the same as stalling at the traffic lights. See Glossary.

'Exactly. We'll stall. And what happens if we stall?'

'We crash.'

'Exactly. The plane stops flying and falls out of the sky unless you take steps to recover. *So make sure you don't.* Keep the air speed at, say a nice, steady 45 knots when you're climbing, and somewhere over 50 in the cruise.' I was sure that what he said made good sense, but the air was so pleasant, and my mood felt so good that I wished he could have relaxed a bit. I had complete confidence that, even if I did inadvertently stall the aircraft, Sean would soon have the situation under control. It was a lovely summer afternoon. Beneath us a tractor was cutting hay, and the scent drifted up. Most of the fields were deep with standing corn which was just turning from green to gold. The view was fantastic—I could almost see the coast—and up here the air was cool and refreshing: there was no doubt that it was the place to be.

'Look at your air speed. Come on, wake up. Now, make a 180° turn to the left, and I don't want to see the bubble move.'

I forced my mind back to the task in hand. Another of Sean's preoccupations was turning out to be the slip indicator: the ball in the horizontal glass tube in the centre of the dashboard. This was supposed to remain central in its window at all times, indicating that the controls—the stick and the rudders—were being used correctly together, or 'balanced', in turns. Attempt a turn with too little rudder, or too much, and the bubble shot off to the right or left. In severely unbalanced cases the bubble disappeared altogether. Since Sean had told me about it, and I had started watching the instrument during turns, I had yet to set eyes on the ball at all.

Sean told me to fill up the Thruster before we packed up after Richard's lesson. 'Fill her up when you put her away and you won't get condensation forming in the tank and water in the fuel next time you fly. Then we'll do your log book, Ants.' Later, in his office, he opened my log book and filled out the first two lines in his firm, careful handwriting. 'Always fill in your log book straight after flying, then you don't forget.' Each of my two lessons was entered separately. There seemed to be a lot of boxes, to do with multi-engines, night and instrument flying, left blank. Under REMARKS, he wrote '1, 2, 3, 4, 5, 6, 7, 8, 9a, 9b, 10a, 10b, 11' which surprised me. I had not been aware of doing anything more than enjoying the view, and dabbing the stick this way and that.

Two hours in the air did not seem much from a whole day devoted to flying. But as I drove us back to Salsingham—the controls of the car felt absurdly firm and precise after the Thruster—I could not remember when I had felt so tired. My skin felt tight, too, where I had caught the sun.

The Watsons had told us there was a swimming pool, and we followed their directions down a path through a wood to a magnificent walled garden lined with peaches and quinces and pears and collapsing glasshouses. On one side through a door of flaking green paint was an oval pool with matching, opaque green water. It felt icy. We decided it was tempting, but not tempting enough.

'Look, Ants, I'm not blind. You can't just *fudge* it and hope I'm not going to notice.' It was lesson four, and we were having air speed problems again. Sean had put on his serious voice. His mood switched disconcertingly from one moment to the next. One minute we were bumbling past the Swaffham radio mast, to the south-west of the airfield, and he was larking about in the passenger seat, shouting 'Aaaaaargh, my bollocks. My bollocks are being zapped by the radio waves. Gemme outta here,' and he would make as if to clamber out of the plane. Then, without warning, he snapped to serious.

To tell the truth, my attention had wandered. Having forgotten, for a few minutes, to keep an eye on the air speed indicator, I had sneaked a look while Sean was in his flippant mode and noticed that it was hovering around the forbidden 40 knot mark. So I had surreptitiously eased the stick forward to lower the nose and raise my speed. Unfortunately this didn't seem to make any difference (I had yet to learn about time-lag in instrument readings). The needle continued to drop, so I had eased the nose down further, hoping Sean would not notice until the reading had recovered, only to receive a sharp reprimand a moment later for incorrect attitude* and losing height.

'Come on. You're meant to be flying *straight* and *level*. That doesn't mean *up* and *down*. This is important. I mean it. So get that silly smirk off your face and stop dicking around.' 'Dicking around' was one of Sean's favourite expressions, employed to cover a multitude of sins: lapses of concentration, imprecise flying, unconfident manipulation of the controls, lax or absent airmanship, starting the engine without chocking the wheels—the reason for the undignified, though not infrequent, sight of a microlight departing, pursued on foot by its unfortunate captain—or, most of all, the antics of other members of the club, usually those of its hapless proprietor Carter. 'Look at him, now,' Sean would say, craning his neck to watch as a distant speck pottered out of the club Portakabin to attend to a fibreglass pond and rockery he was installing by the corner of the hangar. 'A strange, strange man, that. Never stops dicking around, does Carter.'

How much I learned during those early lessons, it is hard to assess, as Sean's instructions, even at his most incensed, impinged little on my happy reverie. Feeling that there was no immediate pressure to prove myself, most of the time I just sailed about the sky in a contented, vacuous daze, savouring the warm air and the fine view. By lesson five, however, on Monday morning, hard evidence was beginning to accrue—or so it felt—of stupidity, incompetence, laziness, hamfisted-ness, mal co-ordination and inability to concentrate, and Sean was beginning to assert himself with some asperity.

I still approached the controls of the Thruster as someone used to the controls of a car. Their effects, however, were bizarely different. In a plane, increasing the throttle *did not* make you go faster, or not by much. It made you go up. Likewise, reducing the revs didn't slow you down;

---

* Not my own; the plane's: attitude, in flying, means something specific—as do many other words, like stall, leg, depression, bank. See Glossary.

it made you lose height. This (needless to say) wasn't quite true: if you held the plane level and 'turned up the wick', then she went a bit faster. Cruising speed was the minimum throttle setting at which it was possible to maintain height.

In flying, two things mattered: speed and height. These were the vital commodities. Speed was what kept you airborne, what kept the air flowing over the wing: drop below the magical 'stall speed' and the wing ceased to be a wing and simply became a piece of debris an uncomfortably long way above the ground. Height, I was learning, was fuel; by putting the nose down, it could always be turned into speed. If things went wrong, height gave you time to recover or to find somewhere to land. It was said to be one of the ironies of aviation that the two things that made your mother think it was dangerous—speed and height—were actually the only things that kept you safe. As an old pilots' saying ran, 'In flying, you need speed, you need height, or you need ideas.'

Then there was the air. Wind, I knew, from Geography at school and *The Microlight Pilot's Handbook*, was air moving from a high pressure area to a lower pressure area. The flyer, of course, was part of the wind (which is why, in a balloon, all is completely still: you are part of the breeze). But, used to looking at the speedometer of a car and getting an accurate reading, it was bemusing to find in a plane that while the air speed might be a steady 55 knots, we might be moving across the ground at 20 knots, or 80 knots. The point being that the moment you were airborne you ceased to be part of the landscape and became part of the air blowing across it.

Turning was another strange one. Again, in a car, you turned the steering wheel when you wanted to go left, then turned it back again to straighten up or go to the right. Always, in the back of your mind, you knew roughly where the wheels were pointing and that they were pointing in the direction you were going. In flying it was not like that at all. Once you had initiated, say, a left turn, by giving it some left stick (plus some left rudder, of course), you did not then hold the stick there, as you would a car steering wheel, until you wanted to straighten up again or go in a new direction. No, having started the plane turning, you then returned the stick to the centre, and the plane *kept turning*. To cancel the turn you applied an equal blat of *opposite stick*. I relate these facts simply and clearly here, as if that is how they presented themselves to me. But whether because Sean never explained it properly, or failed to emphasise it enough, or because my mind was simply overloaded trying to cope with all the other things I was supposed to be thinking about, they did not become clear for a very long time. And until I did understand them, I continued timorously to dab the stick this way then that, holding it in place like a steering wheel as the turn steepened, not having the least comprehension of the consequences of my actions.

Barsham was plainly a forgotten backwater of the RAF, and we had the place pretty much to ourselves. The grid of Nissen huts with their rounded roofs of moulding and mossy asbestos or rusting corrugated iron, Sean told us, provided accommodation for RAF technical staff and training facilities (for such indispensable tasks, I later learnt, as Maintenance Schedule Writing and Spares Forecasting). Despite the fibreglass Spitfire on its plinth at the entrance, there was almost no RAF flying. For all but the last couple of weeks of July, when overspill student pilots from the University Air Squadrons came over from Cranfield to train in the quiet Norfolk skies, the old brick control tower remained locked and empty. The rest of the year the huge expanse of grass (Barsham was reputedly the largest grass airfield in Europe) was shared between the local glider club, the 'Norwich and Eastern' and the fat hares which hid amongst the clumps of clover and daisies.

The glider club operated mainly at weekends, when the field was divided in half by white plastic markers and a big yellow winch on a lorry hauled gliders into the air on one side of the airfield. Meanwhile the aero club, a very sleepy operation, used the other half sporadically running a motley pair of tatty blue-and-white Cessnas. There were a couple of school instructors, recognisable by their white shirts with epaulettes and dark blue trousers, and there was Carter. I never did learn whether Carter was his Christian name or surname. He was fat, with a kind face, and had a fat son called Keith who looked absurdly like him and occasionally manned the radio. Sean paid them no respect. The occasional roar of one of their engines, usually merely to taxi a plane from one position to another, represented the principal excitement of the day. Apart from this the only sounds to break the stillness were the crunch and rumble of the hangar doors morning and evening, the hiss and static of the radio in the Portakabin on the occasions that it was switched on, and the scream of the microlighters' two-strokes. When this faded, as it did soon after take-off, there was just the skylarks, the bells of the round-towered church on the north of the airfield and the occasional distant sound of hammering.

I had never taken a holiday like this. The combination of the weather, the rustic setting, a scheduled activity to give the day some (but not too much) structure, and enough country air and exertion (heaving ten-ton hangar doors, full jerry cans and the Thruster) to stoke ravenous appetites made it seem a world away from advertising, deadlines and the bars and traffic of Wardour Street.

Salsingham, too, had a curiously soul-soothing quality; partly, no doubt, because the place was so extensive. Apart from the two wings (both larger than most large detatched houses), there were stables and kennels, and workshops and barns, and the park with its overgrown lake and boathouse. There was a sleepy somnambulance about the place, as if, when the clock in the pediment on the west wing stopped (at three minutes to two), all influence from the outside world had ceased at the same moment. The flat, right at the top of the house, was spartan but ideal. There was a small kitchen in one of the corner towers, a couple of bedrooms and a sitting room with a view over the lake, behind which the sun set as the ducks came in.

We saw little of the Watsons. Mrs Watson communicated with us mainly by note—irritated ones ticking us off (for bad parking or leaving doors open) alternating with invitations to supper. Occasionally we would encounter Mr Watson, in many ways a Caractacus Potts figure, driving his disintegrating orange Daihatsu, with its flapping rear doors, or carrying a spanner and a roll of electric cable. After helping to round up some escaped cattle, moving some heavy furniture, treating the obstinately opaque green waters of the pool, transferring a car battery and erecting an electric fence, we learnt to dive for cover at his approach. Life at Salsingham, it became clear, was one long, losing battle against an incoming tide of accumulating tasks. Mr Watson had a bumbling, absent-minded manner. He never showed the slightest recognition when he came across us and he never used our names, but as long as he regarded us as a source of assistance, rather than trespassers, I supposed it must be all right.

Now that I was familiar with the basic controls, all lessons took the same form: circuits, circuits and more circuits. The circuit, the core element of instruction in all flying, is an imaginary, rectangular cube of air over an airfield, about 1,000 feet high, and a quarter of a mile or more in its other dimensions, the orientation of which varies daily, sometimes even hourly, to allow for taking off—as nearly as possible—into wind. The direction (left-hand or right-hand) tends to be dictated by local topography. At Barsham it depended on the activities, or not, of the glider club, and we always had to avoid the village, the RAF buildings, two houses to the north of the airfield containing litigious locals and, for safety's sake, low approaches over the gravel pit on the north-east side in case of an untimely engine failure.

Circuits allowed relentless practising of all the essential aspects of control of the aircraft: taxiing, take-off, climbing, levelling off, turning, cruising, following a heading, plotting the approach to land, descending and landing. If it sounds busy, it was: indeed, there seemed to be such an absurd amount to think about that I was always neglecting something. 'Glance at the instruments,' Sean would say. 'Don't *gaze* at them,' as I became transfixed by, say, the needle of the altimeter, or the rev counter, or the air speed indicator, trying to get it to stay in exactly the right position. A helicopter pilot once told me that the kind of person who made a good flyer was someone who, while driving, could wash/wipe the windscreen, re-tune the radio and overtake simultaneously, without letting this in any way interrupt his conversation. I now saw what he meant. In simple 'straight and level' flight I had, simultaneously, to:

- Keep the nose level so I wasn't losing or gaining height.
- Stick to within 4-5° of a given compass heading.
- Maintain a gentle but continuous pressure on the left rudder pedal to counter the torque of the propeller and the effect of the slipstream it put over the right wing on to the fin, so that the ball remained central in the slip indicator.
- Keep a roving eye on the engine temperature, rev counter, altimeter, and air speed gauges—not to mention regular checks of the fuel level.
- Look out, continuously, for birds and other aircraft, and—most importantly—a suitable field for landing in case of engine failure.

This before I contemplated a manoeuvre. Fortunately, we did not have a radio, so I was spared having to keep the 'tower' informed of my actions in the dense and impenetrable jargon of radio-telephony.

The result was that it was never until the end of each lesson that I seemed to get the hang of it, only to find that the hour had pinged by and time was up.

Around the Tuesday a change came over Richard. It was just after he had taken his Air Law exam. Richard, like Lester, had a considerable head start on Dan and me. Having only recently acquired his Private Pilot's Licence in Africa, the Civil Aviation Authority had declared that to be fully 'legal' he need only complete a cross-country flight in a Cessna to validate this licence, and then be 'checked out' in the Thruster. The one thing he had to do first, however, was sit and pass his UK Air Law exam, something I, too, had to do before I could go solo.

Accordingly, we had both been desultorily cramming the air law statutes detailed in *CAP 85: A Guide to Aviation Law, Flight Rules and Procedures for Applicants for the Private Pilot's Licence. CAP 85* was not a racy read. In fact, in both its tone and content it reminded me unpleasantly of my short and lacklustre legal career. It was full of sentences like 'Pilots flying beneath TCA or SRA should use the QNH of an aerodrome situated beneath that area when flying below transition altitude.' However, if we were to get our licences, then learn *CAP 85* we must. So, at spare moments, we had taken to quizzing each other on such essential questions for the single-engined, non-radio daylight pilot as:

What sign does an aircraft marshaller make to indicate to you to open up your starboard engine?

What Secondary Surveillance Radar code on mode 'C' should be used by an aircraft in the event of two-way radio failure?

In level cruise, at the same altitude, at night, what does an anti-collision light together with a green and a white navigation light closing on you on a steady relative bearing of 330° indicate?

Committing the statutes to memory temporarily levelled our relative flying experience, though inevitably Richard was well ahead. The rules of aviation in the UK were not dissimilar to those in Africa and by Monday evening he had felt ready to sit the paper in Sean's office. Naturally, when I saw him afterwards, I asked how it had gone.

'How did what go?'

'You know—the exam. Air Law.'

'Oh that? Messed up a couple of questions.'

'Bad luck. Do you have to do it again?'

'No. You only have to get 70 per cent to pass.'

'You got more than 70 per cent? What did you get?'

'98 per cent. Stupid mistakes too.'

Gone was the shared 'novices-at-this-absurd-activity-together' attitude of before. Nor, over the rest of the evening and the following day, did it return. Outwardly, he was the same as ever, good-humoured, friendly, affable. Only when it came to matters of aviation was his tone altered. It had acquired a didactic note. Where previously he had responded to a casually inane remark about the Thruster being like a tennis ball to land with a sympathetic nod, a murmur of agreement and, perhaps, a close shave that he had had that morning, now he responded seriously, taking the opportunity to dispense some advice that might help me deal with my difficulty. It wasn't that I minded, or that I didn't think it was justified—I was happy to receive all the help I could. But we were no longer equals and, for the first time, I felt the chilly draught of my inexperience and the catching up that had to be done.

Having passed the exam, Tuesday afternoon was scheduled for Richard's qualifying cross-country flight in one of the club Cessnas. He had been checked out in the morning by one of the club instructors, and by the time we went to lunch his superiority had reached a peak. The Thruster and microlighting generally now sounded a very poor relation indeed alongside the 'necessarily more rigorous' disciplines of 'general aviation'. As, after lunch, he prepared his route, drawing lines, measuring angles, confidently turning the dial of his flight calculator as he filled out his flight plan, his involved and excluding air of competence made me feel my inferiority keenly.

'Good luck,' I said, as I went off for my lesson.

'See you later, Antony.'

It was about five o'clock, after an extended lesson with Sean, that I next saw Richard. As I entered the clubhouse, there was the sound of raised voices. 'What the fuck did you think you were doing?' one shouted angrily. 'Think how this makes the club look?' 'Leave it,' said another. 'This is for the CAA.' Three figures with epaulettes on their shoulders were taking it in turns to berate an unhappy-looking fourth person—Richard.

Piecing together what happened afterwards, it seemed that Richard had filed his flight plan and checked out for departure in accordance with standard procedures. Taking off, he struck north-west. Unfortunately, it seemed that he had omitted to check the club notice-board for information about local events, or, once airborne, to change his radio from the Barsham local frequency to the area frequency, Norwich Control or RAF Marham. Oblivious, he had entered the Marham Military Air Traffic Zone panhandle, crossing the approach to the main runway as a pair of Tornadoes were on final approach to land. The RAF, anxious to know who was trespassing in their air space without contacting them at such a time, put out calls on both their own frequency and the Norwich frequency. They were unable to raise Richard, who was by this time circling overhead at Sandringham, an opportunity, he told me, that seemed too good to miss—but unaware that, with the flag indicating royalty in residence, this was prohibited, purple air space. Tiring of this, and still oblivious to the now considerable ground-efforts to contact him, Richard continued round the coast towards Great Yarmouth.

Further trauma was to follow as he crossed the approach to the main runway of Norwich International Airport. Had he called, as he was supposed to, to check Temporary Restricted Airspace, he would have been aware of the Red Arrows coming over that afternoon. As it was, he was overhead as the famous jets, in close formation, were arriving at 1,000 feet across the North Sea. When their on-board radar indicated conflicting traffic, they aborted their approach, but, again, went unnoticed by Richard. Attempts to contact the unidentified Cessna from the ground now became something of an aviation priority in East Anglia, as Norwich air traffic control worked through all the likely frequencies without success. The Cessna's markings were finally reported visually by another plane to Norwich. They identified the plane as belonging to the Norwich and East of England Aero Club, whom they contacted by phone.

Richard, meanwhile—well-pleased with how easily his cross-country was passing off—now turned west for his homeward leg. Unfortunately he opted to do so at 1,200 feet in the busy Cromer Helicopter Corridor to North Denes heliport, prohibited space for fixed-wing traffic. Breezing into the circuit overhead at Barsham Green, perhaps used to non-radio approaches in the Thruster, he neglected to call up the tower. As he could see no other planes in the circuit and the windsock indicated little or no wind, he decided to land as he pleased, forgetting to check the designated direction of take-off and landing displayed in the ground signals area in front of the clubhouse. Hurtling in downwind on the side of the airfield reserved exclusively for the gliding club, in front of a glider on the point of launch, he taxied briskly over to the apron, pulled up and got ready to report a successful flight. It was only then that he discovered that the effect of his actions, broadly speaking, had been like kicking an ants' nest.

Richard's confidence was dented by this incident, but dented less than I might have imagined. As I would discover with flying faux pas, so long as nothing and no one has got hurt, the fuss quickly dies down. By Wednesday lunchtime the pursed lips, shaking heads and mutterings of the club instructors had turned to wisecracks. Richard was told that, so long as he agreed to re-sit his radio-telephony exam, he would not be reported to the CAA and he might consider the matter closed. I received the incident with mixed feelings. On the one hand, it served Richard right; he had only got what he deserved. There was the strangely reassuring comfort of seeing a good friend in trouble, and the overall result was a return to the happy status quo of 'us versus aviation'. On the other hand, if Richard, born administrator and high priest of procedures, could make this kind of cock-up, what hope was there for me?

My concerns, however, had no chance to get any further, as, later on Wednesday, there came a far more dramatic setback: one which brought all our flying to an abrupt halt.

It was about quarter to seven, on another perfect, cloudless summer evening. Richard, now officially checked out to fly the Thruster solo, had gone off on a local flight. Sean was in the hangar briefing a pupil. I was sprawled on the grass outside with a ring binder of loose-leaf pages I had come across in Sean's office entitled *Thrsuter* (sic) *Pilot's and Operator's Handbook*. It was an interesting document. The down-stroke of the 'A' of the 'Thruster Air Services' company logo zoomed with a swoop, a steep climb and a flourish round and through the other words in a graphic representation of a vapour trail, culminating in what was equally unmistakably the silhouette of a jet fighter. It seemed an ambitious image for a company selling a flying machine which had, screwed to the centre of its instrument panel, a plate stating 'ALL AEROBATIC MANOEUVRES STRICTLY FORBIDDEN'. A machine, moreover, which was, even in a brisk tailwind, unlikely to exceed a ground speed of 70 knots.

Anyway, the writing style was breezy, talking, as it did, of a return to the golden age of aviation, where pilots must rediscover the instincts of the seat of their pants rather than relying on fancy instruments. I could almost hear the Australian accent (the Thruster was an Australian design; used, someone had said, to shoot dingos and, fitted with klaxons, to herd sheep): 'Stalls: this little baby has had many a pilot lying six foot under …' when my reveries were interrupted by a flexwing speeding up to the hangar entrance. Leaving the engine still running, the passenger jumped out and rushed into the hangar yelling for Sean.

Something was clearly up. A strict rule of the club was never to have engines running near the open hangar door as it could whip up grit and sand which might damage the machines inside. I could not hear what was said, above the engine. But I saw Sean stiffen, drop what he was doing immediately, and, without bothering to put on his ozee suit or gloves, jump aboard the trike, take the controls from the pilot, and take off from where they were. They were airborne before they had even left the tarmac apron for the grass of the airfield.

I got up and walked over to the figure left behind. 'What's up?'

'There's a Thruster down in a cornfield. Looked like the one we'd seen round here.'

The sentence took a moment to sink in, as my mind searched furiously for ways to explain, parry, reject or somehow defuse the information it contained. A fearsome, disorientating dread washed over me, accompanied by a slightly sick nausea. This was joined, it must be said, by a pulse of pure excitement, stabbing through the gentle glow of the evening.

It *had* to be Richard.

There were no other Thrusters. Not round here, anyway. In any case, the man had said as much. '*Looked like the one we'd seen round here.*'

I stared, slightly deranged, at the hangar in the yellow evening sunlight, the dangling windsock, the club Cessnas, the warm green of the landing field, all so friendly and charming a moment before. Now, I noticed them again. They looked different, dangerous, threatening … as if they were the final image of flying I was to take away with me as my memory singled out this moment for saving and filing with a burnt-in time code. Not because it was contented like the one before, but because this was when I heard that Richard had been killed.

Had he? That was the question. Was his body, even at that moment, slumped in the smashed wreckage of the Thruster?

'Was … was the pilot okay?'

'Couldn't see. Looked as if the machine had nosed over.'

This wasn't part of the plan. This wasn't supposed to happen.

Thoughts flooded through my head. What could have happened? Had the Thruster broken up in mid-air? Christ, how horrifying was that? I had been in it only an hour before: it might have been me. Had everyone been right after all? Were these machines just death traps?

Why had we trusted them? Were we out of our minds? Placing our lives in the hands of a company who could not even spell their name right on the cover of the handbook?

And, round and round, again and again: Richard. Could he really be dead? No more Richard. What would I do without him? Who would be my best mate? What about our flying plans? What about our holiday? Who would I share the flat with? What would I say to his parents?

Of course, if he really *were* dead … it did give our hobby quite an exotic, *boulevardier* ring … and it certainly highlighted the risks we were facing —and consequently our extraordinary courage to have taken up such an activity—not to mention providing an eminently good reason to give up … *tchaaargh* … how could I think such things? About Richard … my *best* mate. At a time when he *may be dead*.

DEAD.

I felt ashamed I had pinched his bacon at breakfast without telling him. What a childish and odious thing to have done. The maddening impotence of my situation took hold. All I could do was hang about, waiting for further information. If he *weren't* dead, what shape was he likely to be in? What was the most likely injury from a flying accident? Spine presumably. Jesus. And the ambulance had not even been *called* yet. There wasn't even anyone I could talk to. I did not know what to do. I certainly couldn't continue reading the Thruster Handbook. It no longer seemed an amusing example of the quirky charms of amateurism. It had become a chilling testament to the idiocy of not doing things properly.

For fifteen minutes I paced about in an agony of lonely imaginings, until one of the white-shirted Cessna instructors came out of the Portakabin. I had seen him around but had never spoken to him before. 'You Tony?' His face and voice were kind and reassuring. 'Sean's been on the radio. It's OK. Your mate's had an accident but he's fine.' He paused, then gave a sniff. 'Doesn't have much luck, does he?'

It would be wrong to say that the news of Richard's survival came as a blow. But it would be equally wrong to say that it was not in some way anti-climactic. Perhaps preparing myself for the worst, as a defence mechanism, I had decided that Richard was definitely dead, or—at the very least—badly injured. Now, as I sat down on the ground again, the planes, the hangar, the summer evening all came up for emotional re-evaluation in the light of this information update. Relief flooded over me, and I felt exhausted. But, now that his survival was not in doubt, I also felt annoyed at having been put through the trauma. Now that the drama was over, all that remained was tedious information gathering and—no doubt—clearing up. There was a sense of let-down; and, with it, of irritation. Richard was okay, I told myself. That was the main thing. He was fine. But our plane? Was *that* fine? A flood of less charitable thoughts entered my head. Was the machine damaged? If so, how badly? Did it mean we would miss any flying tomorrow? At that moment, Sean arrived back.

'Ugh!' he groaned, shaking his head mournfully. 'Why did he have to choose standing corn? There are lovely fields all round here, and he chose one of standing corn. Phwah! She was running lovely as well. Come on.' He slung a battered metal tool box into the back of his van. 'I dunno. You boys.'

It took some time to locate Richard from the deep lanes running between high hedges that divided the fields to the south-east of Barsham Green village. At length Sean spotted a yellow combine through the hedge which he remembered was working nearby and we parked in a gateway.

When Sean had flown over, Richard had been standing beside the plane, waving. It had been impossible to see how much damage had been done to the plane. Now I could just see the tail of the stricken Thruster sticking up over the standing corn, with Richard, expressionless, alongside. Sean grabbed his tool box and I followed his clanking progress round the edge of the field, brushing flies and insects from my face and arms.

The Thruster was a sorry sight. Her propeller was broken, splintered at both ends. Several spars were bent. The pod was torn and gashed on one side. Dust, straw and heads of corn littered the cockpit. With the arrival of the combine from the adjoining field—the farmer obligingly cut a swathe up to and around the Thruster—clouds more dust and chaff were blown into every nook they had not already reached. 'She lost all power,' began Richard. 'I went as far as I could but I couldn't maintain height.'

'They're so reliable, these engines. So reliable,' said Sean, shaking his head and making what point I'm not sure as he set to with a spanner. 'Are you sure you weren't hearing things?'

I do not know whether I was expecting some kind of apology or, at least, some word of regret from Richard. If I was, I didn't get it.

'So it didn't exactly fail,' I said, realizing, as I said it, that it was perhaps not the most helpful comment to have made. Irritated by Richard's bland lack of remorse or—I suppose—injury, I wanted to prompt some reaction out of him. He said nothing. 'Well, so long as you're all right. That's the main thing,' I said, viciously.

It was nine thirty and getting dark before we dropped our sad freight—de-rigged, on the farmer's trailer—back at the hangar. She looked very forlorn as, in the darkening gloom, we laid the wings on the dusty cement of the hangar floor, then manhandled the pod and fuselage into a corner. I wanted Sean to reassure me that the Thruster could be mended tomorrow and we could be flying again by tomorrow afternoon, that I could still get my licence by the end of next week. He saw my face. 'Look, this is flying. It happens. At least no one got hurt.'

As Richard and I drove home neither of us spoke. Partly it was tiredness. But there was an unresolved heaviness between us, something more than tiredness and disappointment. Nor was anything said next morning, when we watched Sean, notebook in hand, pick carefully over the Thruster to order up the necessary parts. In fact, neither of us ever mentioned the incident again.

We were now at a loose end. We had booked two weeks holiday and it was only Thursday of the first week. It was going to take a couple of days at least for the replacement parts to arrive, a couple more after that for Sean to find time to fit them (this was his busiest time of year). I was bitterly disappointed. We debated reading by the pool at Salsingham. But on Friday morning we were discovered by Mr Watson and, after assisting him to clear a land drain, it became clear that lasting peace was not to be found there.

Over the next few days we drove up to the north Norfolk coast near Holkham, drank in pubs and walked on the beach. We joined the queues of cars that threaded their way around the Broads. We visited Houghton Hall. We went to see films in Norwich. It was fine; if only it was what we had wanted to be doing. As if to taunt us, the heat wave continued: each morning dawned insolently cloudless, windless and perfect. By the following Tuesday night, Sean had the Thruster back in one piece. The pod was still cracked like an eggshell in two places, with splints of glass fibre poking out of the tear. Straw and stray seeds of corn were still lodged in corners and crevices. The wings and tail had picked up a number of minor scuffs and gashes and streaks of oil and grime in transit.

We had four days of holiday left, but by then the weather had turned. The sky was overcast and the wind had got up. It was too blustery, Sean said, for novice instruction. I fitted in two more lessons, mainly at my insistence, but I seemed to have forgotten everything. With just eight hours recorded in my log book, I returned to London.

Despite the disappointment of the holiday, the sun seemed to have come back out on life. Advertising was booming. Creative departments, which had an evocative (pre-digital) aroma of Magic Markers, Spraymount and ArtClean were exciting places to work. My days alternated pleasantly between flirting with three minxy secretaries, sitting in our Chinatown office with my feet on the desk trying to shoehorn celebrities I wished to meet into scripts, and trying to swing location shoots. I spent happy periods pottering in Soho and got out of the office on periodic factory visits or to one of the sound studios, editing suites or post-production facilities sprinkled through the basements of Soho. When times were quiet, I went to matinée cinema performances in Leicester Square. Voice-over recordings gave me the chance to patronise famous actors like John Hurt and Ian Holm ('Bit more emphasis on the 'U' please, John. Equip-*U*-Office Equipment. *That's it*, John, you've got it').

We now automatically headed for Norfolk every weekend unless there was an overpowering reason not to. For some reason, the image from *Out of Africa* where Meryl Streep reaches back for Robert Redford's hand in the flying scene above the clouds had lodged in my head. Already, I had visions of the Thruster carrying myself and a young model or actress that I might shortly meet on a shoot or at a casting session, plus a bottle or two of champagne and, perhaps, a few blinis, to a quiet area of Holkham beach. A slightly different version found us amongst the cow parsley of a shaded but sun-dappled corner of some unknowing farmer's field, wrestling for the last morsel of a ripe peach as the juice ran down our chins. All that lay between me and these promising daydreams was the minimum twenty-five hours of flying time (with instructor or supervised solo), my General Flight Test, and a few straightforward multiple-choice ground exams. I imagine some similar idea was in Richard's head.

Accordingly, we fell into a more-or-less standard routine. On Friday night we would drive up to Salsingham, ready for me to take a lesson with Sean the next morning. In the afternoon I would switch to the passenger seat, and Richard, now fully legal, and I would head off together on a cross-country flight. On Sunday the process would be repeated, after which, tired but fulfilled, we would head back to London. This was the idea anyway but the weather did not return to the clement skies of our summer holiday, and with Sean a lot busier at weekends it was hard to determine how instructive these weekends were. With less time to become immersed in the flying, I often arrived for my lesson still distracted by the week's unsolved advertising problems and unmet deadlines. The period between putting away the Thruster on Sunday evening, and getting back into the cockpit (if all went well) the following Saturday morning, seemed like a lifetime.

By the end of August I could take off and fly straight and level pretty competently (as, Richard pointed out, anyone could). I could feel if the nose was too high or too low. I could do gentle and medium turns, both climbing and descending. And I could do full power steep turns sufficiently accurately that the ball of the slip indicator remained roughly central in its window, and I felt the blast of air of my own wake as I completed the turn (Sean's more rough and ready definition of a perfect turn). Descending, I didn't need to check the air speed indicator to know when I was going between 50-55 knots: I could feel by the back pressure on the stick.

However, when it came to landing, everything went to pieces.

I just could not get it right. Some people, I suppose, simply have a better sense of space and distance than others. I found the whole exercise of gauging an even, controlled descent from an altitude of around 1,000 feet down to a few feet off the ground at a specified spot in the landscape, by co-ordinated adjustment of throttle, ailerons, elevators and rudder, virtually impossible. Even if I did manage it, once I was down to near ground level, getting the Thruster smoothly onto the turf was another matter altogether. All might be well down to fifteen or ten feet from the ground. Sean would say something encouraging like 'Nice. Very nice. That's a perfect approach. This is going to be good, I can feel it.' Then, when we were a foot or two from the ground, it would all go wrong. I would flare out (the action of rounding from a descending attitude to a level one just above the surface of the runway) too early, stall too high above the ground, crash down and bounce. I would flare out too late, slam into the ground, and bounce. Even if I flared out just right, and got the wheels onto the ground, she just would not stay there. With a mind of her own she would leap into the air again in a series of terrific balloons and kangaroo-like bounces. Each time Sean would have to take over and bring her back under control. Lesson after lesson went by doing nothing but landings, landings and landings.

At one stage I thought I had it, and so did Sean. 'One more like that,' he would say, 'and you can go solo.' Then I would mess up the next one. It became a familiar routine. Each lesson he would say, 'Right. We'll get you solo this time Ants,' and the end of the lesson would come and the matter wouldn't be mentioned again. At other times he would say, doubtfully, 'I don't know, Ants, maybe I should send you solo. It might be the best way.'

It began to depress me. My knowledge—buttressed by Sean's repeated assurances—that the Thruster was, even by tail-dragger standards, an exceptionally difficult plane to land, had made it an exciting challenge to start with. But any reassurance that had conferred had long since begun to ring hollow. The others, including Dan, had all gone solo ages ago.

I constructed reasons and explanations for myself. Richard had already done his licence. So had Mr Watson. Dan, living in Norfolk, had access to the plane in good weather on a regular basis, while I had to take my chances at weekends: in any one hour lesson I got, at the most (by the time I had completed each circuit), only eight attempts at landing. But the fact remained that I had now done eleven hours of flying—twenty-five if you included my hours in Africa—and I still hadn't gone solo. It had become an issue. In every account of learning to fly that I had read, the subject had gone solo in a quarter of the time. Roald Dahl in *Going Solo* had done it in seven hours forty minutes. Cecil Lewis in *Sagittarius Rising* had soloed his Maurice Farman Longhorn after an hour and twenty minutes. *An hour and twenty minutes.* I even recalled that James Herriot had learnt to fly and when I looked up *Vet in a Spin* I discovered *he* had done it in nine hours. In the Battle of Britain seventeen-year-olds—*seventeen*-year-olds—were flying Spitfires—*Spitfires*—after the time I had been flying. I began to feel resentful and bitter. Why did the plane have to be stuck in Norfolk? Why was I saddled with such a lousy instructor? Why was I pouring money into this pointless activity?

I had almost accepted that landing aeroplanes was one of those talents, like rolling hose-pipes or folding maps, that either you had or hadn't when, one showery Saturday morning on the last day of August, I did three passable landings in succession—and Sean told me to take her up alone. 'Remember, with only one, she'll climb much faster,' he said. I felt far from confident.

Sean was right. Without a passenger aboard I seemed to be in the air almost before the throttle was fully open. She leapt off the ground, and once airborne *seemed* much lighter too, bouncing around a lot more. I was at 800 feet, the height at which I normally executed a gentle climbing turn into the crosswind leg, before I was two thirds of the way down the runway. It felt hideously lonely looking to my right and seeing, where Sean should have been, just an empty seat, with the safety harness buckled across it. By the time I reached the point where I normally turned crosswind I was already at 1,200 feet and hurriedly realised that I should be levelling off. I reduced the power to the usual 5,700 rpm, but the Thruster continued to climb furiously—1,250, 1,300, 1,400 feet. I had to reduce the power to 5,000 rpm before the altimeter needle finally held steady. As I repeated Sean's rule to myself ('Attitude, Power, Trim'), for the first time I remembered the trimmer; I had forgotten to set it at all. Already it was time to turn onto the downwind leg. And—what was I thinking of?—I was almost halfway round the circuit and I hadn't given a thought to what would happen if the engine failed. I should have been scouring the ground for suitable fields. And this is what I was busy doing when, quite suddenly, I was engulfed in cloud.

I didn't see it coming. It must have been some low stuff, sweeping across on the breeze, as it had been all morning. I must have climbed into its path by levelling off so high.

Had I kept my head I might have guessed that, if I only lost a little height or maintained my heading for a few moments, I must soon get clear. But I was in no mood for keeping my head: this was my first solo. Suddenly engulfed in a dense, impenetrable white-out, my stripped, disorientated senses had not a clue what to do. Utterly blind, I could not think where I was supposed to look, or concentrate on anything. I scanned the instruments desperately for clues. But my mind refused to tell me what information was relevant and what was not. Which dial could help? What information mattered? The readings began to leap out at me as my eyes flicked frantically from one to another. Not to stall, that was the main thing; so I opened the throttle and lowered the nose.

After a few seconds more, the only thing that became sharply clear was that I was going to crash—in my mind the cloud extended infinitely, in all directions—so I braced myself for the impact. My only other clear sensation was that I was about to fall out of the left-hand side of the cockpit: I could actually feel my weight against the strap of the harness. To level the plane, I applied hard right stick. Knowing I should accompany this with some right rudder, for a moment I became transfixed by trying to centre the ball in the slip indicator. I steeled myself for the inevitable.

Then, as suddenly as it arrived, the cloud was gone. I was spiralling in a near vertical right-hand turn over the centre of what should have been my final approach. There was the airfield directly ahead. My spell of blind flying must have lasted a matter of thirty or forty seconds at the most.

I levelled the wings, reduced the power and got her down. It was not great. I bounced a couple of times. But I got her down. Panting, and soaked with sweat, the relief was overwhelming. I had done it. It had been close, but I had gone solo and brought the aircraft and myself back in one piece. The cloud which had contributed so much grief had disappeared as fast as it had come, and already, as I started to taxi back to the hangar, the sun was shining. Everything seemed so normal and ordinary and safe now I was back on the ground. There was Sean standing by the hangar chatting to someone; it didn't look as if he had even noticed my drama. There was a Cessna, starting its engine. The terror in the clouds of just a few minutes before seemed from another world. It felt ridiculous and absurd to feel so shaken. 'There you are, Ants, wasn't so bad was it?' said Sean.

'No problem,' I said.

I could not manage a smile.

The flight entry in my log book for 31 August at 11.40 was the first where, in the 'Captain' column, the word 'SELF' appeared, instead of Sean's name. The flight lasted ten minutes. In the 'Remarks' column, Sean wrote in his characteristic handwriting, '17a', which consultation of the necessary manuals would reveal as 'solo flight'. It ought to have been a red-letter day, the most significant of any pilot's training, and it was, in a way. I had done it, it was true. I was equal with the others again. On the other hand, it had not been quite the neat, clean, tidy line between the uncertainty of the past and the promise of the future that I might have hoped. I had winged it, and I knew it.

Sean suggested that I have lunch, then afterwards go out and do an hour or two of circuits and bumps to consolidate the good work. But by three o'clock the showery weather had set in, the wind was gusty, and, almost relieved, I had to call it a day.

The next day, the first of September, was fine and clear. As I took off to do some circuits, it felt almost normal to be alone in the Thruster. I did two circuits; the landings went all right, and I began to relax. But on my third circuit, as I came in to land, the machine went into a series of the old, kangaroo bounds. They were hard ones, too, each one sending her bucking and vaulting back into the air, higher and higher. Uncertain what to do, I jabbed the stick this way, then that, in an effort to regain control. To no avail. The bounces seemed to get bigger and more and more uneven, as the Thruster crashed heavily down first on one wheel, then the other. One descent was so dramatic that I thought she might go right over onto her nose. I cut the engine completely, and finally she came to rest.

It had been close, there was no question of that: I had been lucky to get away with it. I got out, started the engine and made to taxi back to the hangar. However, I found that I had to rev the engine nearly to full throttle to get her to move at all. The controls, too, had become stiff and awkward. She would not taxi in a straight line: only in an ungainly crabbing motion to the right. Distraught and furious with self-hatred, engine screaming to overcome the resistance, I finally got her to the hangar where I sheepishly confessed to my 'hard' landing. Sean cast an expert eye over her, ducking his head over and under the pod. He narrowed his eyes. He wagged the stick backwards and forwards. He chewed his bottom lip. Then he made his pronouncement.

'A write-off,' he said. 'If not, a complete rebuild.'

He was right. To my innocent eye the plane might hardly have looked damaged, but closer inspection revealed the awful truth. Almost every spar and strut and joining plate was very slightly wrenched out of true, or bore the tiny tell-tale stretch marks, whitening or slight distortion that indicated buckling, twisting, fatigue or strain. Several people in the clubhouse, it transpired, had enjoyed a ring-side view of my performance, and with grinding teeth I contemplated what they must have said to each other. 'Thought you were going to go over there for a moment,' said one with a smile. 'Didn't really hold off enough, did you?' said another. I didn't know what he meant, but the cautious confidence which had followed my solo flight of the day before, evaporated. I felt humiliated and ashamed. The thought of confessing to the Watsons made me squirm. It was hardly as if there were mitigating cirumstances: it was a perfect, still, summer's day, in a nearly new machine, performing faultlessly on the largest grass airfield in Europe. And I had written off the plane. What a pilot.

For me personally, of course, the implications were severer still. I might have gone solo, but what was the gain? With flying suspended for the foreseeable future, the incontrovertible evidence remained: I still could not land.

The Cows Just Got Smaller

New Rules of the Air 1998

Rule 1: If it is not too windy, it will be too wet to fly today.

Rule 2: If it is not too windy or too wet, it will be too unstable to fly today.

Rule 3: If it is not too windy, too wet or too unstable, it will be too cold to fly today.

Rule 4: If it is not too windy, too wet, too unstable or too cold, the visibility will be too low to fly today.

Rule 5: If it is not too windy, too wet, too unstable, too cold or too murky to fly today, the aircraft will be unserviceable.

Rule 6: If it is calm, dry, stable, warm and clear today, and the aircraft is serviceable, you will have unbreakable commitments elsewhere.

Professor B. J. Brinkworth, *Microlight Flying*, November 1998

For weeks the mere thought of flying made me miserable and depressed. Mr Watson's stupefied, 'What? Not *again!*' when I had informed him that the Thruster would be out of action 'for a short time', still rang witheringly in my ears. The first invoices of what Sean promised would be a considerable repair bill had already come in, and I was having seriously to entertain the possibility that landing the machine was altogether beyond me (I wasn't sure how keen I was to get back into the cockpit, anyway). In fact, if it had been possible to back out of the whole project at that point, pay off the Watsons, and bail out,

I might have done so. Unfortunately, it wasn't.

There had already been far too much easy talk about our aerial exploits, both to the girls at work and amongst my friends. The Watsons—especially Mr Watson—Salsingham, Sean, Carter, the Thruster, the 'Norwich and Eastern'—all were rich seams to mine in banter and chat, and mined they had been, to capacity. The London flat, *The Rachel Papers*-fashion, had become 'propped' with flying paraphernalia: photographs of us and the Thruster taken on our July holiday, Barsham Green, Salsingham, the Thruster in the cornfield. One of our big 1:500,000 aviation charts of the south of England decorated the kitchen wall, and very impressive it looked, with all its control zones and airways (especially around Heathrow and Gatwick). Books with titles like *Advanced Aerobatics*, *Bush Pilot*, *Mountain Flying* and *Weather for Pilots* had found their way onto the table in the living room, along with one of our rulers graduated in nautical miles. A flight calculator sat on the stereo. In the bathroom, *Flightline* had joined the rumpled soaked-and-dried-out copies of *The Face* and Richard's copies of the *Spectator*.

The two awkward incidents that neither of us mentioned to each other, we found ways of glossing over to friends. Richard's accident was a typical example of the kind of life-threatening situation that these machines routinely placed one in; the tacit implication being that only quick reflexes and presence of mind had saved him. Our present lack of an aircraft—with its absence of a single mitigating circumstance— merely served to underline what dogs to handle they were, even under the very best flying conditions.

And it worked. Already we had acquired a gratifying whiff of romantic daring and amateur enterprise, which we made no attempt to play down. Microlighting was still an eccentric novelty sport. We had become known as 'the aviators'. People talked about us. I was too far down the runway—so to speak—to pull out. I was 'committed'. Besides, from a purely personal angle, it would have been unacceptable to admit defeat now. The Thruster had begun to annoy me. I could still hear Geoff's stinging challenge from the

Popham trip: 'a lot of people find it impossible … only a few can learn to land a tail-dragger'.

It was November before the Thruster was ready. After the two months back in London, the Watsons and the events of the summer had already become as remote and unreal as a half-remembered dream. Even Richard had disappeared from my life, having been sent away to a regional branch of the bank for one of his interminable training courses. But Guy Fawkes day, a Saturday, found me standing in the hangar with Sean—my first solo trip to Norfolk—inspecting the repaired Thruster.

The cockpit had been completely rebuilt. There were new aluminium spars, new wing struts and, in place of the former 'flimsy' (Sean's word, not mine) aluminium main axle linking the leaf springs of the undercarriage—the part which took the brunt of the strain of any heavy landing—he had inserted a stout box-sectioned girder of mild steel. 'To stop you culling her again, hopefully,' he said. Even with all her new parts, the Thruster still bore signs of her skirmishes. Sean had not had time to repair the gashes in the pod from Richard's accident (there were still grains of corn, chaff and straw in nooks and crevices), and the wings, from their second sojourn on the hangar floor, had acquired more smears of oil and grime.

It was the first time I had been to Norfolk since the summer, and Barsham was a very different place. The sky was the colour of grubby pillowcases, the ground was sodden and most of the leaves were off the trees. The air smelled of damp and autumn, and the big windsock twirled and flapped restlessly.

The flying conditions, Sean said, were borderline, but having come all the way up, I insisted we try. He said it was too gusty to practise landings, and directed me away from the airfield to practise general handling. What little technique I had acquired over the summer seemed to have deserted me, as the machine bucked and rocked in the gusts. Sean kept having to take the controls to steady her. After twenty minutes he said, 'This is pointless, Ants. You're not going to learn a thing,' and the lesson was abandoned. 'Look, we'll try again this afternoon, if you want. The wind may have dropped a bit by then.' But by three o'clock it was hardly better, and though we went up for a full hour this time, I was only left more confused. By four, as we came back over the airfield, car headlights were visible on the A47 and yellow lights shone from the windows of the houses in Barsham village and the outlying farms.

On Sunday, I called Sean from Salsingham after breakfast. The row of poplars in front of the north front of the house—my wind index— still rustled unceasingly, but I was determinedly hopeful that conditions might be better at Barsham. I would learn in due course what a naïve hope this was. If the poplars even twitched at Salsingham, it meant that at Barsham, with its huge expanse of open ground, there would be a stiff breeze; if they were rustling, it would be blowing a gale. Sean sounded as if he was still in bed. 'Ants, look out of the window. Look, it's not my fault. It's just the way it goes.'

I had not considered the weather as an obstacle to flying before—or, indeed, in relation to anything before. Nor had it struck me that, in winter, flying time would be dramatically reduced by the shorter period of daylight. All the flying I had done so far, both in Africa and earlier in the year, had been in fair weather. Through August it had never been so bad that Sean had cancelled a lesson (though sometimes he had suggested waiting until the evening when the wind dropped). September and October had been settled and fine, in London anyway. While obviously some days were *better* than others for flying, the almost complete weather-dependence of the activity had not occurred to me.

And so began an inordinately frustrating period. Impatient to sort out my landing problems, I determinedly headed for Norfolk at every possible opportunity. From Wednesday onwards, I would telephone Weathercall daily, to listen to the three-day forecast for East Anglia. It was, invariably, utterly noncommittal. The recorded voice (which I came to know like an old friend) told me of unending 'areas of low pressure coming in from the Atlantic'. On television these became translated, by Ian McCaskill, into handy catch-all symbols of a cloud, with a bit of a cheery yellow sun peeping out behind, plus—to cover every option—two fat raindrops. The key piece of information that I required—wind strength—was not supplied. On the ground at Barsham Green, this could mean anything at all, from howling Fenland gales to nondescript East Anglian murk (a regional speciality I now learnt) whereby the fields and hedgerows beyond the windsock on the far side of the airfield faded away into white winter gloom. Every Friday I would call Sean and he would say, 'Dunno, Ants. It's very unsettled at the moment, so it's hard to say. Check the forecast, you might be all right'. This, because it was not an emphatic no, I would take as an OK, and set out.

What motivated this almost deranged determination to head for Norfolk under such blatantly unpromising circumstances? The fact was that my mission had acquired a new urgency since Richard had become officially 'legal' to fly the Thruster. With his seduction platform up and running, he was already making vigorous attempts to exploit it, issuing casual invitations for flying weekends to practically everyone he met. I, on the other hand—still unable to fly except as Sean's pupil (or Richard's passenger)—had, as yet, little to gain: for me, the Thruster remained no more than an irksome cost centre, racking up regular and substantial overheads. (Even in London, if Richard were present, the extent to which I could talk up my role with our new toy was greatly restricted. Several times, girls had turned from Richard to me with a half-purred, 'And you fly too?' To which, under Richard's self-satisfied gaze, I was forced into circuitous, defensive explanations, by the end of which all interest had long since evaporated. The situation was highlighted in the last weekend in November, when Richard's pretty nineteen-year-old sister, up visiting friends at the University of East Anglia, brought several of them over to Barsham to check out her brother's new toy. As if Richard's salacious satisfaction at this prospect were not enough to endure, my own position of 'flying partner'—hardly above passenger—permitting me only to assist in such menial chores as cranking open the hangar doors, man-handling the Thruster, refuelling, engine-starting and, apart from that, simply to act as general ground stooge, fielding banal questions from adolescent men, was intolerable. Richard, meanwhile, soaked up wide-eyed attention, gasps of delight and clinging female hands in the air. Accordingly, until this situation could be rectified, my former London life at weekends, was placed on unconditional hold—and strangely, I did not miss it a bit.

'This was an illegal flight by an unqualified man flying an unpermitted aircraft,' read Richard. *'The aircraft took off and flew into a tree. Witnesses state that the pilot lost control within seconds of the aircraft leaving the ground. The pilot, a 71-year-old man, was taken to hospital with serious injuries.'*

Richard had recently discovered the *Accident Survey*. Rummaging in my 'flight bag' (a large carrier bag) for something, the yellow A5 inserts had fallen out of the copies of *Flightline*. I had seen them when I flicked briefly through the magazine, knew that I probably ought to read them (the most substantial section of the magazine was usually the Obituaries), but had written them off, with their statistics, dry tables of data and summaries of circumstances, as beyond my scope. Richard, at home with such things, was immediately interested. He flicked to another entry.

'Hmm … this one's in italics. Wonder what that means?' Frowning slightly, he referred back to the front of the document. 'Ah, italics mean the accident was fatal. Where was I? Yes.' He continued: *'It appears that two men, without flying experience, came across this machine on a country walk and decided to fly the aircraft without instruction. It seems they experienced difficulty starting the engine, during which an air filter was replaced with half a Fairy Liquid bottle.*

Eventually the engine was started and one of the men attempted a take off. The aircraft rose steeply before nosing over and impacting heavily with the ground. Like further details? It's all here. *Licence: none. Hours as Pilot-in-Command: 0. Hours on Type: 37 seconds.* Are they trying to be funny?'

Most of the time not spent hanging about or waiting on the weather on flying weekends was spent in the car: the journey to Salsingham from London might take anything from three to four hours, depending on traffic. That was eight hours return. The journey from Salsingham to Barsham, up to half an hour each way and made at least twice on a typical flying weekend, added a couple more hours.

Fortunately, neither Richard nor I minded spending protracted periods in the car; it was how we had spent several holidays travelling in Europe and Africa. But now, from Richard's point of view, the benefits of spending winter weekends in Norfolk were less obvious. With no central heating, the damp in the flat at Salsingham, despite Lester's best double-glazing efforts with polythene sheeting and insulating tape, was all-pervading. It was dark. We could see our breath from our beds in the morning. It had been a considerable achievement to get him to accompany me again so soon.

'…*After completing maintenance work on his engine, the student decided to take the aircraft without its wing for a trial run. The throttle jammed in the open position and the aircraft accelerated. The aircraft went through a fence at the end of a field, across a small B road and into a hedge. The aircraft flipped onto its rear and was severely damaged …*'

I envied Richard's self-assurance in the cockpit. He appeared to have complete and unshakeable faith in his own abilities—a faith he maintained in the face of any amount of evidence to the contrary. Only this morning, returning from a cross-country flight, despite my nervous and urgent warnings that we were low on fuel, he had embarked on a lengthy circuit 'joining procedure' with the result that we did indeed run out on our final descent. We had no alternative but to make a forced landing (in full view of the clubhouse), one field short of the aerodrome.

'... *the pilot did not notice that his passenger was wearing a scarf.
During the flight the scarf entangled around the engine pulley*...'

Two weekends ago, there had been the so-called Dashboard
Incident. Sean had warned us repeatedly of the hazards of taxiing on
tarmac rather than grass (we had to follow the tarmac peri-track round
the field to reach the appropriate runway). 'The tail-wheel's very
ineffective and, with no brakes, she'll just run and run, even after you
cut the power,' he was always saying. 'Just remember, you can't go too
slowly on tarmac.' I had been interested to note the brisk pace that
Richard had set as we taxied out; the little tail-wheel twitching and
shimmying in protest behind. When the moment came to turn onto
our runway, Richard had cut the revs, pressed the rudder-pedal and—
predictably—nothing had happened. We continued in a straight line,
mounted a small bank and nosed into the drainage ditch which ran
alongside the peri-track. After clambering out, we lifted the Thruster
out with some difficulty and set her back on the tarmac. As we did so,
there was a faint metallic chime as a screw rolled out of the base of the
pod onto the tarmac. After searching for several minutes for its origin,
without success, I had resigned myself to a tedious return to the hangar
to seek Sean's assistance, when Richard (who had been clicking his
tongue and muttering about wasting time), suddenly clamped his hand
firmly down on the wing, and barked: 'As Pilot-in-Command of this
aircraft, I pronounce it safe to fly.' We had started the engine,
clambered back aboard, rebuckled our harnesses and taken off. At 800
feet the dashboard had fallen off.

'... *injury: one cow*...'

Sean, too, was an unknown quantity. With flying time squeezed by
weather and light, even I had begun to conclude that the 'maybe-it'll-
be-better-tomorrow' attitude of my flying instructor and my
timetabled, deadline-driven office life were irreconcilable. I was used
to a world where things had to be done, and by a certain time. Flying,
it was clear, would be subject to no such scheduling. I didn't help
myself in this regard. Perhaps because of the capriciousness of the
weather, I acquired the notion that it hardly mattered what time I

showed up for my lesson, even if it were booked for a specific time. Having always found it hard to be on time, I would forget that it could as easily take thirty-five minutes as fifteen to get to Barsham from Salsingham, by the time I had got stuck behind a tractor most of the way. The Barsham security system might add another ten minutes. Getting the plane out, refuelling and 'pre-flighting' might add another twenty minutes.

Sometimes Sean would have got the Thruster out and be waiting impatiently to go. He would cut short my apologies with a terse, 'It's your money, Antony,' and then, I thought, would deliberately make me taxi more slowly to the take-off point, linger for hours on my checks, before cutting the lesson at exactly an hour after the officially booked starting time. At other times he couldn't seem to care less. 'Take your time, Ants,' he would say. 'There's no rush. Never hurry anything to do with flying. Want a cup of coffee before we go?' And he would loaf around the hangar chatting to the mechanics and club members and other oddballs who always seemed to be loitering, whether or not he had a string of other students booked. Entries in my log book from that period indicate that hardly a lesson lasted the full hour; most were abandoned after twenty minutes or less. On some weekends, getting airborne at all seemed like an achievement.

'...*After a severe frost the night before, the pilot landed on an unprepared field that had often been used in the past. Although the pilot avoided most of the molehills he hit one that was frozen solid. This tore off the drag link and the undercarriage collapsed and went through the propeller. The aircraft slid down the field on the remains of its undercarriage ...*'

I wrenched my mind back to what Richard was saying. Frost! That was what I wanted. A real, old-fashioned, brick-hard, rime-coated, see-your-breath-and-put-some-colour-in-your-cheeks sort of day. Flying in frost seemed to be the next flying ambition to which I could reasonably aspire. Was it so much to ask? In December? I fancied the idea of dressing up in thermals and scarves, breathing in the freezing air, and seeing how the landscape looked from above, white and bare with eddying wood smoke. When would that happen? Instead, here we were, once again, beneath bone marrow skies in the damp and murk and rain and wind.

'Do you think these people have a death wish?' said Richard. 'Or is life just cheaper to them?' He turned and looked at me in bewilderment. 'What makes them do things like this? Who are these people?'

It was the end of January before I managed to persuade Richard to accompany me to Norfolk again. I had marketed it as the ideal head-clearing, cobweb-blowing, post-Christmas recovery plan. Wise from before, he was not easily convinced, but eventually, as it was January and there was nothing else to do, he had agreed.

And, once again, the weather let us down.

Saturday, a day that blue skies had been promised after some early fog, was certainly foggy—a blanket pea-souper so thick that even trying to navigate from Salsingham to Barsham was out of the question. We mooched gloomily about the flat. Richard sat by the sitting room window, wearing his flying suit to keep warm, reading. I rummaged in the half-light of the corridor outside. It was stacked with junk: mattresses, lampshades, assorted chairs, old televisions, table football, jigsaw puzzles, blackboards, birdcages, antlers, headless teddy bears, ancient skis. There were shelves and shelves of books: one was devoted to twenty-eight copies of the Bible, on the next, alongside each other, were *The Concise History of Hertfordshire* (three vast volumes), *The Balfour Declaration*, *The Last of the Just*, *The Perennial Philosophy*, *Intelligent Use of the Microscope*, *Himalayan Campaign*.

The fog was so thick that we could not even go for a walk. It took an hour and four near-crashes to get down the drive and into Salsingham to the pub for lunch. By the time it got dark, around quarter past four, there was no doubt that we had begun to get on each other's nerves. We watched television all evening by ourselves downstairs (the Watsons were away). On Sunday, I got up and peered hopefully out of the window at quarter to eight. The fog had lifted, but now the row of poplars were not so much rustling as flexing like Russian gymnasts, meaning it must be blowing like a hurricane over at Barsham. I had been too embarrassed to call Sean and admit I was up again, and for once I was glad.

By lunchtime we had cabin fever and were climbing the walls with boredom. I felt guilty about having dragged Richard up; he was furious that he had let himself be duped into coming. After lunch at the pub we decided to drive over to Barsham just to have a look at the Thruster, to give us something to do, before we started back to London.

The airfield was deserted. The clubhouse Portakabin was locked and the car park was just a sweep of puddled tarmac, without even Sean's red van in evidence. The big twelve-foot wind sock, 500 yards away, stood out at right angles. Occasional mighty gusts made it flap and billow, making deep, crunching 'ruc-ruc' sounds from its heavy material, as if an invisible hand were trying to tear it off its pole. We wandered out onto the landing field. The temperature was mild, but the wind was howling, yanking our hair at the roots. There was no way it was going to let up today. The school Cessnas had been put away inside the hangar: all except for one, which was rocking and pitching on its tie-downs. The whole place was closed up.

The little metal side door into the hangar seemed to be locked when I tried it, but Richard managed to haul it open. The suction effect sent the machines inside rocking on their landing gear. It slammed behind us with a resounding metallic crash. We picked our way around in the dingy half-light, listening to the moan and whine of the wind, the twenty ton hangar doors rocking and creaking on their runners. There was a smell of grease and aero oil. I was studying the new arrivals: an autogyro and a helicopter and some kind of foreign biplane, which had Russian (or some Slavic language) on its gauges and warning plates. I had been looking at these for a few minutes when I noticed that Richard was moving machines around.

'What's up?'

He ignored the question. I felt a beat of unease somewhere deep in the pit of my stomach. Now that I watched, he wasn't just nudging planes to and fro: his actions were firm and decisive. His chin was set. He had that look he sometimes got. I repeated my question. Again, he ignored it. Unease seeped through me. The third time I asked he answered shortly, 'What does it look as if I'm doing?'

I laughed nervously.

'Can't imagine. If I didn't know you were more intelligent, I might have thought you were trying to get the Thruster out.' I gave another half-derisive, half-pleading laugh.

'Out of my way please.' As a sort of subconscious protest, I suppose, I was standing in front of the machine.

'Look. Christ, Rick. What are you playing at?' I put on what I hoped was a calming, reasonable, wheedling tone. 'It's blowing a fucking gale. Thirty knots, probably gusting fifty. The Thrasher's only made of string and balsa wood.'

Richard continued what he was doing as if I wasn't there.

'Antony, I'm not asking you to come flying.'

And that, I'm afraid, is Richard for you: ninety-five per cent bank manager, five per cent psycho. That use of my Christian name meant he was serious. I knew from long experience the futility of trying to stop him or argue once he was in a mood like this. It would only harden his resolve. But what to do? It was plainly insane to go flying. But—and this was the question that was already hammering in my head—*what if it turned out to be OK?* What if he went up and came back safely while I, who had tried to talk him out of it, waited nervously on the ground? He would have taken the initiative. He would have the adventure to tell. Meanwhile, where would I be?

The bastard, I thought. The mad bastard.

The hangar doors were almost impossible to open, the wind was forcing them back so hard against their runners. The moment the two central doors were prized apart, it was like releasing a vacuum. There was a rattle as grit and dust were whipped off the fairing and hurled against the metal skins of the aircraft inside. The wind through the opening moaned like an organ pipe. As I helped him push poor G-MVOY out onto the concrete, it was as if that cumbrous, heavy, awkward shape had come alive. She bucked and rocked as we tried to hold her down with one hand, while struggling into our suits and helmets with the other.

Yes, 'we'. Oddly, once I realised that I had no option but to accompany him, my qualms had passed and, in a gun-to-the-head way, I had almost began to enjoy myself. 'Why not?' was my thinking. If he smashed up the plane, it wasn't my problem. In fact, it was nothing to do with me. He was the one with the pilot's licence. I was a mere passenger; an innocent party. Besides, maybe he *did* know what he was doing; maybe he *had* been up in conditions like these before, though I doubted it. I felt a glorious abrogation of responsibility. And, to give Richard his due, all boredom and listlessness had certainly disappeared from the afternoon. That said, as I plugged in the helmet intercom, once the engine was running, it seemed wise to confirm this power shift.

'Madness. Insanity.'

It found its mark.

'Get out.'

'No.' Somehow my resolve softened his manner.

'All right then. Here goes.'

As he turned the machine into the wind a gust round the edge of the hangar caught the starboard wing, briefly tipping us onto the left wheel. We balanced, swaying crazily, for a second or two—the port wing tip just inches from the ground—but finally Richard's full right stick plonked us heavily down again. He turned us squarely into wind ready to begin the taxi past the club buildings and paraphernalia to the take-off area. However, as he gingerly opened the throttle to begin the taxi, we were away. We simply lifted off, vertically; there was no forward movement. 'What the—?' said Richard, but, seeing we were off, opened the throttle fully. The effect was as if we had been at the farthest range of travel of a mighty stretch of bungee, or in the shaft of a rocket-powered lift. The hangar, the Portakabin, our parked car; they receded beneath us as if by auto-zoom. As, I think, a fighter pilot once put it, 'the cows just got smaller'. We jumped, lurched and bucked. I grabbed the A-frame bar for support. The altimeter read 1,000 feet in less than twenty seconds, yet we had made no forward progress at all. In fact, I noticed that in terms of ground motion, we still hadn't crossed the taxi-way onto the take-off strip.

After ten minutes of this, at full throttle, Richard executed a 180° turn. There was no mistaking our progress now. We slewed round and then shot downwind at about 100 mph, over the trees and gravel pits at the east end of the landing field.

'Is this wise? Will we ever get back?' I shouted into the intercom. Richard tried another 180° turn back onto our original heading. We skidded and yawed round in another wide arc.

'The wind must be stronger up here. Maybe we should lose some height,' I shouted. Richard closed the throttle to idle, but the Thruster, apparently now beyond the control of intermediate agencies, showed no inclination to descend.

Until, quite suddenly, the wind abated completely.

Caught unawares, hanging ludicrously in limbo, we nearly stalled, before Richard slammed the nose forward and we dropped like an anvil some three hundred feet. Just as he slammed the power back on, another gust caught us. With a sickening lurch, we were hurled back up to where we had been. The airframe creaked and groaned alarmingly, and the wing struts alternately slackened, then hauled, on their joints: the wings were practically flapping. I swallowed hard and gripped the A-frame tighter. I was not sure that the Thruster could take this kind of punishment. What was more unsettling was that we appeared to be making no headway at all. Checking our forward motion against a mark on the ground—I chose the gravel heap alongside the lake below us—it became clear that we were actually going backwards. This meant that the wind must be over sixty knots. Seventy-five miles an hour. The words from *The Microlight Pilot's Handbook* hammered in my temples. 'It is better to be on the ground wishing to God you were in the air, than in the air wishing to God you were on the ground.'

What was one supposed to do? Reverse to a flat field? 'Hover' until the wind dropped? The thought prompted me to check the level of fuel in the tank behind us. I had not thought of doing this before: partly because there were so many other matters on my mind; partly because we were, after all, only going up for a 'bumble' for a few minutes. At first I couldn't see the level in the tank at all, the liquid was sloshing around so much. I eventually estimated that we had just less than a quarter of a tank, or about twenty minutes. Richard had the engine screaming at full revs now, stick hard forward, his jaw jutting determinedly.

It took us every bit of twenty minutes, but finally the airfield perimeter fence was beneath us. We went down as we had come up— vertically. It was as if we were being lowered by a crane operated by a drunk, releasing the cable in great spools, periodically winding us back up 200 feet, then dropping us down 250 again. The moment our wheels made contact with the ground, which they did without turning at all, I jumped out and clung onto the wing to stop her blowing over. It took another fifteen fraught minutes to walk her back to the hangar, bucking and twisting, me hanging onto the end of the wing with all my strength. By the time we reached the hangar, I was sweating, despite the wind. Richard cut the engine, we shoved her inside, cranked the doors shut and, apart from my breathing, all was peace and quiet.

'Splendid, Antony,' said Richard companionably, blowing his nose into a large white handkerchief. 'What an excellent afternoon's flying.'

As we left the airfield we passed Sean's red van coming the other way. We stopped alongside each other.

'What the Hell are you boys doing here?' he said, astonished. 'God, you never give up, do you? What … *thinking of doing a little flying, were you?*' He gave a shout of laughter, then a pitying shake of his head. We smiled back.

'Just out of interest,' I said. '*Could* a Thruster go up in conditions like these?'

'Come on, Ants, use your head. What do *you* think? Look at the bloody windsock. That's a forty or fifty mile an hour wind. I've just come up to make sure everything's OK. Nothing's flying in or out of here. Oh, you boys. You do make me laugh.'

I had not been to the Science Museum since I was a child. My chief— in fact, only—recollection was the gigantic landing wheels of an airliner, and I was pleased to see that this was the first exhibit that greeted me in the main foyer: though they looked a good deal smaller than I remembered. Upstairs, in Flight, I strode briskly past the opening series of displays. Their subjects were balloons, feather-covered gliders, devices with flapping wings—and they carried rather lengthier explanations than I felt up to dealing with. High up above, however, suspended from the roof, as I had hoped, was a machine that looked remarkably like the Thruster.

I had been privately planning to visit the museum since I had read, in a flight test from *Pilot* magazine pinned on Sean's office wall, that the Thruster was 'reminiscent of the Santos-Dumont *Demoiselle*'. I liked the idea of our flying being connected with that of the early pioneers, and the name had stuck in my mind. More importantly, I think I hoped that the experiences of the early pioneers might assist perhaps with my own landing difficulties.

Most of the early planes plainly shared characteristics with fixed-wing microlights. They looked awkward and fragile, were completely unstreamlined and had no instruments. Even I could see how basic the control systems were—and every one was different. There were no ailerons, just wires to twist the wings. Some seemed to have the 'tail-plane' out in front, others behind, some had both. The ones which had it in the familiar position, behind, had no fixed 'fin' in front of the rudder mechanism: the whole surface moved. The airframes looked as delicate as paper lampshades; the engines crude and heavy. The craftsmanship, however, was of a different league: no sharp edges and crude finishes; just hulls of polished wood like a boat's and beautiful, dark, beeswaxed propellers, carved from blocks of mahogany.

I could find no mention of Santos-Dumont or his *Demoiselle*. But the plane that vaguely resembled the Thruster turned out to be a monoplane like the one in which Louis Blériot had crossed the Channel for the first time in July 1909. There was a photograph of the great man taken shortly after his moment of glory, standing in front of his wrecked machine at Dover, hands on hips, chest puffed out, looking as smug as can be—and a rather more telling one, evidently taken moments before his departure from France. Even given that Blériot seemed habitually to wear a slightly startled expression, if ever there were a picture of woe, this was it. The man was in a dreadful state—a bundle of tormented apprehension alongside his *soignée* rival, Hubert Latham, who was casually leaning forward for a light, in another nearby photograph. For a moment I felt a curl of disdain towards Blériot— until I remembered which of the two men had made history.

Under any other circumstances, I would have probably proceeded to the far end of the gallery, to the Spitfire, helicopter, flying boat and Harrier jump jet. But now I lingered where I was. There was a case of early instruments, like turn-and-bank indicators, air speed indicators, altimeters and rate-of-climb indicators, dating from around 1910. There were smudgy black-and-white photographs of the kind of machines I recognised from the early pages of books about flight. The scenes looked familiar: the big, open, fenceless fields (like Barsham Green); the murky, washed-out skies; the knots of people standing around the machines, tinkering; the crashes—especially the crashes— with their forlorn heaps of bent metal, broken propellers and crumpled wings. There was a plaque alongside Amy Johnson's bi-plane, with a quote she had once made: 'There is nothing more wonderful or thrilling than going up into the skies in a tiny plane at peace with everyone, and exactly free to do what you want and go where you will.' I wondered if it was a sensation I would ever know.

A big, ancient twin-engined biplane turned out to be the machine in which Lieutenant John Alcock and Captain Arthur Whitten Brown had crossed the Atlantic for the first time in 1919. I had actually visited the spot in Connemara where they had crash-landed in a bog. Now, it was hard to see how two men could possibly have squeezed into the absurd little cockpit. The plaque explained how, in a heavy storm cloud, they had lost all sense of balance and entered a spiral dive. With no idea what to do, it seemed as if nothing could save them as they plunged towards the ocean. When they finally fell out of the murk, sixty feet above the waves, the water seemed to be standing up sideways, almost vertically—until, in the nick of time, Alcock recovered his balance, righted them, and they were saved. It was an experience, following my first solo, with which I could feel considerable affinity. I had got as far as examining the air intakes of the two big Rolls-Royce engines, which the limping Brown had apparently clambered out onto the wing to clear snow from (in a storm, 8,000 feet above the Atlantic), when I noticed that it was five o'clock, and I should be back at work.

In the gift shop I bought a big book called *The Complete Book of Aircraft and Flight*, and *Sky Fever*, the autobiography of Sir Geoffrey de Havilland, because, when I opened it at random, it contained an account of the author teaching himself to fly in 1909. I felt strangely furtive as I emerged from the building into a torrential shower, and, skulking by the entrance, I felt almost embarrassed in case someone I knew recognised me. I did not mention my visit to anyone.

Over the next few days I read the books and began, with difficulty, to identify the difference between the designs of the early pioneers. I tried to trace the connection between the achievements of the Wright brothers in Kitty Hawk, North Carolina and the largely independent work of the French, or France-based European pioneers—Santos-Dumont, Voisin, Blériot, Ferber, Farman, Esbault-Pelterie and the rest—with their bushy moustaches.

Two things struck me. First was how fast it had all happened: little more than a decade from the Wright brothers' first, tense, twelve-second powered hop on 17 December 1903, to the more or less fully-formed bi- and triplanes, able to perform upside down, loops, rolls, and other aerobatics of the later stages of the First World War. The height record, for example, leapt from 500 feet, hardly above the tree tops, at

BEFORE

© Hulton Getty

© Hulton Getty

AFTER

the first great air rally at Reims in 1909, to 10,500 feet a year later.

Practically every day of those exciting early years brought new experiences astonishingly similar to those I had either recently acquired or shortly hoped to acquire: the first landing without crashing; the first landing on wheels (the Wright brothers used rails and skids); the first proper turn; the first flight in gusty winds (Latham's speciality). In Europe, Henri Farman flew the first full circle, to great acclaim, in January 1908. Shortly afterwards he flew the first official 'journey': the twenty-seven kilometres from his field at Camp Chalons to Reims.

Farman's turn was accomplished by means of rudder alone. Until 1908, this ungainly and inefficient method was the only effective way the Europeans had of turning. It was the Wrights—bicycle repairers by trade—who mastered the idea of banking, like on a bicycle. This they did by twisting the wings, or 'wing-warping'. It was not until Wilbur Wright visited Le Mans in 1908 and demonstrated their system that the French (who by this time had vastly better engines) mastered control of the air. In July 1909, when Blériot wave-hopped through the Channel fog to collect the *Daily Mail*'s £1,000 prize, he was using, effectively, the modern 'stick and rudder' system of controls (though, amazingly, no compass). Thereafter Blériot became the world's most successful aircraft manufacturer and the French lead continued. French designs pioneered most of the modern control features: tail-planes, stabilisers, fins, wing dihedral, rear elevators, rudders (which is why so many words referring to parts of aircraft are still French—*fuselage*, *ailerons*, *Pitot*, even *pilot*).

Meanwhile the 'firsts' continued: first passenger; first female passenger; first landing on water; first night flight; first cross-wind landing; first flight above clouds. First experience of fog. In *Sky Fever*, Geoffrey de Havilland described how, on a murky autumn day at Farnborough in 1913, he took off for a short test flight 'to see if the weather was good enough,' only immediately to lose sight of the ground—and everything else—until trees and chimney-pots on houses suddenly loomed up in front of his nose and had to be jumped. 'I understood,' he wrote, 'as never before, the meaning of fear.'

By 1913, Adolphe Pégoud, a French ace, was flying upside down and demonstrating rolls and bunts (half outside loops). Then twenty-six-year-old Lt Petr Nikolaevich Nesterov of the Imperial Russian Air Service performed the first complete loop on 9 September, beating Pégoud by twelve days. Again, in *Sky Fever*, the quiet, self-effacing, countryside-loving Geoffrey de Havilland described how, around the same time, he took his plane up one morning and, without instruction, preparation, helmet, safety harness, parachute, or ever having seen it done before, did a loop himself. 'It had been a strange and interesting experience, and had proved easy to accomplish.'

It all brought home the courage of the pioneers. With no knowledge of wing-loading or stresses, catastrophic and fatal mid-air collapse was the norm as they experimented. Yet they persevered, getting themselves into manoeuvres like the spin, from which there was no known method of recovery, then calmly trying to extricate themselves, carefully remembering the exact sequence of their actions—on the off chance that they survived to report the experiment. (The first lucky, and accidental, recovery from a spin was in 1911.)

None of the books contained much solace for my own difficulties. But Richard, catching me unawares in the flat with my eyes shut, holding the bread knife like a joy-stick said: 'If it's any consolation, Ants, I was lucky to get my licence in Africa. Lindsay hustled me through because she knew I was leaving the next week. And though I went solo in a Cessna in a couple of hours, it took more than twice that before I did it in the Thruster.'

Nor did the books say much about Santos-Dumont's *Demoiselle* (though a photograph indicated that it looked like the machine flown by the Frenchman in *Those Magnificent Men in Their Flying Machines*) apart from the fact that it was the first plane to be sold in 'kit' form, thereby qualifying it as the first attempt to put private flying on a wider footing. What I wanted to know was why, given that in all my favourite sci-fi movies* private aerial buggies were the standard mode of

---

* *Metropolis, Things to Come, Bladerunner, Brazil.*

transport, this had not happened? But amateur flying got little attention, alongside the sexier chapters of aviation history like fighter planes, helicopters, bombers, the jet engine, breaking the sound barrier and getting to the moon. So one rainy Saturday, I decided to take the matter into my own hands; I went to the Royal Aeronautical Society library to find out.

'Flying for all,' it rapidly became clear, was aviation's one still unconsummated ambition.* If Santos-Dumont's *Demoiselle* of 1908 (so-called because the Japanese silk stretched over its bamboo frame gave it the transparent elegance of a 'young girl' or 'dragonfly') was where the idea began, it also highlighted the difficulties ahead. Like other planes of the time, the *Demoiselle* was highly unstable, requiring absolutely calm weather and could only carry the lightest of pilots— Alberto Santos-Dumont had the advantage of weighing just 49 kg 'without shoes and gloves'.† In short, the *Demoiselle*, like every other plane, was completely impractical; and, though the advertised price in England of £300 was far less than for any other production aircraft, it was still way out of most people's league.

After the First World War, 'barnstormers'—de-mobbed pilots in ex-war planes flying round the countryside—introduced the idea of flying to a wider public, and the potential of private flying began to sink in. But, despite several Air Ministry-backed competitions no-one could come up with a practical two-seater for anything less than perfect

---

* As I write, the papers are full of the latest scam: a strap-on personal helicopter called a SoloTrek, not to mention various webbed 'bat-wing' gliding suits and ruck-sacks with snap-out wings.

† Interesting fact: to enable Santos-Dumont to tell the time while he was flying, when his hands were not free to consult a pocket watch, his friend Louis Cartier made him a watch on a leather strap, the first ever wrist-watch.

weather. Until, in 1925, Geoffrey de Havilland produced his two-seat Moth bi-plane.*

Inspired by his love of natural history, de Havilland made its wings fold back—like a moth's—so that it could be stored in a barn or garage and towed by a car. It was sturdy. It was easy-to-fly. The production version was so economical to run that it prompted a boom in private and club flying across the world. In May 1930, when Amy Johnson flew one to Australia, it became world famous. The Moth, so the story went, inaugurated the golden age of private flying.

Except that it didn't, *really*. Certainly a lot were sold (more than 9,000 of its successor, the Tiger Moth, which became the standard trainer). And, compared to anything else, it was certainly elegant, practical and reliable: a handsome hand-built wood-and-cloth bi-plane made by an accomplished aircraft manufacturer. But it wasn't cheap to make, and, at £595, it cost about five times as much as a car and more than an average suburban family house.

And that was how things stood until the saga of the Flying Flea. The Flea was a baby aeroplane devised and built by a Frenchman, Henri Mignet, in his workshop. In 1934 he wrote a book describing his design, how he came to it, giving accurate plans and instructions for its construction and tips on how to fly it. He published it under the title *Pou-du-Ciel* (at the time the French nickname for the mass market Ford car was the *Pou-de-la-Route*) plainly hoping it would, likewise, become the affordable family plane that had been sought for so long. And it nearly did. The design was simple, required only cheap, everyday materials and was (deliberately) small enough to be assembled in a Paris apartment. The idea was so romantic, and Mignet's enthusiastic style so infectious that when the book was translated into English the following year, under the title *The Flying Flea*, six thousand copies sold in a month. Here, finally, was a set of foolproof instructions on how to build a plane from tea chests and string. People everywhere began botching together Fleas, adapting materials and tweaking

---

* The one in *Out of Africa* and the one that did not crash in *The English Patient*.

Mignet's design as they saw fit—and, like fleas, they perished. Following a series of accidents, the French authorities put a *Pou-du-Ciel* in a wind tunnel and discovered that if it entered a dive at an angle of more than 15°, the nose could not be raised to prevent a crash. By the time the Second World War broke out, Mignet had remedied the design (and he remains the patron saint of 'homebuilders') but the Flea never recovered.

The key development for wider private flying came in the 1950s when the American company Cessna launched their 150 trainer-tourer. Instead of a stick, it had a steering wheel—or, at least, a 'yoke' that looked much like one; its interior was designed to look like a car's and, most importantly, it was not a Dreaded Tail-Dragger. Instead, with its 'Land-o-matic' tricycle undercarriage, it was advertised as the easiest plane to land that there had ever been. It was supposed to initiate the safe, traffic-hopping era of the modern age, and over the next thirty years, its slightly larger sibling, the 172 did become the most mass-produced aircraft in history after the German Me 109. Except, of course, it was still far too expensive for most people.

It was an American aeronautical engineer, Francis Rogallo, trying to solve the problem of getting the Apollo capsule back to earth with more dignity than a parachuted splashdown, who came up with the delta flexwing design that begat modern hang-gliding. When someone added an engine, 'microlighting' was born. An explosion of home-build kits and factory-finished, ultra-light machines followed—'three-axis' and 'flexwing'—exploiting all the new materials and technologies of the age: and with it, as the first practical two-seat trainer, came the Thruster.

The Thruster seemed to satisfy almost every one of the necessary criteria of an 'aircraft for all'. It had both Mignet's *sine qua non*s for touring: side-by-side seating and a high wing to allow a good view of the countryside. It was compact. It cost less than a hatchback and ran on unleaded petrol. It took off and landed in a very short space. It could fly in wind and most weather. It would not spin. It was stable and would naturally recover if pilots just closed their eyes and folded their arms. In fact, the more you left it alone, the better it flew. Why, then, was it not the panacea that science fiction had sought for so long? And there, of course, *I* could supply the answer.

The bastard was impossible to land.

How to Land a Plane

Should the aeronaut decide to return to *terra firma*, he should close the control valve of the motor. This will cause the apparatus to assume what is known as the gliding position, except in the case of those flying machines which are inherently unstable. The latter will assume the position known as 'involuntary spin' and will return to earth without further action on the part of the aeronaut.

From 'How to Fly an Aeroplane',
flying manual of the 1911 Curtiss Pusher.

What is a good landing? A good landing is a landing from which the pilot can walk away unaided.

Flying adage.

By the end of February I had had enough of London. The weather had turned lousy again. It had been persistently dreary and wet for a month and showed no signs of settling. Blue skies and frost seemed to be a quaint memory, and I was fed up. Unless there was a reason to stay in London, I usually drove to my parents, in Somerset, at weekends. There I could lie in for hours, laze in front of the television with the papers, recover from the excesses of London living and be a child again. My mother would feed me up with steaming casseroles and roasts and crumbles until I could hardly move.

To prevent alimentary seizure, I would go for long walks with my father. Our favourite route was from the lonely, windswept Glider

Station above Cheddar Gorge, along the top of the bleak Mendip escarpment towards Black Down. Here the wind howled straight in off the Atlantic and, both south and west, were some of the finest views in southern England. Below us were the Somerset Levels with their rhynes and dykes, the smoke from the chimneys of villages like Westbury and Draycott curling into hanging fronds of mist. On a clear day you could see to the Quantocks and Exmoor. To the right was Brean Down, Steepholme, and, across the Severn, Wales. To the left was Wells and the Wiltshire Downs. If the weather was not clear, as was usually the case, the view was better still: huge thunderclouds heaping and boiling up out to sea; straggly wisps of low cloud hanging in the middle distance; mist or haze (according to season) lying between the hedgerows and walls running away beneath us. Sometimes blanket fog filled the whole vale, with just Brent Knoll and Glastonbury Tor floating above the cloud.

As a scene, it had everything: scale, variety, beauty, drama. And all I could think, as our noses reddened in the chilly February air, was what would it be like to *fly* over landscape like this? On two successive weekends, the Atlantic winds blew the skies clear of clouds and I felt mounting frustration that the Thruster was stuck in Norfolk. Who wanted to fly there? The country there was two-dimensional; boring, empty and featureless. *This* was the place to have a plane. An hour's flight here could take in coastline and island, lowland and upland, cathedral and suspension bridge, lake and combe, gorges, grassy hills, barrows, deserted mineries ...

It had become a habit to look up when I heard the sound of a propeller-driven plane droning overhead. If indoors, I would even go outside to watch, until it was out of sight. On the Saturday morning of the second clear weekend, at the beginning of March, the customary stillness was disturbed by an unusually loud, high-pitched engine note. Hurrying outside to investigate, I found, to my astonished surprise, not 500 feet above me, a yellow Thruster.

Apart from at Popham, I had never seen another Thruster. Microlights were still rare, and Thrusters accounted for a tiny proportion of microlights. Now, here was someone *else's* Thruster over *my* patch. Rushing for my car keys, I chased it six or seven miles, as far as the Glider Station, where, after circling around for a bit, it came in to land amongst the sheep. Two old buffers in tweed caps climbed out, both in their fifties or sixties. They kept the machine down at Marston Mallet, they said; on a disused airfield on the Levels. There was an instructor there called Ken.

My zest for life was magically restored as I drove down to Marston Mallet after lunch. I had got hold of Ken and arranged a lesson for two o'clock, and the new season and next chapter of my flying seemed poised to begin.

The airfield was deserted. It was part of what was evidently once a much bigger wartime aerodrome, with a section of the old peri-track now used as the runway, with a parallel strip of grass alongside. The presence of an old Thruster, tied down under covers behind a barn, indicated that I was in the right place. But other than that there were no planes or cars or signs of human life at all, other than a locked caravan, faded and green with mould.

Wandering around, I was wondering which part of our arrangement could possibly have been misunderstood when a burbling noise behind made me turn round, to see an old aeroplane glide gently in to land. It pulled up, parked, and, after a few moments of rummaging, a big figure climbed out clutching a flask and a packet of sandwiches. He nudged the door to, with his chin, as if it were a hatchback. 'You must be Tony,' he said, in a husky West Country burr. Ken, it turned out, was a farmer's son from another part of Somerset. He flew up to give lessons.

Keen to demonstrate my good airmanship as we taxied out, I asked Ken where the windsock was. 'Windsock, Tony? Don't think we've got one of those.' He made it sound as if I had enquired about runway lights, or the Executive Lounge. He gently depressed the left rudder pedal of his dual controls. 'I should use this runway,' he added. I began to explain that I felt confident about most areas, but landing was still a problem. He held up a vast hand. 'Let's see how we get on, shall we.' Still keen to impress, I asked whether he thought the engine was warmed up enough to take off.

'Don't worry, Tony. I'll tell you if it stops.'

Ken had a robust attitude to basic training. There was one thing and only one thing that the novice pilot needed to know, above all things: how to land in the event of engine failure. Sean's instruction in this area had been mainly theoretical. He would periodically say, 'Right, where would you land now?' Then, a few minutes later, 'And now?' with occasional pieces of advice like 'Always know which way the wind is coming from—draw an arrow on your map if need be—and always choose a field within 180° arc in front of you. *Never* turn back to the airfield; you won't make it.' Very occasionally he would, unexpectedly, cut the throttle to idle, usually followed by a shout of 'Get the nose down!' as he grabbed the stick and shoved it forward. (Because the Thruster was so light, there was no momentum to keep her going if her engine cut out: unless you immediately put her into what amounted to a shallow dive—to keep the air flowing over the wings—she would stall. Heavier planes had more momentum to keep them going, so tended to glide better.) Sometimes Sean would make me point out my chosen field, check that it was orientated into wind, and we would go down as low as thirty or forty feet before he would say 'OK. You're in.' Then he would open the throttle and we would climb away. Increasingly, once he was happy that I was getting the nose down fast enough, he would re-open the throttle after just a few seconds.

We had climbed to about 1,500 feet when Ken pulled the same trick, without warning cutting the throttle to idle. 'Oops, Tony. There goes the engine.' Determined not to be accused of failing to 'get the nose down', I shoved the stick hard forward and held it there. In a more or less vertical dive, in fact. No one was going to tell me I was risking a stall.

'Mmm. This is interesting,' murmured Ken, as the view ahead became the ground directly beneath us. It was the first time he had registered any emotion. 'Very interesting indeed,' he repeated softly, as I kept the stick hard forward. I levelled out a little as we descended through 200 feet … 100 feet … 50 feet, waiting for Ken to re-open the throttle. He did nothing.

'Do you want me to… actually to *land*?' I was sure it must be illegal to land in farmers' fields, particularly ones with cattle in. We were approaching hedgerow height.

'Seems sensible, Tony. If we're not to crash.' Ken gripped the A-frame tube firmly with his gloved right hand, but still made no attempt to touch the throttle or take the stick. 30 feet … 20 … 10. I remained calm. Two could play at this game. It was a matter of who blinked first. He *had* to open the throttle. There was no way I could land: it was a completely unsuitable field, for one thing. Far too small, full of cattle, long grass, trees at the end—and I had not lined up my approach properly. Come on, I thought. You could be leaving it too late here. You're about to mess this up, Ken.

Suddenly, with awful conviction, I realised he was not going to open the throttle. *I had to land.*

It was a devastating moment. Suddenly, I realised why I had not been ready to go solo; why Sean had hesitated and hesitated. I had not taken responsibility. Knowing Ken was there to take over, as Sean always did, I had relied on his doing so. I cursed not taking more trouble, not picking a better field, not lining up my approach sensibly, not touching down earlier to give myself more room. We were already more than halfway down the field by the time we slid below hedgerow height. It was one of the lush rectangular water meadows which line the dykes on the Levels, edged at the far end with a row of pollarded willows along a wide water-filled rhyne. Grazing cattle looked up at the noise of the idling engine, then turned with wheezing coughs of alarm to gallumph out of our approach path. As the wheels touched down in the wet tussocks, my only thought was *we aren't going to make it*. The willows were just fifty yards ahead, rushing towards us. I cut the engine completely. There was a splattering as the tyres rolled through the wet cow pats, and a *thruppa thruppa thruppa* as they flicked dollops of gloop onto the underside of the wings. The heavy tussocks were helping to slow us, but not enough. At the last moment, as we were about to career into the willow trunks, Ken stamped on the left rudder pedal and we wheeled hard round to the left to bump to a juddering halt.

'Well, Tony. We're alive,' he boomed cheerfully.

'That was OK?' I inquired nervously.

'Appalling, Tony. The worst I've ever seen.'

Once we had re-started the engine and buckled ourselves back into our seats, I taxied her carefully through the soaking grass to the far end of the field, ready for our take-off run. The left wheel flicked water liberally over my outside thigh, which felt icy in the chill of the propeller blast. Yet, bizarre as it might seem, I felt elated. I had done it, and I could do it again. It gave me confidence. As we took off, the engine fought to haul us skyward. It made a hell of a difference having two heavy people aboard. If I weighed twelve and a half stone, Ken must have weighed nearer fourteen or fifteen. After quarter of a mile we were still only at about 200 feet, with the nose pointing steeply up.

'Think you've got that, then, Tony?' said Ken. 'Good.'

And he leant forward and flicked off the main power switch. The engine went dead.

'That damned engine, Tony. And on take-off too.'

An engine failure during take-off is one of the most dangerous things that can happen in a Thruster. There is no re-starting the engine once airborne. You are caught, at low speed, in a dangerously 'nose-high' or steeply climbing attitude. To prevent the plane stalling disastrously you have to react like lightning. I got the stick forward in the nick of time, just as the controls were beginning to go dangerously mushy. After an agonising pause, the rude, brutal silence left by the engine finally filled with the whistle and moan of air rushing over the wing and the wires, and the stick firmed up. I had only one option— straight ahead; it was a larger field than the one we had just left. It was then a matter of split seconds before the ground was rushing up to meet us, and I could level out and bounce to an unsteady halt. I wondered what the proper procedure was, on discovering that your flying instructor was a lunatic.

'Mmm. Not disastrous, Tony.'

Then we did it again. And again. And again.

Ken showed me how to pick the best field (which meant the biggest) and how to prepare a proper approach, calmly and without losing excessive height. He taught me how, once the nose was down and a glide established, to take my time. 'No need for anything manic. 50-55 knots, that's all. No need for the Stuka bit.' He rammed the stick forward to demonstrate what I had done and cupped his hand over his mouth in imitation of a klaxon in a submarine movie: 'Wooooop! Wooooop! Dive! Dive! ... You're just squandering height: you've got nearly a minute, from 1,000 feet.' He showed me how to spot invisible telegraph and electricity wires by looking for the poles that carried them. He showed me how to set up an approach circuit so as always to keep my chosen field on my side of the cockpit. And he showed me how to get into position on my final approach while I had height in hand, then serpentine to and fro to lose it. 'There are plenty of ways of shortening the glide, Tony. But no-one's invented a way to stretch it yet.'

Then, and only then, did Ken attend to the quality of the landing itself. 'Paddle those rudder pedals, now, to keep her straight,' he said, as I lined up my approach. 'Go on, paddle away and keep paddling.' To demonstrate, he paddled the pedals himself, yawing the nose this way then that. 'See? That's how to keep her straight. Now, just reduce the power gently and fly down the runway, a couple of inches above the surface, keep her flying now—no, don't try to land—that's right, keep her flying, keep her flying, keep her fly... and ... whoops ... there you go.'

And suddenly it clicked. I started to land perfectly every time. More importantly, I began to know how to do it perfectly every time. The secret? It was so simple that I couldn't believe no-one had told me before. It applies to all tail-dragger aircraft, which means that it applies even more to 'trike' undercarriage planes, which are, by comparison, a doddle. It is (by definition) universal, applying equally to 747s*, MiGs, Mustangs or Cessnas as much as to Thrusters. The secret, the key piece of information that had eluded me for so long was as follows:

Make no attempt to land.

I'll say it again: *make no attempt to land the plane.* Simply line yourself up to fly down the runway, paddling the rudder pedals to keep yourself straight. Fly down the runway just a few inches above the surface, gradually reducing the power, but without ever actually touching the wheels onto the ground. Then just 'hold off'—the pilot's term for attempting to keep her flying while reducing the power so that she cannot—and continue to hold off as you fly along the runway. Paddle the rudders to keep her straight. Hold off some more, until there is simply not an atom of flight left in her. Paddle. Hold off. Hold off. Hold off. Paddle to keep her nice and straight. And suddenly you will find you have landed and are running along the ground without even realising it. The bit that nobody tells you is that the plane lands itself.

I could put forward many reasons why it took me so long to learn a skill that most people, given similar opportunities, would probably have acquired in a tenth of the time. Perhaps I do, simply, have less feel for flying than anyone else who has ever flown. Perhaps it was because Sean, a naturally brilliant pilot (whose dazzling aerobatic displays, as he practised competition routines in his muscular Pitts Special bi-plane, regularly rattled the clubhouse windows), could not conceive of

* Not so, apparently—you'll scrape the tail on the runway.

anyone having such elementary difficulties. Perhaps it was simple lack of faith in my own competence. There is no doubt that five years in an advertising creative department did not help here. From my first day of employment, I had been tacitly encouraged to behave like a delinquent; 'creatives' were expected to throw tantrums, storm out of meetings, be rude, break things, lose train and plane tickets and generally be intransigent,* objectionable, and display *virtuoso* incompetence (and disdain) for workaday tasks. Thus could be perpetuated the myth of specialness of the creative people who generated the one product that an advertising agency has to sell. The difficult nature of the creative temperament had to be indulged at all times if the agency were to continue to deliver the services of such rare and gifted talents—or so the myth ran. Anyway, it was a position far too agreeable not to abuse fully, with the result that, even if you started out, as I did, a perfectly respectable middle-class adult, after a few years I had reduced myself to cradle levels of imbecility.

It was May before I returned to Norfolk, and for the first time, I no longer felt a stranger at the Thruster's controls. There seemed to be less that I had to struggle to concentrate on. Information and action had become reflex. I found I was looking at the right instruments at the right moment, already doing what had to be done, topping up information levels rather than groping in the dark. A phrase from a flying book came back to me: 'You don't get into a Spitfire; you buckle it on.' I wasn't, perhaps, quite at that stage yet. But I could see where the author was coming from.

Scarcely able to believe the improvement, Sean approved me to go solo again. The same afternoon I spent a wildly happy hour doing circuits and bumps, wallowing in my new confidence and skill. As the overcast sky cleared to a beautiful, still early summer evening, one of the club Cessnas joined me in the circuit. Afterwards, as I was putting the Thruster away, Sean came up. 'Just talking to Vic,' he said (referring to

---

* 'How many copywriters does it take to change a light bulb?' 'Change? I'm not changing anything.'

one of the club instructors). 'Said he was in the circuit with the old Thrasher.' Sean brushed some dead flies casually from the propeller with his hand. 'Said whoever was flying it was doing some nice landings.'

It was the greatest compliment I could ever remember receiving.

Never Eat Shredded Wheat

I couldn't but be conscious of the *single* sparking plug which adorned each cylinder just ahead of my nose. For hadn't my outspoken friend, Mr Grey, of *The Aeroplane*, just produced a powerful leading article damning what he called 'pop-bottle aviation', and briefly summarising cross country flying on two cylinders as 'delay action suicide'?

Flying For Fun, An Affair with an Aeroplane, Jack Parham, 1935

If the Air Ministry is going to allow people in the too-light aeroplanes to break their necks they ought to be compelled to keep inside the boundary of the aerodrome. There they can crash and burn up to their heart's content without anybody worrying much, so long as their next-of-kin replace the divots.

Charles Grey, Editor, *The Aeroplane*, 28 August 1935

'One for you, Tony, I think.' Richard was scanning the latest *Accident Survey*: '*The pilot's right foot jammed to the side of the steering bar on the landing roll-out and as a result, his left foot forced the brake hard on. The aircraft tipped over. The pilot reports he was wearing a new pair of heavy thermal boots at the time.*'

I had recently invested in a new pair of boots. I had selected them specifically for flying. They were leather-lined, padded with Thinsulate and had soft padded leather collars. Three brass eyelets and three D rings meant they laced up to my calves, protecting the chilly area around my ankles where the draughts seemed to howl however many pairs of 'stockings' I put on.

I had awarded them to myself for learning how to land. My feet were size $10\frac{1}{2}$ but I had ordered 11s to allow for a couple of pairs of thick socks. It had struck me when the assistant brought them out that they looked large, but I decided they were too good to miss. Now, trying them in the Thruster up at Barsham I discovered, to Richard's delight, that they were a shade too big to slide easily into the stirrups of the rudder pedals.

The boots were significant. Since learning how to land, everything had changed. Gone was the joyless, slightly deranged obsession with landing. In its place, a new world of exciting possibilities had opened up: namely, cross-country flying. The idea of taking off from Barsham and *arriving somewhere else* seemed almost impossibly exotic. In my mind there was still no connection between the arduous activity that took place in the cockpit of the Thruster over Barsham, and a practicable means of transport, with all its romantic requirements in terms of meteorology and navigation.

This had knock-on effects. First was that I began to see my world entirely in terms of its aviation potential. Cycling across Hyde Park to work each morning, I landed between the twin avenues of trees of Rotten Row (blissfully unaware of the perils of rotor effect), on the wide road which runs along the Serpentine (I decided the Thruster's wings would just clear the bollards and litter bins) and (uphill) on the Broad Walk. As I felt my skill improve, I restricted myself to landing on the narrow tarmac footpaths, dropping my wheels precisely where the paths crossed. I landed on the South Carriage Drive, Kensington Gore, Knightsbridge and the south-west end of Piccadilly. After a late session drinking after work (and in a moment of clear traffic and a light east wind) I touched down on the Knightsbridge approach to Hyde Park corner, taxied through the underpass and took off again on the ramp up to Piccadilly (impossible, on recent inspection, due—amongst many things—to the overhead streetlamps; I must have been drunk).

Wherever I saw an open area of dirt, gravel, grass, pasture, lawn, track or tarmac, I yearned to be touching down on it. On the M4, I found myself doing field-by-field appraisals for clear approaches, gradient, telegraph wires and pylons, making allowances for direction of seed-bed and carefully noting obstacles like lone trees or water troughs.

I now had to get on with my 'ground school' in meteorology and navigation. Since my Air Law exam, the only text-book information that I had made a conscious effort to acquire was the phonetic alphabet—information irrelevant to the pilot of a non-radio aircraft— chiefly to add a note of authenticity to my expanding range of aviation- themed Walter Mitty fantasies (these varied from Air-Sea helicopter rescue, carrier work in the Falklands, stealing Me 109s as an escaped prisoner-of-war, and prizing flying boats off tricky reaches of the Congo). I began to acquaint myself with details of pressure systems and air masses. I read of fronts and occlusions and adiabatic lapse rates and Coriolis Effect (something to do with the direction water goes down plug-holes). I drank in this information, and soon could have reproduced many of the diagrams from the text books, but making any useful connection between them and the conditions I encountered when I put my nose out of the door each morning was trickier.

Broadly, I could see that high pressure was Good, in that it was associated with fine weather, clear skies, and the sort of days that made you want to turn up the radio. Lows, on the other hand, were Bad: they brought unsettled, drab, dour, damp, wet, non-flying days of the kind when a hearty deep breath did nothing and you felt apathetic, listless and bored. But then I was foxed when high pressure also brought murk and haze and white skies, and low pressure brought sunny intervals with blue skies.

My existence, by my mid-twenties, had become completely severed from the natural world. I had not given the seasons a thought since being instructed to write poems about them at primary school.*

Although I had grown up in a Somerset village, I never felt particularly rural or part of the countryside, and since coming to London, even that limited influence had gone, to a point where I had become almost completely insulated from all environmental, solar or planetary cycles. As my life was conducted in brightly-lit, air-conditioned offices, tubes, buses, trains, taxis, bars, pubs and flats, the weather was neither here nor there. I did not own a waterproof (if it was raining, I did not bicycle). My job hardly helped, demanding, as it did, the creation of Christmas campaigns featuring snow and reindeer in June, and ads for Pimm's or Barley Water (usually featuring half-baked jokes about the rain) in winter. If I left London, I never looked at a map; I just followed timetables or sign-posts. Consequently I had no sense of direction. If pressed, I could not have said in which direction the sun rose and set without a nagging fear that I was getting it the wrong way round.

But now little, everyday things began to acquire a new significance: steam rising; condensation on a window; the sun in my eyes; a McDonalds wrapper blowing down the street; birds landing on my mother's birdtable; spoilers and the aerodynamic styling of new cars. As crocuses, then daffodils, began to appear in Hyde Park, leaves began to appear on the trees, and the air felt warmer—especially the air—flying made all these things interesting and relevant.

As autumn and winter had brought their new weather systems, I had been amazed how the *feel* of different kinds of air had changed. Last year, flying in the heat of the July midday sun, the air had felt as bumpy and jarring as driving down a rutted track. In the evenings, this tended to settle and soften, and the feel became smooth and velvety. Flying then was like sliding down the fast lane in a limo. On muggy, oppressive, white-skied August days it had been different again: dilute, slippery and wallowy. The controls had felt mushy and

---

* 'Season of mists and mellow fruitfulness, close bosom friend of the maturing sun ... did you write this, Woodward?'

   'Yes, sir.'

   'See me afterwards, Woodward.'

slow to respond. Then, on a frosty, blue-skied day (I had finally caught one with Ken), it had felt as crisp and firm as the rime-coated grass, yet perfectly smooth. The controls had seemed to 'grip' better and the Thruster felt twice as responsive.

Now Sean showed me, as midday bumps began to appear once more in the early summer sunshine, how the low, fluffy cumulus clouds were like flags, marking columns of rising warm air. Beneath them, I could expect bumps but could also get free lift from the thermal. I liked this idea that the sky was not a meaningless swirl, but a sort of forensic trail to be decoded. I became wary of being too specifically assertive with my new lore, however, after drawing a girl's attention to some fine, lenticular clouds over Barsham—*altocumulus lenticularis* I may have called them—only to be informed by Sean (who I had not realised was within earshot) that these occurred only in the proximity of mountains.

Some set-up was necessary to hold a map in place in the cockpit. The only commercially available knee-boards were very lightweight affairs, designed for pilots in enclosed, draught-proof, heated cabins. They were nowhere near robust enough for the blustery cockpit of the Thruster. However, as the microlighting market was too tiny to be worth catering for, we were left to improvise.

After a recce visit to the 'Pilot Shop' in Pimlico to inspect the commercial designs, I bought the best quality foolscap-sized hardboard clipboard I could find, with a strong, spring-loaded metal clip. I had a matching piece of hardboard cut by a local timber yard. Then I joined the two along their long sides with a wide strip of glued canvas, creating a stout, folding board with the clip on the top right-hand side when it was opened. To the reverse of the clipboard I glued two strips of wood of triangular section, roughly three inches apart. These held in place, at right angles, a five-inch wide band of heavy gauge elastic, to the end of which I stitched Velcro. Thus, once in the cockpit, the board fitted into position on top of my right thigh, and fastened securely by stretching the elastic round my leg.

While at the haberdashers I had also bought a length of knicker elastic. This I cut and stitched to length so that it would 'snap' tightly across the corners of the open board, so that a map, once folded to display the required route, could not flutter or flap in even the breeziest conditions.

From a mail order catalogue of flying accessories, I ordered a sixty-minute stopwatch, with a bolt-on clip to hold it, to time my 'waypoints' along my route. This the maintenance man at work drilled and fixed at the top left-hand corner of the opened board. The catalogue itself was a source of wonder: there seemed to be no end to the array of aviation-linked merchandise available, from the severely practical—in-flight pee bottles, flares, lifejackets and survival kits—to compass ash trays, altimeter desk sets, flight instrument coasters and Mile High tie-pins. I ordered a couple of spring-mounted pen-holders for good measure, and super-glued them to the back, plus some marker pens and chinagraph pencils to go in them, also a *Pooleys Flight Guide*.

I had been impressed by the mass of complex-looking information printed on the professional knee-boards: check lists, call signs, Morse code, ground signals, quadrantal and semicircular rules. Most of these had no relevance for the non-radio microlight pilot, but I had the agency studio design and set the information onto a sheet of A4 anyway, which I laminated and glued to the front. For some time after, the board, and some laminated, 'wipe-clean' Flight Plans I designed to go with it, became my favourite possessions. I would turn them over, trying to think of little improvements, snapping the elastic and clicking the stopwatch.

When I saw Dan's map-board—he had evidently devoted as much thought to the matter as I—I was irritated to see that it was rather better than mine. He had used heavier gauge canvas, included pockets inside, a digital timer, and, in place of my elastic leg strap, had stitched on a leather belt. When I asked Richard what he planned to do about a map-board, he said that he planned to use mine.

A number of new skills were needed for cross-country flying, starting with the efficient recognition of landmarks from the air—such as the destination airfield: 'It's right there, right in front of us,' Sean would say, as we overflew another stretch of identical countryside south of Barsham. 'Jesus. It's in front of your nose.' There was map-reading, and checking for wind strength and direction en route by looking out for smoke or ripples on water. There was crosswind landing. And, most importantly, there was the ability to follow a tolerably accurate compass heading.

Almost every aspect of the compass I found baffling. For a start, (though I had not revealed this to Sean), I could not remember the order of the points of the compass without repeating to myself, on each and every occasion, 'Never Eat Shredded Wheat'. Sean's instructions, along the lines of 'Turn to starboard 60°. What will your new heading be?' made my head seize as I tried to picture the compass in my head, do the arithmetic to work out my new heading, then initiate the manoeuvre. Even if I got it right, he had only to phrase his next order using the points of the compass—'Right, turn anticlockwise, onto an easterly heading'—to throw me again.

Part of my problem, I think, was that the compass didn't look like a compass to me. It was panel-mounted in the dashboard, so that only a 30° arc—or a maximum of one 'point'—showed through the little window. I was used to compasses being round, with the whole face visible. In all but the stillest air, the instrument shook and bounced so much that I was never sure in which direction it was trying to go. 'Push the stick left, and the compass moves right,' Sean would say. 'Push the stick right, and the compass moves left.' But somehow, though I had heard him say this a dozen times, it did not seem to work. There was just sufficient lag in the compass's response, jumping wildly as it was, that I would get cold feet when it did not respond, try to correct myself, over-correct, and our course would proceed in a series of ungainly zigzags. 'Don't *stare* at the compass,' Sean would say. 'Find a point on the horizon to aim at and you'll find you'll keep your bearing naturally.' I would try to do this (not so easy in featureless Norfolk), and he would say, 'Look at the compass, Ants. Where's your heading?'

Finally, quite by accident, he supplied the piece of information I had been missing. It just slipped out. 'Ants, *the compass is stationary*. It's the plane that moves around it.' This had not occurred to me. The last thing the compass had ever seemed to be was stationary. After that I had no more compass problems.

The syllabus required the student pilot to complete 'two solo cross country flights of at least forty nautical miles,' each to include 'an out-landing … at a site at least fifteen nautical miles from the take-off point.' For my first 'qualifying' cross-country I had settled on a northerly route. I was to land at Little Snoring, scarcely fifteen miles north of Barsham, then head west to Oulton (an ex-wartime airfield which, like so many in Norfolk, was now a pig farm). If I missed Oulton, there was always the more readily recognizable brick bulk of Blickling Hall nearby—then back to Barsham again. It was a cloudless, pale blue village-fête-and-cricket-match June day with a light seven knot north-westerly breeze. As I set my course from Barsham, my new map-board strapped to my knee, my heart was pounding in my ear. I had spent almost an hour selecting and circling my way-points, timing them and laboriously calculating wind drift on the Flight Calculator along my 'track required'. These Sean had approved. (Actually, what he had said was 'Jesus, Ants, what *are* you doing? There's hardly enough wind to bother with all that. You do make a meal of everything'.)

I was about ten minutes out of Barsham, just past the big Victorian mansion in the woods to the north of the airfield, when the engine failed.

It did not stop dead (though I did not always mention this when I was telling the story afterwards): it just kept cutting to a muffled sound and losing power sufficiently that, during the muffled phases, I could not maintain height. Then it would pick up. Then, just as I thought it was all right, the underpowered phase would cut in again. At first, I could not comprehend what was happening. The engine had been running perfectly a moment before. What could conceivably have gone wrong? I reached behind my seat and pumped the rubber fuel bulb, the only thing I could think of to do. It made no difference. The underpowered phases started to become more frequent. This cannot be happening, I thought: not on my first cross-country.

The phases began to get longer so that I was losing height rapidly. I looked urgently around for somewhere to land.

I wanted to panic. It was my right to panic. As the engine missed, picked up, missed again, I distinctly heard a whining child's voice casting around for someone to blame, someone else to take over. *I'm going to fuck this up* the voice said, *I'm going to smash the machine and kill myself. That'll show you.*

There was a huge field right below me, with a soft seed bed as the surface. The wind was coming from the north-west, from the direction of the Wash, which, conveniently, was also exactly the direction in which the seed bed had been drilled. I began to hear another voice. *Why make the fuss? Just do it. There's a big field right underneath. Why not just land?*

The approaches were clear all round. There were no wires or trees or buildings. (I checked where the gate was: would the ambulance get over the bump?) I got into position at one end, then serpented to and fro, as Ken had shown me, to lose height. The engine was still periodically kicking in with short bursts of power, then relapsing, so, as I lined up my final approach I closed the throttle completely. I remained completely calm, though I may have held my breath. I kept my approach steep and a few seconds later made a perfect engine-off landing, putting the wheels gently down between the rows of the crop.

As she rolled to a halt, I felt a charge of euphoria.

I felt, in fact, better than at any moment I could remember. I was stuck in a field in the middle of nowhere, with the promise of endless hassle and inconvenience ahead, not to mention the fact that I would not, after all, be completing one of my qualifying cross-countries. Yet I felt no frustration or irritation at all. I felt great. *I could do it.* I was safely down and, what's more, a 'greaser', bang into wind. Not a hint of a bounce. Sheer skill had prevailed—and icy *sang froid*, of course. But then, that was what this activity demanded. I was a natural. I had found my *métier*. What a perfect day! What a guy! I was still buckled in, shaking my head incredulously at my own brilliance, when I heard a voice behind me.

'Hope you've brought your wallet with you in that fancy machine.'

A battered Land-Cruiser had driven up from nowhere and a burly figure in wellies and muddy moleskin trousers was getting out of it. I presumed, correctly it turned out, that this was the owner of the field. For the first time it struck me that there was another light in which my momentous achievement could be viewed.

'Hope I haven't damaged too many cabbages…' I began apologetically. There was no answering friendliness in his voice.

'Two, maybe four tonnes,' he said shortly. 'And it's beet. Not cabbages.' He regarded me as he might an aphid on his crop. 'You clearly know even less about farming than you do about flying.'

I could not see how two light wheel prints running for fifty or sixty yards with (rather than across) the direction of the seed bed could amount to such awesome damage. But I had yet to understand that farmers have a tendency to exaggerate such matters until blame has been properly apportioned and admitted.

I apologised. I explained that it had been a life-or-death situation. I promised to make good any losses he sustained.

He had lost interest. He was disgustedly, distractedly, pulling handfuls of weeds from between the rows of beet. It was making him increasingly angry and resentful. For the first (and only) time it has ever happened, I saw an opportunity.

'If you don't mind me saying so, if you used a different adjuvant you'd eradicate all those weeds.'

When you spend your working day analysing and minutely interrogating the benefits of a range of very specific products, you cannot help finding yourself in possession of nuggets of curiously specialised information. I know, for example, that an avocado pear is not a pear but a berry, and that a peanut is not a nut but a pulse. I know that if you do not specify exactly what you want when sending flowers, your bunch is likely to consist of one rose, five carnations and a cloud of gypsophila. I know that most people do not like the taste of coffee, though they adore the smell and the idea of it. I know that nuclear power stations in this country are incredibly safe because their switches are kept open by electricity, so in the event of a power failure they all close automatically by gravity. And I happened to know, because I had recently been writing advertisements for it, that if a fluazifop-P-butyl-based herbicide was mixed with a particular ionic adjuvant, it would work exactly ten times as effectively.

He gave me a frown of surprise.

'Just out.' I continued. 'Better surfactants, better emulsifiable oils, better activators. It also means a little goes a lot further. Application rates are right down, it's better for the environment. And it works out miles cheaper.'

'But how ... how come you ...' His attitude had changed considerably. By the time I had finished he was nodding his head thoughtfully.

'Well, how about that, then? Yes. Yes. Indeed. Well. Look, we should be getting back to the farm. 'Spect you'll be ready for a nip of whisky after your experience.'

From the farmhouse kitchen, where his wife plied me with cups of tea and home-made cake, we called Sean, whose red van was soon on the scene.

'Nicely into wind, Ants. Just right,' he said approvingly as he pumped the fuel pump, switched on the ignition, and pulled the starter cord. The engine fired immediately, and for a moment I dreaded that it was going to run perfectly. But as Sean was about to attempt a take off, to my relief the ignition started breaking up again. I say ignition wisely, because that was what Sean diagnosed as the trouble. But he could not isolate the fault. In the end we had to dismantle the Thruster and, for a second time, she returned to Barsham by road. I did not mind. I was still glowing. Far better, in fact, than if I had merely completed a successful cross-country. As for the farmer, he could not have been more helpful, providing a tractor and trailer to carry the dismantled carcass. He would not hear of any compensation.

Flying was never quite the same after that. There had been a breach of trust. Up until that day, I had always assumed it would be something *I* did that would crash the Thruster. I had not seriously considered the possibility of mechanical failure. Precautionary landings were no longer drills for improbable emergency. They were a hard, necessary reality.

It took weeks to rectify the problem. The Thruster was one of the few remaining piston-engined aircraft still fitted with single ignition. Almost all aero engines, since the 1950s, have had dual ignition: a double electrical system, including two magnetos and two spark plugs at the top of each cylinder, so that if one goes down, there is always a backup. Although Sean knew the trouble was electrical, he didn't know exactly where or what it was. He replaced one part after another. But that still did not do it, so eventually he had to take the engine off and send it away to the Cyclone Hovercraft Company, who imported it. They couldn't find out what was wrong either, and passed it on to the electrical supplier. In the end the cause never was isolated. The electrical supplier replaced the whole system, from plugs to alternator, asserting vaguely that vibration was the cause, and returned the engine enclosing a large bill.

So it was not until the third Saturday in August that I next made it up to Barsham Green. It was a baking weekend, and the summer felt well past its best, the verges bleached and dusty. In the morning, I sat my 'Meteorology and Navigation' and 'Engine and Airframes (Technical Aspects)' exams. Sean installed me in his office, prudently removing sale copies of *The Microlight Pilot's Handbook* and other textbooks from the shelf where they were usually stored, and any other sources of reference I might be tempted to consult. Also, having overheard Richard's admission that, during his exams in Africa, he had made strategic visits to the lavatory, where he had taken the precaution of secreting the necessary textbook behind the cistern, he forbade me to leave the room until I was finished. Fortunately, however, he did not disconnect his telephone. When I was stuck, I telephoned Richard, sitting outside in the car with *The Microlight Pilot's Handbook*, for assistance. I scored 98 per cent and 100 per cent and felt very satisfied with my morning's work.

After lunch, as I wheeled the Thruster out of the hangar, I could not help feeling mildly apprehensive. Sean sensed this. 'Tell you what, Ants,' he said. 'You've never seen how high the old Thrasher can go, have you? Why don't you stay over the airfield and go as high as you can? That way if you're not happy, and in the remote chance you *do* get another engine failure, you'll always know you can just glide down. Make sure you alternate the way you're turning every now and again so you don't get dizzy. And look around inside the cockpit from time to time to prevent yourself getting vertigo.'

There was no wind. After taking off I turned right into the circuit, then headed over to an adjoining field where a farmer was burning his stubble. I kept the nose up, with the air speed indicator at exactly 45 knots for maximum rate of climb. I was at 1,500 feet when I crossed the flames of the stubble, and, as I caught the thermal, it was as if a shoulder had come up beneath and heaved me upwards. I throttled back to a relaxed 4,000 revs, turned a tight circle over the main area of flames, and settled back to watch the altimeter wind steadily clockwise.

If I strayed too far from the flames below I could feel myself falling out of the thermal, so I maintained a steady climbing turn, first one way, then the other. At 1,800 feet a buzzard joined me, circling not fifteen feet away, waiting, I suppose, for mice or rabbits to be driven out by the flames below with lazy twitchings of its outstretched wings. As I gained height, the haze from the burning stubble seemed to get thicker and dirtier.

By 4,000 feet there was no sensation of forward (or, in fact, any) movement: I seemed to be stationary over a carpet of countryside spread as far as the sea. All warmth in the air had gone. At 6,500 feet I suddenly broke out through a layer of petrol-coloured haze into deep, clear blue sky. Now, the air was much colder, and below me, through the murk, it looked almost dark.*

By 8,000 feet I could see the whole of East Anglia. I could make out Norwich Airport, Sizewell B, The Wash. I began to feel acutely and chronically unstable, as if I were floating outside the atmosphere in a bath tub which might tip up at any moment. I could see why Sean had told me to focus on things inside the cockpit. The absence of any external reference points with which to calibrate my middle distance vision was disorientating. There were no clouds, so it was either the instrument dials, two feet away; or the ground, which was one-and-a-half miles away. It was a view I had only ever seen from the window seat of an airliner, when I usually had a drink, a newspaper and a packet of nuts in my hand. I felt very alone.

With such an enormous field of view it was hard to tell if I was still over the airfield or not. If I looked down and concentrated, I could make out the black hangar—a minute dot, far below. I focussed on the instrument panel again and felt better. I was hardly climbing at all now

---

* I had been up to about 5,000 feet on trips with Richard, but probably, if you're not a flyer, such figures won't mean much. As a guide, circuit height—between 800 and 1,000 feet—is between the height of the top of the spire of Salisbury Cathedral and the top of Canary Wharf tower in London Docklands. The point when you encounter clouds after take-off from Heathrow on a typical, overcast day is 1,500-2,000 feet. Five minutes after take-off in a passenger jet you are at 7,000-10,000 feet. Returning across the Channel to Heathrow, as you cross the English coast you are at about 15,000 feet.

and had started to feel intensely cold. I was, in fact, wearing almost every garment I had brought to Norfolk—with the result that I had been sweating profusely on the ground. Now my fingers and toes were completely numb and the rest of me felt naked. My climb rate had tailed off completely. The altimeter read 11,800 feet and I seemed to be winding round in a level turn.

I had been amazed to read, in *Diary of an Unknown Aviator*, that First World War pilots routinely went up to 20,000 feet and higher, in open-cockpit planes over the trenches without heated suits or down jackets or oxygen, let alone pressurised cabins. That was higher than Mount Kilimanjaro, most of the Alps or even the Andes. 'Gosh, it's unpleasant fighting at that altitude,' noted the anonymous diarist. 'The slightest movement exhausts you, your engine has no pep and splutters; it's hard to keep a decent formation, and you lose five hundred feet on a turn.' Plainly pilots were hardier in those days.

I wanted, if I could, to get the needle to touch 12,000 feet. But I had been up in outer space turning and turning for half an hour without noticeably gaining height. I couldn't see the fuel level any more, I was well over two miles above the ground, and I was freezing. I decided to call it a day.

Whether emboldened by my little adventure, euphoric, bored or simply light-headed from oxygen starvation, I then took it into my head to do something inexplicable. I deliberately reached forward to the main power ON/OFF toggle switch on the dashboard, and flicked it to OFF. The roar of the engine stopped dead. In surreal silence, the propeller flickered into visibility. Unable to believe what I had done, I tried to rectify the madness; hardly had the noise died away, before I had flicked the switch back to ON again. Too late, of course.

The propeller began to windmill slowly. As I established a glide, the sound of the rushing air in the wires increased. My position was not particularly dangerous, so long as I kept my head. Like any plane, the Thruster would glide, albeit like an anvil. It was just a staggeringly idiotic thing to have done. It meant that I had one chance and one only at my landing. There could be no overshooting if I touched down late.

No burst of power if I undershot and came in too low, or got caught by a patch of sink, on finals. No going around if I felt like another go.

Through the windscreen I could see the pull-start cord of the engine, twitching in the air-flow. It was almost within reach, if only the windscreen were not between us. I toyed with the idea of climbing out round the outside of the pod to pull it, and had actually got as far as releasing my seat harness, when it occurred to me that it would probably be easier to smash the windscreen. However some experimental thumps against the Perspex with my padded, ski-gloved fist made it clear that this was not a practical option—besides, my attempts were making the plane rock wildly.

Another thought occurred. Could I, perhaps, bump-start the engine, like a car? If I put the plane into a Stuka nosedive, it might just be possible to force the propeller round fast enough, if the ignition were on, to get the engine to fire. There was that section in *The Right Stuff* where Yeager had to restart the main engine of the NF-104. 'To relight the engine you have to put the ship nose down into a dive and force air through the intake duct and start the engine windmilling to build up the rpms.' Did the same apply to a propeller engine?* Why the hell hadn't I found this kind of thing out? Rather than cheating in exams on which my life might depend?

It took ages to descend; well over quarter of an hour at a steady 750 feet per minute. It seemed far longer—perhaps because I was impatient to get the landing over with—but as I finally passed down through 5,000 feet, then 4,000 feet, then 3,000 feet, the air warmed up and I felt I was once again re-joining a life-bearing planet. The Thruster no longer felt rocky and unstable. By 1,200 feet, almost down to circuit height, everything felt familiar again. I flexed my fingers and toes to make sure they still worked, joined the circuit on the base leg, swept round onto finals and touched down exactly on the key-shaped bald patch of grass which Sean told me he made students aim for when he cut the engine in their flying test. Then I climbed out of the cockpit,

* No.

started the engine, and taxied back to the hangar. 'All right Ants?' called Sean, as I put the Thruster away.

My next cross-country was on 15th September, a flawless Battle of Britain day. In fact, as I learned on the radio on the way up, *the* Battle of Britain day: the Fiftieth Anniversary. I had been enjoying a preview of the scheduled fly-past by the RAF Memorial Flight, down The Mall and over the Queen on the balcony of Buckingham Palace. However, apart from mildly regretting that I was out of London on the one day I might have got the chance to see and hear a real Spitfire and Lancaster I didn't give the matter serious thought.

So I was surprised when Sean came up as I was in the final stages of my pre-flight checks. 'Checked the board for NOTAMs?' he asked. Sean had a habit of saying unsettling things like this just as I was all set to go. The answer to his question was that I had not checked the board for NOTAMs, for the simple reason that I had not the faintest idea what NOTAMs were.

Whenever I tried to look at the Club notice board I would find my eyes beginning to glaze and become gripped by a rising queasiness. The dog-eared state of most of the notices meant it was impossible to tell what was current and might be relevant, and what had been there for months or even years and no one had bothered to remove. There were quite a few notices of which I understood not a single word. Metfaxes routinely contained sentences like 'GEN 8 KM IN RA OR DZ, WITH 5/8STSC 500 FT/5000, AND 2/8ACAS 10000 FT/14000.' In fact, the acronyms and abbreviations seemed limitless.*

---

* Try this by no means comprehensive selection: AAL, ACC, A/C, A/D, ADF, ADR, ADT, AFIS, AFTN, AG, AGL, A/G, AIAA, AIC, AIP, AIS, ALT, AME, AMSL, ANO, AOA, Ap, APAPI, APP, ASR, ATA, ATC, ATCC, ATD, ATIS, ATS, ATSOCAS, ATSU, ATZ, AVGAS, AVTUR, AWY, BAA, BAUA, BCPL,

Did everyone else know what they stood for? Did the Norwich and Eastern instructors, in epaulettes, know, for example? If I buttonholed Carter and asked him what OAC, RIS and VORTAC stood for, would he be able to tell me? I found it hard to believe that he would. Yet I felt even more unsettled by the possibility that he might. I had a hazy idea that NOTAMs were sort of official bulletins from the CAA, sent out daily or weekly (or maybe hourly) to airports and airfields. But I had decided they were something for professional pilots and had gratefully written them off as beyond my scope.

'It's OK, I'm only going to Priory Farm,' I reassured Sean.

'Check the board,' said Sean. 'There's a Battle of Britain fly-past going on today. Half Norfolk's a no-fly area this morning.'

How a fly-past in London, however grand or official, could possibly affect my half-hour bumble across the north Norfolk countryside, I could not even guess (though the thought that, as a pilot, I came under the jurisdiction of such an event was flattering). I had no idea where NOTAMs were posted in the clubhouse, or what they looked like. What I did know was that searching the four walls of hieroglyphics might take a month. I was wondering whether to risk asking Carter's son Keith, who was on the radio, and receive a sneering, sarcastic reply,

C, CAA, CAS CAVOK, CDF, C of A, C of E, C of T, CHAPI, CMATZ, CO, c/s, CTA, Ctl, CTR, DAAIS, DACS, DERA, DH, DME, E, EAT, EET, ETA, ETD, FFA, FAT, FBU, FIC, FIG, FIR, FIS, FL, GCA, GLS, GMC, GMP, GMT, Gn, GVS, H24, HF, HIRTA, HJ, HMR, HN, HO, HP, HPZ, HTA, HX, IAP, IAS, ICAO, IFR, ILS, IMC, IR, ISWL, JAR, JB, LARS, Lctr, LDA, LFA, LITAS, LLZ, LTMA, M, Mag, MARAS, MATZ, MDH, MDZ, MEDA, MEF, MET, METAR, Mil, MKR, MM, MNM, MSD, MTWA, FL, N, NATS, NATSU, NDB, NDB(L), NM, NOTAM, OAC, OCA, OCH, OM, OPMET, O/R, O/T, P, PAPIS, PAR, PIC, PN, PNR, PPL, PPR, QDM, QFE, QFU, QGH, QNH, QTE, R, RAC, RAD, RAS, RCC, RCL, REIL, RIS, RT, RVR, S, SAL, SAR, SFC, SID, SIGMET, SR, SRA, SRZ, SS, SSR, STAR, SVFR, TACAN, TAF, TCA, TDME, Thr/Thld, TMA, TORA, TVOR, TWR, UFN, UIR, UKAIP, UNL, UTC, VAD, VASIS, VDF, VFR, VHF, VMC, VOLMET, VOR, VORTAC, VRP...

when fortunately one of the Cessna instructors came in with his pupil.

'I think it's OK now,' he was saying, striding purposefully up to a board on the opposite side of the room to the one I had been looking at. 'These fly-pasts only take about three quarters of an hour to assemble.' He smoothed flat the curling corners of a sheet as his eyes scanned the paragraphs. 'Yes, 10.45 to 11.30. You're clear.'

'Fine,' I called to Sean. 'All clear from 11.30.'

'Well, keep a good look out.'

The day was so warm I was wearing just a tee-shirt and shorts beneath my ozee suit. As I took off, I could smell the grass where a tractor was mowing the verges along the lanes around Barsham. I felt relaxed and seemed hardly to have turned onto my heading of 170° when, keeping the disused railway line on my right, the big, pitted runways of Tibenham Airfield appeared straight ahead. Priory Farm was to the left, the wind sock twitching straight down the runway. I swept round in a tidy circuit and landed, taxied up to the small blister hangar and switched off the engine.

The sensation of having left one place and arrived at another, entirely by my own work, without signpost or timetable or any contact with the earth, was extraordinary. It was like materialising from nowhere. I had stared at some abstract lines on a piece of paper, listened to the weather forecast, done some calculations with ruler, protractor and flight calculator, obeyed the indications of two or three dials on my instrument panel and now, here I was: literally out of the blue. The fact that I had visited Priory Farm numerous times before with Sean was not the point. I had wrought this magic all by myself.

For some time I was overcome by my own powers. I explored the barns and outhouses; the place was deserted. I 'signed in', writing my name and G-MVOY into an old exercise book in the caravan, refusing to allow the fact that the previous entry was also the Thruster (Sean taking a student out), from the day before, to dent my sense of pioneering endeavour. And I made a mental note to enter 'Priory Farm, Tibenham', into the AERODROMES VISITED section at the front of my log book that evening. With that, I zipped myself back into my ozee suit, and took off on the reciprocal leg back to Barsham.

I had climbed to 500 feet, and was about to set my heading to 350°, when four Tornadoes passed underneath me.

I nearly swallowed my tongue with surprise. They were so close that I could see the faces of the pilot and navigator, or what was visible of their faces around their Darth Vader masks. I could see their helmets coolly tilting from side to side as they chatted. I could see the rivets and the small, stencilled capital lettering painted onto the grey fuselage beneath the canopy. I could see the luminous read-outs on the instrument panels in front of them. I could almost hear their conversation.

The experience was made more freakish by the silence. There was no roar of jet engines. True, I had the steady WAAAAARRRRGGGHH of the two-stroke in my ear, but the planes appeared to be moving in complete silence. The noise came a moment later: a crashing, rolling thunderclap that engulfed and drowned the puny Rotax, scoring my eardrums. Instinctively, I yanked the stick back hard. All I could think was 'gain height, gain height'—anything to get clear of the dreaded 'wake turbulence'.

Wake turbulence is the churned and chopped-up air which passing aeroplanes and helicopters leave behind them: it is the reason that planes queuing to take off do so at discreet intervals. On big, heavy or powerful machines it is tremendous and very dangerous. The turbulence from giants like a Hercules transport plane or a Chinook helicopter could flip a small plane upside down. It tended to be worse from propeller-driven aircraft or choppers than from jets, which were 'cleaner'. But I had heard that someone in a Cessna flying through the flight path of a passenger airliner which had passed more than *fifteen minutes* before was still thrown all over the place. So I was taking no chances. I threw the throttle open and hauled the nose up into the steepest climb she could manage, waiting any second to be flipped over onto my back. As I did so, four more Tornadoes passed above me.

If the first encounter had been close, this time it was a great deal closer. It felt so close that the wing fabric might be cut by all the sharp, pointy bits that jet fighters have underneath. There must have been fifty feet between us, but it seemed like two.

Nor was that it. Quite suddenly the whole sky seemed to be dark with aircraft. Not just Tornadoes, but F 1-11s, and a couple of giant Hercules transports, too. They can't see me, I thought. They're all going too fast. This is it. Heart pounding, engine screaming, controls crossed, I clung on to the stick wondering what to do.

As it happened, I did not have to do anything. As suddenly as they had appeared, the planes were gone. The Tornadoes, locked in formation, curved round in a huge arc and disappeared off into the distance. The two Hercules trundled off to the north-east. The F 1-11s headed south. I decided that if the wake turbulence was going to get me it would have done so by now. The pilots must have known what they were doing, I decided, and, high-spirited as they returned to their bases after their fly-past, decided to have some fun. Bastards.

It was my first close encounter with another aircraft. During lessons, I had been used to seeing—and had almost come to regard with affection—the gawky A10 'Tankbusters' (soon to become famous in the Gulf War) from USAF Lakenheath, which sauntered about, practising sighting-up on tractors. And quite often we saw the dark, fast-moving shapes of F1-11 fighters. But Sean had said not to worry; they always kept their distance, and to date they always had.

No-one seemed much interested in my tale back at Barsham. Sean was out with a pupil. The other instructors just laughed. 'That'll teach you,' sneered Keith, though I wasn't sure *what* it was supposed to teach me. Even Sean, when I told him later, just sniffed 'I told you Ants. Keep a good look out.' I felt inclined to point out that one could scan the skies like an eagle, but what difference would it make?*

A few weeks later, by chance, I met an American colonel from the USAF Eighth, based at Lakenheath. He gave me a woven cap badge

---

* Military aircraft can practise low flying more or less where and when they please, and there are not many precautions you can take—except, as Sean said, keep a good look out.

embroidered '48TFW Deployed—When Diplomacy Fails'. I recounted the incident, suggesting that the Tornado pilots had been having some fun. Speaking in the quiet, measured voice of someone used to thinking before he spoke, he said, 'No, they don't do things like that. Too damn easy to make a mistake. No, you wouldn't appear on their radar. To pick you up, it would be set so fine it would pick up every damn flock of birds, and every car on the road. Nope. They wouldn't have seen you. That's what happened.' He sipped his drink impassively. 'Yeah, that's what happened. You were lucky.'

Natural Born Tinkerers

If you can nail together a packing case, you can construct an aeroplane.

Henri Mignet, *The Flying Flea*, 1935

They built a weird machine,
The strangest engine ever seen,
And they'd quite forgotten that the thing was rotten,
And they shoved it in a flying machine.

They called them RAF 2Cs, on the RAF BE 2C

I was furious with Lester. It was a perfect evening, the last Sunday in September, and I was pacing up and down the grass outside the black hangar, fuming. I had driven all the way over to Barsham Green from the Midlands, to take my General Flying Test—or at least a mock-GFT which, Sean had said, if I did well enough he would count as the real thing. Indeed, after initial doubts Sean had become almost encouraging. The sun was shining from a cloudless sky. There was no wind. The visibility was perfect. I had spent the whole day in mental and physical preparation, going through the necessary manoeuvres in my head. I had eaten a light lunch, drunk nothing, and arrived at Barsham in good time. To find the Thruster gone.

At first I thought Sean must be out giving a lesson or a trial flight, but a few moments later he arrived in his red van and was equally mystified. The explanation emerged from Carter: Lester had taken it that morning.

121

Lester had passed his GFT a week or two before (with his hundreds of flying hours, he didn't need to complete the statutory minimum twenty-five hours required of Dan and me). Although Dan had not yet taken his GFT, I knew he was about to, and the certainty that he would sail through, leaving me once again, the sad loser left trailing had acted as a catalyst to my own niggardly progress.

The situation was particularly maddening because this was probably the last opportunity I would have to take my test before the weather turned. I had even called to warn them I would be coming.* I tried calling Salsingham, but to no avail; the phone just rang and rang with its usual distant and old-fashioned echo. Where could he be? It was the first time I had felt irritated and thwarted by anyone in the syndicate other than Richard. I tried to factor into the equation the fact that the Watsons had put up with considerable Thruster 'downtime' due to my own actions. But it did not alter the fact that while those were a hazard, this was plain selfishness. Didn't Lester realise what a slog and expense it was to get to Norfolk? I did not live here. After bitching to Sean along these lines for twenty minutes, I was wondering whether there was anything to do but head back to London, when a characteristic, high-pitched whine became audible and the unmistakeable silhouette of the Thruster appeared in the sky.

I was so torn between preparing a speech for Lester and trying to re-psych myself for my GFT that I wasn't paying much attention as he landed. But Sean, cocking his head critically one way then the other as the Thruster taxied up, said, 'Oh no. What's he gone and done?'

Now that he said it, there *was* something strange about the way the Thruster was moving. It was leaning a little too much on one side, crabbing slightly as it taxied. As it came to a halt and Lester stopped the engine, I saw that the bolt holding on the left-hand wheel was far too long, rusty and bent.

'What the—?' Sean began, springing over and crouching down to

* In all the time we had had the Thruster, this was our first, and, it would turn out, last, timetabling clash.

examine the new arrangement. 'What's going on here?'

'Where the Hell have you been, Lester—?' I said.

'Sorry. 'Fraid I had a bit of an accident,' said Lester, with an apologetic smile. 'Nothing serious. The axle-pin sheared and I had to replace the bolt. That's why I'm a little late.'

'Oh *no*,' said Sean, with a groan.

'It's perfectly safe, Sean; perfectly safe. It's a jury rig,' Lester asserted authoritatively. The substitute bolt was four or five inches over-length, a deficiency Lester had remedied with an assembly of washers and nuts, of mixed size, origin and age—mostly, it appeared, from the workshop floor. These had been used to pad out the excess length of the exposed shaft to the part where the thread began. Sean inspected the unscheduled modification disdainfully.

'It's a bloody mess. That's what it is,' he said, clicking his tongue and groaning again. 'What happened?'

'I'm so sorry, Antony. I do apologise,' said Lester, turning to me, then looking at his watch. 'But I'm sure there's still time for a flight now, if you're quick—'

'No one's flying anywhere in this,' said Sean finally.

'But Sean, it's perfectly all right, I assure you,' Lester persisted, though not quite so confidently as before. 'It's perfectly sound; a jury rig.' He repeated the phrase for emphasis, something I had noticed he did occasionally, if he suspected there was a danger his interlocutor might not be accepting his point of view. 'Perfectly safe. I'm a trained engineer, you know. It's a jury rig,' he repeated, sadly.

'You know what this smacks of?' Sean said, cocking his head this way then that as he inspected Lester's handiwork. 'I'll tell you. It smacks of *Lester*. This is an aircraft we're talking about, not a bloody lawn mower. Unapproved mods are illegal. Besides—' He was now craning his head underneath the Thruster. It was interesting to hear the censure in his voice. Though only a year or two older than us, he cut effortlessly through the generation gap between himself and Lester. Richard and I, the same age as Lester's children, less experienced as pilots, guests in his house and disciples of his lifestyle, had only recently summoned the courage to use his Christian name (not, I am sure, that he noticed). The idea of addressing him in this manner was unthinkable.

'Besides —' said Sean straightening up. 'You may well have buckled the whole frame. How did you do it, anyway?'

It turned out that Lester had flown over to Salsingham to see if any of the fields were suitable for landing. A large stubble field to the north-west of the house had looked all right, so after a couple of approaches he had decided to land. Unfortunately, just after touchdown, the left-hand wheel had hit a tractor rut, spinning the machine round and shearing the-axle pin. It had taken all afternoon, with his daughter Seph's help, to prop the Thruster onto a bale of straw, and get the wheel back on.

Strangely, as I left for London, I was not as disappointed as I might have been. True, my chances of getting my GFT before next summer had dwindled to zero, but, frankly, they had been minimal, anyway: the time when I felt genuinely competent to take charge of a plane single-handed still seemed a long way off.

I was pleased that the Watsons had had an accident, at last. There had been, up to now, a mild but mounting air of censure from Dan and Lester and even, recently, from Rhona, Seph and the rest of the family: Richard and I did not take enough care; we did not do it right; things went wrong for us; we damaged the Thruster. Now, at least, Lester had evened things up a little. As I turned out of the airfield, the last thing I heard was Lester's voice carrying plaintively over the skylarks. 'But it's a jury rig, Sean. Perfectly safe. A jury rig ...'

I told Richard about the incident and, for a time afterwards, whenever we came across any bodged or obviously Heath Robinson contrivance, we would nod sagely, catch each other's eye and murmur, 'Jury rig. Perfectly sound.' But, laugh as we might, this superficially trivial episode weighed on my mind. Had I been faced with Lester's position

I would have had no option but to telephone Sean, explain the situation, then wait for him to arrive with his tools and expertise. Lester's attitude demonstrated an ability to deal with a problem rather than pass it on. His jury rig might not have been perfect, but it worked well enough to get him back to the airfield. As for Sean's sneering—well, it was his job to do that.

The technical and mechanical aspects of shoestring aviation had concerned me from the start. Sooner or later, if I were ever to fly safely and confidently out of Sean's catchment area, I was going to have to come to grips with it. All my safety checks and maintenance procedures on the Thruster I was doing by rote or letter, rather than from understanding—a typical consequence of which had been the recent Duckham's oil fiasco. Early on, Sean had impressed upon us the importance of using Duckham's oil to mix into the 'two-stroke mixture' of petrol and oil on which the Thruster's engine ran. Knowing nothing about oils, engines—or flying—but naturally anxious to take whatever steps were necessary to promote the smooth and consistent running of the engine in the air, we had taken Sean at his word and gone to inordinate lengths to procure Duckham's oil. It soon transpired that Duckham's, more expensive than regular oils, was stocked by a minority of retailers. Having discovered these many, as they sold out, did not re-stock. Gradually, we found ourselves driving further and further, to motorcycle centres, specialist motor parts stores or distant service stations (often consuming much of Saturday morning in the process) to secure supplies of the precious blue fluid. This continued until the day when our supplies finally ran out just as I was due for a lesson. I told Sean the problem, and his response was to wander round the hangar, picking up nameless grimy old three-quarters empty pots of different oils—none Duckham's—which he then tipped, without measuring, into the tank of the Thruster. 'That ought to do it,' he said. 'Slosh some petrol in on that.' I was appalled.

'I thought you said we had to use Duckham's.'

'Yes, Duckham's is a good oil, Ants.'

'Yes, but I thought you said we had to use it. Nothing else would do.'

'Come on, stop fussing. There was life before Duckham's, Ants. We should be in the air by now.'

So after that we bought any old oil, and it didn't seem to make any difference—the point being that, knowing next to nothing of mechanical matters, let alone the theory and practice of flying, it was hard to gauge what mattered and what did not. Every lesson began with a 'pre-flight check', consisting, essentially, of a visual once-over of the aircraft. The idea was that any dents or damage inflicted by other hangar users, or vandals, or worn or damaged wires or parts, or dirty or perished fuel lines, and so on, could be picked up before they failed in less convenient circumstances. I could see that this principle was sound enough, but, at the same time, how could *I* be trusted to know whether a part was serviceable or not?

I would wander round the aircraft, as instructed, prodding at the wing fabric, twanging the control wires, running my hands over the ailerons, glaring at the engine block. Would a large pigeon-dropping on the rear elevator affect the airflow? Did a soft left tyre matter? Would it send me somersaulting on landing? Why was there a bunch of multi-coloured, apparently loose electrical wires up by the engine? Shouldn't they be connected to something? Did the clearly visible grunge in the fuel line matter? It always seemed to be there, yet the engine carried on running well enough. My inspection felt fraudulent and pointless.

I had recently seen an article in *National Geographic* about the Eighth Air Force in Britain during the war. In it there had been a photograph of a Flying Fortress bomber which had collided with another Flying Fortress in formation and one of the propellers of the second Fortress had chewed a vast, fifteen-foot chunk out of the first Fortress's port wing. There was practically no wing left; just the leading edge and the engine. Yet it carried on, dropped its bombs on the target and returned safely home. How was that possible? And given that it was possible, *why* was it possible? How much of the wing did you need? Another plane had lost its entire stabiliser and rudder, yet made it home too. There was a picture of it. Bombers apparently regularly came back with four hundred flak holes. How important could sponging dead flies off the propeller blades be—as Sean regularly insisted we do—when planes could fly when they were perforated like a shower head?

As for the engine, if it didn't start within five or six pulls, I could not help imputing human characteristics (a hang-over from childhood Saturdays spent trying to coax my father's bloody-minded rotary mower into life). I would plead and wheedle, threaten and curse. If it still would not start, I had one diagnosis up my sleeve: that it was 'flooded', and needed a rest. Indeed, of all the mechanical areas that frightened me, engines frightened me most. The way they worked— that they worked at all—seemed so inherently improbable; so many complicated actions, all dependent on numerous other, equally complicated and unlikely mechanisms.

This was not to say that I could not appreciate and admire fine machinery when I saw it—from a strictly aesthetic point of view. I could stare into the cutaway Spitfire engine that I once came across in an aero club; mesmerised by the bewitching assembly of (I later discovered) 10,000 parts. The double bank of cylinders, six either side, with its gleaming pistons and camshafts, was as awesome as any sculpture, while the bald facts of the caption, tersely Biro-ed onto a piece of torn card, moved me so much that I wrote it down.* I liked to

---

* *Rolls-Royce Merlin: V12, liquid-cooled; capacity, 27 litres; four valves per cylinder. Generated output 1,800 hp at 3,000 rpm. Powered Spitfire, Hurricane and, later, American P-15 Mustang fighters (as well as Mosquito and Lancaster bombers). The most advanced and powerful engine of its time, the Merlin's performance was little short of phenomenal. In combat, pilots were permitted to push the throttle 'through the gate' for up to a maximum of three minutes, producing a near-impossible boost pressure of +27.5 lbs per inch². The Daimler-Benz Db 601 engine, which powered the Spitfire's main rival, the German Messerschmitt Me-109, was considerably larger (35.7 litres); performance of the two fighters, however, was similar. Throughout the war there was enormous pressure on piston engine development. The Merlin more than doubled its power from 1,000 hp in 1939 to over 2,100 hp by 1944, mainly through improvements in supercharging. There was no sacrifice in reliability.*

imagine an Me-109 diving out of the sun onto the Spitfire, pumping a stream of tracer and exploding cannon shells, and the Spitfire pilot ramming his throttle 'through the gate', knowing the engine would respond. In a documentary, I heard an American Second World War veteran who flew Merlin-powered P-51 Mustangs, say, with infinite affection, 'That bird; she just hummed.'

'She just hummed.' The soothing phrase kept coming back to me. What I wanted to know was, why, a full half-century after Henry Royce had perfected the finest piston aero engine in history, a similar epithet could not be applied to the Rotax 503, the 'lump' bolted to the front of the Thruster? The Rotax was a two-stroke engine, the kind found in chainsaws, Strimmers, cheap outboards and bottom-of-the-range motorbikes; in short, everything (apart from hammer drills) that makes the worst noise of modern life. Two-strokes were the simplest kind of internal combustion engine. They revved furiously and generated enormous power for their weight, so they were ideal for anything where weight was at a premium. But the racket meant that even the shortest time flying resulted in ringing ears. Longer flights ended with throbbing headaches. Codeine-aspirins and Ibuprofen Extra Strength were as indispensable flying kit as maps and spare batteries, while the vibration meant that the engine continually appeared to be trying to wrench itself off its flimsy mounts. And the failures—well they were insufferable.*

Now I was being forced to concern myself with the technicalities of engines as well as airframes. Microlight engines and control systems were not hidden tidily away behind screwed down metal cowlings, like on 'proper' planes: they were there for the tinkering. And everyone I had met who flew microlights loved nothing more than to tinker with them. Microlighters were natural born tinkerers. They liked nothing better than to roll up their sleeves and get busy with a spanner. The vast

---

* I did finally discover why microlight engines were less reliable than car and bike engines: they work harder. Cars spend most of their life pottering down to the shops, not at 80 mph. With aero engines, it is 80mph pretty much all the time.

majority carried out their own servicing and maintenance. Several people I had met at Barsham or on cross-countries to Priory Farm had *built their own aircraft*. A twilight world seemed to exist, reminiscent of the early pioneers of aviation, behind suburban garage doors, of accountants slaving late into the night by the glare of single bulbs, building flying machines in a toxic atmosphere of sawdust, fibre-glass, glue and formaldehyde.

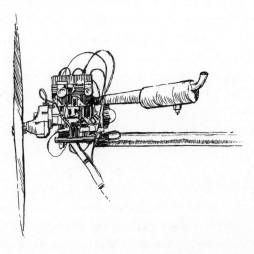

The most worrying aspect was that I had yet to meet anyone who flew microlights who was *not* like this. Those few I had met—Sean's students, or people at other airfields—all seemed to have technical jobs: they were airline pilots, engineers, mechanics, maths teachers, RAF ground-crew, quantity surveyors, accountants, lab technicians, air-traffic controllers, lighting-cameramen. Often their interest had begun with radio-modelling. They adored gadgets. They all had mobiles, laptops, Psion Organisers, Leatherman tools, GPSs (and, later, Palm Pilots and email addresses) years before everyone else. Their planes would be rigged with improvised fuel gauges and electronic timers, video camera brackets and reserve fuel tanks. And it seemed always to have been so. I had recently seen a television film called *Flying for Fun*, the true story of an army officer in the Thirties buying and bumbling about in an old plane. A more heart-warming tale of accessible amateurism could hardly be imagined, and I hurried out to buy the book it was based on; only to come across the sentence 'I bought a feeler gauge and religiously checked valve stem clearances before flying.'

Richard, I knew, was in the same boat as me, the difference being that he did not think so. (As a student, his Renault 4, a notorious swine, was always overheating and cutting out. He would throw up the bonnet and rummage in the engine. Once I had watched what he did during these performances: all it consisted of was joggling pieces of wire and prodding things; strangely, it quite often worked.)

Lester and Dan definitely fell into the category. Lester was an engineer by training and a tinkerer by nature. He was never happier than when fiddling with an electric fence or the swimming pool heating system or a car engine that was not working. He was endlessly pottering in and out of the large workshop off the main hall. Dan was the same. In his free time he made elegant steel sculptures and funky steel-and-glass CD racks out of off-cut 'T' girders and mild steel tubing left over at the engineering works. Only the week before I had been admiring the neat welds and shot-blasted finish of his latest creation.

Part of the problem was separating my fears and prejudices from the reality. Having assumed that anything to do with aircraft servicing was beyond me, I had gradually begun to see that there was, in fact, no magic to the Thruster. Its control mechanisms, when I only took the trouble to understand them, were no more complicated than those of a bicycle. It was only the consequences of their failure that were more severe. The only defence against that, of course, was to check more carefully. Richard, interestingly, seldom did any checking at all; he seemed to regard the whole process as in some way *effete*, or underhand (perhaps a subconscious rebellion against the demands of his day job). 'Antony,' I once overheard him saying, with unconcealed scorn, 'is incredibly anal about his checks.'

The fact that Lester had broken our monopoly on accidents was reassuring. But two other incidents, occurring at much the same time, also served to increase my confidence in this area. As it happened, I did make it back up to Norfolk a week or two later, by which time, as I suspected, Dan had sailed through his GFT. Dan had always been the golden boy of the four of us (as Sean never seemed to tire of reminding us: 'He's a good little pilot, Dan; he could teach you a thing or two'). Nothing ever went wrong for him. The engine never missed, let alone failed. He never did heavy landings. He plotted his routes methodically, and did not get lost.

On this occasion Dan had just returned from a flight. He, Richard, Sean and I were standing around the Thruster while I conducted my pre-flight with its usual nervous thoroughness. 'Come on, Ants, it'll be dark if you don't hurry up,' Sean was saying. As I was going over the tail-plane, however, I spotted a hairline fracture in the main weld connecting the steel frame of the tail-plane assembly, almost certainly a consequence of a heavy landing. I called Sean over: the fracture was hard to make out, nearly hidden, as it was, by the fabric covering the tail fin. 'There's nothing there, Ants, it's all perfectly—' And then he saw it. 'Shit. Yes. See what you mean. Nasty. Well-spotted, Ants. That's good airmanship, that is. You should be proud of that. I'll take the tail off and get it re-welded this afternoon.'

Any disappointment I might have felt at missing my flight was countered a minute later by a second buttress to my confidence. We were about to trundle the Thruster into the hangar. Dan and Sean were looking at the engine when Dan's gaze dropped down and alighted on the static vent, the right-angled copper tube that kept the air pressure constant for the air speed indicator. It protruded, as it does on many planes (even passenger jets), at a right-angle from the side of the cockpit.

'I wonder what this copper tube does' he said absently.

I stared at him. Richard stared at him. Sean stared at him.

'What did you say?' said Sean.

'I said, I was wondering what this copper tube does,' repeated Dan, examining the static vent curiously. 'D'you think it's anything important?'

We continued to stare at him. Dan, the natural; Dan, who had just got his licence; Dan, who had never been ticked off for ignorance or bad airmanship; Dan, who never put a foot wrong, in his second year of flying, had just looked at the static vent—correction, had just *noticed* the static vent—and asked what it did. To me, it was a moment of epiphany. It meant only one thing; I was not the only one.

He knew nothing either.

Pilot-in-Command

I see no reason why the determined aviator need be put off by longish grass if he is prepared to be a little adventurous ... Make two or three fast runs up and down the field to blow water from the grass ... but beware of filling the pitot head with water or grass seeds ... A ski ramp is used by the Navy to launch its Harriers from ships. You can borrow this technique by using a hump in your field at the take-off point. Experience of this sort should be gained gradually and not all in one morning.

Geoffrey Farr, *Country Flying*, 1981.

Autumn arrived in London that year as punctually as summer had done, on the first of October. The three previous days were emphatically summer: baking tee-shirt-and-shorts weather with blue skies (apart from vapour trails and some high cirrus). Now there was a heavy dew across Hyde Park and a whiff of damp. The leaves on the trees had not changed colour yet, but suddenly they looked tired and jaded through the haze. With the change of season, my urban life received a seismic blow.

It was an unspoken fact that girls were the reason for acquiring the Thruster and getting into flying. And girls, if it came down to it, were pretty much all my life was about. When I arrived in London, I had quite a few ready-made friends who arrived from college with me. Advertising was a sociable industry. There was seldom any shortage of opportunity to try and get lucky. I tended to chase and fall in love with girls who refused to go out with me, and form grudging, ungracious temporary relationships with girls who chose me. Consequently my love-life felt perpetually transient and unsatisfying, never going anywhere because I would not allow it to. The more regular and settled a relationship became, the more uneasy and trapped and pressed up against a glass ceiling I felt: and the more unthinkable any kind of long-term future became. As, one by one, most of my friends settled into steady relationships, living with their partner, having children, obstinate singledom or marriage—I told myself that there was no hurry. Girls were a game. There was a lifetime to meet the right person.

As with my flying, I believed, I was still firmly at the experimental, information-gathering stage. With every new girl that I met whom I fancied, there was usually one particular reason or feature that I fell for. Whether or not I got anywhere with her, that feature would quietly, subconsciously, be added to the ideal of feminine perfection in my mind that I was, sometime—in, say, the next three to five years—going to meet and settle down with. Each new contact or conquest, naturally, made my ideal slightly more so, and slightly less attainable. Thus, I required B's sense of humour and intelligence; T's sophistication and immaculate taste; E's rock-chick style; J's generosity; A's kissing and dancing; K's drive and ambition and cosmopolitan chic; E's tits, S's cute little bum; J's friends and family; T's wide-eyed, flirty, fluffy-chicken vulnerability which made me feel so male; R's energy and mad spontaneity; S's rapacious sexual appetite, butterfly touch and automatic orgasms—which pretty well ruined sex with anyone else for years. And so on.

I knew from experience, if I thought about it (which I did not), that many of the features were mutually exclusive: that sexiness was inversely proportional to affection, that the seriously beautiful were almost invariably abysmal lovers. Yet in my mind I had no problem reconciling that my insolent temptress who would drive me mad with desire, would also be unswervingly loyal, adoring, supportive and faithful.

To this array of charms and talents I soon found myself adding details from daily experience, like the green eyes of the girl in the post office or someone I spotted in a bus on the way to work. These, in due course, were supplemented by pleasing images from the media: the soulful beauty of Mazarine Mitterrand at her father's funeral; the muscle tone of the peasant girl in *The Name of the Rose*, the attitude of Anne Parillaud in *Nikita*, the insolence of Linda Fiorentino in *The Last Seduction*, the sheer beauty of Ingrid Bergman in *Casablanca*; invariably over-ridden by the heroine I fancied in the most recent blockbuster (at time of writing, still Milla Jovovich). Who was I to merit such a creature, you might ask, and why should she find me attractive? Good questions—and I certainly didn't consider them.

I knew that I should have known better. I, after all, worked in advertising. I knew how false media representations were of pretty well everything. I knew how much we tweaked, flipped, retouched, stretched, cleaned, buffed up and generally 'enhanced' every image we made, how much effort and trouble we took to make things more interesting than they were. I spent my working week seeing cars being weighted to sit more prettily on their suspension, brushing carrots with Three-in-One oil so that they glistened nicely, removing lines from already near-perfect faces. Yet, flicking through magazine features consisting of pages of semi-naked models and actresses, quotes like 'You've got to keep trying things—especially when it comes to sex,' would lodge in my mind. And I would look at my own relationships and find them wanting.

I was now in my late twenties. I knew that I was luckier than most, that I was a victim of the 'I want it, I want it all, and I want it now' generation and after two painful and protracted separations, separated by long periods of nothing, I was beginning to consider the depressing possibility that maybe, just maybe, I was being a little unrealistic in my expectations. When, as I say, a seismic heave occurred.

I met her.

It happened at an interview for a new job. Following a bit of luck the previous year with a campaign to advertise Mauritius, I had won some awards. Suddenly I found myself approached by headhunters to see if I was interested in moving companies. One of the agencies that was interested was one where I had long dreamed of working. Everyone in advertising had. It was by a wide margin *the* place to work. Its campaigns were cleverer or wittier or more stylish or had funkier soundtracks than anyone else's. The company had cool, high-tech offices in Soho. The girls who worked there were legendarily beautiful. Now they had seen my 'book' (a copywriter's or art director's 'book' is a portfolio-plus-showreel of their best work) and they wanted to see *me*. And, in advertising, if they wanted to see me, that meant that the job was in the bag. For a 'creative', the job interview is neither here nor there: it's a formality, to check that you are not a psychopath—even if you are, there's no reason why it should necessarily prove an obstacle. While it might not mean much of a step up financially, in kudos, as a name for my CV and chips to be cashed in the future, it was a dream. Another agency also happened to be interested, so I decided to go along to see them first as a dry run.

The second agency was also in Soho. I knew I did not want a job there. I did not like their work, offices, style, image, or the look of the partners, whose photographs periodically appeared in *Campaign*. Worse, they had the reputation for being a fearsome sweat-shop. I was going along purely for the ego massage because they had shown an interest, and so that I had an alternative up my sleeve for negotiating purposes when it came to the interview that mattered the following week. All my suspicions were confirmed as I waited in their reception, nonchalantly turning the pages of the *Evening Standard*, and trying not to be too obvious as I admired the buttocks of a girl leaning over—unnecessarily far over—the reception desk, whose face I could not see. After a few minutes I was told by the receptionist to take the lift to the sixth floor. As the lift doors were closing the girl with the buttocks slid in.

She leant grumpily against the wall, slumped her shoulders, raised her eyebrows, shook her hair and then flicked it back, puffed out her cheeks in a mock sigh, arched her back inwards, pressing her shoulders and kicking her left foot back against the lift wall, chewed her chewing gum with her mouth open looking dead ahead, paused, grunted, then, for one millisecond, locked her eyes onto mine and I found myself looking directly into laser green irises. She half-smiled, made a pout like a spoilt toddler, stamped her foot, shook her head again, and shrugged.

That was the sum total of our communication. The display indicated the sixth floor, the doors opened, and I found myself dreading her walking out of my life. The art director I was meeting was waiting. He smiled at her and turned to me. 'Company perk,' he said. At that moment she turned her head back over her shoulder and looked back; not hurriedly, not sneakily, nor flirtatiously, but with half a hint of a smile.

I was offered a job. I accepted. I called the headhunter to cancel my appointment with the agency I had dreamed of working at for seven years.

This was not typical behaviour. For the most part I am a solid, depressingly focussed Capricorn with all the leaden characteristics of that plodding sign. I was well aware of how absurdly I was behaving, but I could not help it. Lift Girl had become the only thing that mattered. I had never been so sure of anything than that she was the girl for me. The decision did not even require any decision-making. It was the only option. It was easy.

It would be inaccurate to say that I enjoyed my first few weeks at the new company. There was a moment of panic early on, when, after Lift Girl's non-appearance for two weeks, I feared she had left. It turned out that she was on holiday and when finally I did encounter her in a corridor the following Tuesday, my instincts was confirmed when my pulse nearly seized—even before I recognised who it was with the perfect tan. I tried to catch her eye as she brushed past, and had to remind myself that she did not have a clue who I was.

Every man has their own seduction formula. Mine was always to strike early and impertinently fast. It very frequently worked, and if it did not, if I got brushed off—well, it hardly needed to be taken personally. As a strategy, it had a number of advantages. It cut out the tricky, time-consuming 'getting to know each other' bit. It exposed time-wasters and attention-seekers early on. It permitted minimal exposure of sensitive male pride. It maximised clear, unclouded judgment, because I did not yet care. Somehow, though, now that the stakes were higher, such an approach seemed inappropriate.

For several weeks I showed iron self-control while I completed my information-gathering. I engineered no more than a trip every other day to the floor and area where she sat. I initiated a flirting campaign with one of the secretaries who sat nearest to her. To Lift Girl, when we met, I showed friendliness, but thereafter complete indifference. In fact, I ignored her. While almost everyone else missed no opportunity to cluster round her desk for flirtatious chats, I avoided her. I asked nobody about her, while absorbing whatever details came my way (she was an account manager; she had been at the agency two years; she had a boyfriend but she didn't seem to be that keen on him; she had snogged one other person at the agency at the last Christmas party).

It was, if I say so myself, a remarkable campaign. Gradually, I suspected (but hardly dared to believe) she began to appear on my floor more than, strictly, she needed to. She would hover about in the area outside my office. Eventually, in an amazingly fortuitous piece of luck, she came into my office as I was doing some tedious cheque-writing for a pile of gas, telephone and electricity bills. At that moment, the uppermost invoice was a hangarage bill Dan had forwarded to me. Sean had, unusually, typed it on headed Norwich and East of England Aero Club paper and it happened to be facing in her direction. It caught her eye. 'Hey,' she said. 'Do you fly?'

'Mmm,' I said absently. (I was too immersed in what I was doing to have much attention to spare for gossip.) For a millisecond, this appeared to floor her, but she recovered immediately.

'Got to go. See you.' And she skipped out.

Two nights later, in the pub, the secretary who sat near her said, ' So what's this I hear about you having your own plane?' and I knew I was on my way.

After that our encounters started to become more frequent, and more flirtatious. Cheeky messages would appear on my desk when I was away. The Friday before Christmas, the entire company of 130 was flown to Paris for lunch at La Coupole. (The agency had had a good year: this was advertising at the end of the 1980s.) At a club in the evening we found each other dancing and had a delirious, sweat-soaked, post-dance snog. I floated through the following week and Christmas, my head full of private daydreams—clubbing, making love, watching TV, flying together. A week later, back at work in the New Year and after a trip to the pub, my resolve weakened by drink, I tried for another kiss. She turned abruptly away. 'What are you doing?' she said coolly. 'Hope you didn't get the wrong idea before,' she went on. 'That was a party kiss. Nothing serious.' She paused, before adding the chilling words: 'I mean, I really like you. But not like that.'

I was still numb with misery when Dan called a few days later and suggested a weekend at Salsingham to help prepare a landing strip. The weather since Christmas had been too miserable to justify a trip to Norfolk, but now any distraction was welcome. The intention had always been that as soon as we all had our licences, the Thruster would be moved permanently to Salsingham. Hangaring her at Barsham Green was inconvenient in that it meant at least a twenty-minute drive at the beginning and end of the day's flying. Further time was wasted painstakingly moving aircraft to and fro to extricate her. Invariably, over a period of a week or more, she had found her way right to the very back. And storage in a large and crowded hangar carried with it the constant risk of 'hangar rash'—the minor abrasions incurred by part of one aircraft rubbing up against another. Finally, there were the exorbitant quarterly hangar charges meted out by Sean. Accordingly, with Lester, Richard and Dan now qualified, and our third flying summer round the corner, the question arose as to where would be the most suitable place for a strip to be planted. A small hangar would then be erected by Lester's engineering works.

There had been considerable debate as to the best site: selecting a suitable field was less easy than it might sound. Even planes with as good short take-off and landing capability as the Thruster needed at least 300 yards of clear runway for safety, orientated, ideally, in the direction of the prevailing wind (from the south-west, in Britain). In practical terms this amounted to a big field.

The approaches needed to be clear of trees, cables, wires, hedges, tall buildings or other obstacles, or anyone or anything likely to be disturbed by the noise of a plane taking off or landing. The land had to be free-draining and exempt from any agricultural vagaries of crop growth and harvesting or livestock. Finally there was the question of gradient and surface. Even in topographically-challenged Norfolk, once sites were critically assessed on a field-by-field basis, it was amazing how few were flat enough, and without hollows, dips, ridges or obstacles of some kind.

The obvious way to pick promising fields was from the air, and Lester and Dan had made a couple of reconnaissance flights. Lester's initial suggestion had been a thirty-acre field to the north-east of the house. Here, in his earlier flying days, he told us, he had landed his Gemini after flying back from Africa and, on trying to take off again, had only just managed to clear the tall poplars on the northern perimeter. 'We knew it was going to be tight, so we took everything we could out,' he told us—he often used the royal 'we'—'seats, radio, everything. The tank was only a quarter full. We only just made it. We *clipped* the top of the poplars.' Upon these slender indications of promise, Lester had attempted to land the Thruster in the same field in the summer, causing the sheared axle that led to the jury rig.

It was now the last Saturday in January and the four of us were squelching round the sodden pastures to the south-west of Salsingham Hall. The house stood on a low hill, with the land around falling away in a shallow valley to the lake, now silted up and overgrown with willows, rushes and nettles. From the lake, a sluice overflow let water into a stream which ran along the valley to the west of the house and under the brick hump-backed bridge which carried the Salsingham road. It was an undeniably picturesque spot but now two things struck me. First were two oaks, solitary, but massive, spreading themselves luxuriously over on one side of the field. What high-jinks, I wondered, might they cause, in terms of rotor effect, turbulence, and the other nameless mysteries of localised air flows of which I had read but otherwise knew nothing? Secondly, there was the matter of four raised concrete storm drains which butted up six inches or so above the level of the field at 150-yard intervals.

'What about these, Dad?' asked Dan, bumping the toe of his boot against the edge of the raised concrete. Expecting to hear that the proud masonry could be trimmed down until it was flush with the surface of the grass I was mildly surprised by Lester's response.

'Go round them, of course.'

'What about the trees?' said Dan.

'What about the trees?' said Lester, impatiently.

'Well, between them, it's not giving us much leeway.'

'It's perfectly all right.'

I caught a quizzical look from Richard but was still too intimidated by Lester's experience as a flying veteran to voice my own doubts. I think we were both glad when Dan put our thoughts into words.

'Dad, does seem a shame we can't find somewhere a little straighter and flatter, with a bit more room.'

In the end, a field on the far side of the river was chosen, reached across a deep ford where the sluice of the lake overflowed. It didn't look very suitable to me. It was on a pronounced upward gradient into the direction of the prevailing wind and, with a hollow dip followed by a hump, it was far from level.

We spent the rest of the morning trailing up and down behind a tractor in the drizzle, picking up flints and surface stones—a task of infinite duration as there were just as many as we cared to look for.

Then we shovelled sand and gravel into any ruts and hollows, an exercise rendered nearly pointless because the ground was so soft after weeks of rain that, fast as we filled them, the wheels of the tractor created new ones. The high point of the day came after lunch, when Lester pressed the other house guests—a distinguished-looking Indian in turban and full sherwani, and a man who did not seem to be a Red Indian but was called Shining Bird—into joining the work party. They tried to excuse themselves, but Lester was having none of it.

We were now an accepted part of the establishment when we were at Salsingham—a position not acquired without a certain learning curve. Having made the early mistake of assuming that the Watsons periodically communicated with each other, I had occasionally turned up following arrangements made through Lester or Dan, to encounter such a hurricane of wrath from Rhona that, on one occasion, I thought it must be the end of the Salsingham Syndicate. (This non-communicating aspect of the Watson family—perhaps a consequence of living in such a large house—was highlighted one Saturday morning when Lester, after a piece of toast, glanced at his watch and said 'I must be off,' eliciting no response from anyone; a final, head-round-the-door 'See you, then,' a few moments later, prompted Dan to inquire absently where his father was going; his destination was revealed to be China.) Experience, however, had shown the consequences of Rhona's explosions to be short-lived—on one occasion her tirade even ended with 'Right, let's get a drink'—and once we realised this, and made sure to make and confirm all arrangements with her, she seemed to come to regard us with tolerant affection. When this, in due course, evolved into a state of permanent mild irritation, I knew that we had, effectively, become family.

Lying in my bath in the half-light (the only functioning bulb was twenty watts), I ruminated on my emotional difficulties. For the past few weeks I had been blundering through life in a 'just woken' state of emotional disorientation. My real problem with Lift Girl was not knowing where I had gone wrong. It had all been, up until that disastrous moment, such an exemplary campaign. The more I looked at it, the more flawless it seemed. She had made the running, not I. So why, the moment I reciprocated, the *volte face*? Was it to test me? It didn't sound like a test: it sounded painfully, dismally matter-of-fact. Whichever way I looked at it, the only possible bad tactic seemed to be that, by trying to kiss her again, I had revealed that I fancied her—so, apparently, ending her interest in me. Was that it? Was that really the full extent of her interest? It hardly augured well. If that were the case, then what was my plan from here? Damage limitation? How grim was that? Either way, the maddening thing was that I had, of course, now revealed my position. I had shown my hand. There was no going back on that score. The only way of recovery seemed to be to show that I did not care that much.

I would withdraw. I would avoid her floor as much as possible, and all her normal haunts. As she was exceptionally adept at interjecting herself into my company as if by accident, I would have to be wary of this and develop my defences. At meetings where I knew she would be present, I would arrive late, be careful not to catch her eye, and, perhaps, leave early. Or I would keep myself surrounded by a protective ring of people I knew. I would force her to come to me in such a way that she could not disguise it, or dress it up as something else. And if she didn't? Well, in that case, it hardly bore thinking about, but there was nothing to be done anyway. Strengthened by this battle plan, my face glowing healthily after my bath and the cold air and rain, and starving from my exertions, I went downstairs. Lester was dispensing glasses of cider from a gallon plastic drum, in a range of dramatically assorted glassware.

'What do you think Mubarak should do?' was his unsettling opener; a gambit which led to a sticky conversation about the politics of water wars in the Middle East. The difficulties of surveying with eighteenth-century instruments followed, then comparative finger techniques for organ and harpsichord, before I finally managed to steer him onto the safer ground of flying stories. He told me about the time he nearly crashed in the Rift Valley: how he was caught by the same treacherous downdraughts that Beryl Markham's instructor introduced her to in *West with the Night*. 'It was very alarming,' he said calmly—the first time I had heard him acknowledge that flying carried any risk at all—'Very alarming. When we landed back at Wilson, my friend got out of the plane and he was shaking—literally shaking. His wife was there to meet him and the first thing he said to her, pointing at me, was "That man just tried to kill me".'

'What did you say?' I asked.

'I said, "Nonsense. I just saved his life".'

I was first up next morning. I couldn't be bothered with my contact lenses, so put on a pair of glasses and headed down to the kitchen to make myself a cup of coffee. In due course, Lester pottered in. Never at his most communicative at that hour, I made a casual remark about how much we needed some decent flying weather to get airborne again. This appeared to wrong-foot Lester, who blinked at me, a little uncertainly.

'Good Heavens,' he said finally. 'Are you an aviator?'

'Sûr le valise, chaps? Got everything you need?'

'Sûr le valise, Jim'

It was Jim's pet expression, and we had been 'on the case' now for nearly three weeks. Jim was Head of Traffic at work—the person responsible for hassling creative teams to make sure that work was produced in time to meet deadlines. The phrase sounded so friendly and innocuous—yet its underlying meaning was so not. In those simple words were contained everything most fearful and pressurised and grim about working in advertising—when things weren't going well. We had already asked for more time and been given a grudging three days, followed by an even more grudging two further days. And still we had not come up with anything satisfactory for a disagreeable brief for dried packet soup (with real pasta!). For three weeks my life, thoughts and dreams had been dogged by packet soup. I had drunk litres of the noxious brew. I had held it, smelled it, sipped it, gulped it, spilt it, watched it steam, burnt my lips and tongue on it, sieved the dried vegetables (and real pasta!) through my teeth, stared at the plastic sachet of what appeared to be toe-nail clippings, eventually tipping the contents onto my layout pad, marshalling them into rows and flicking them one-by-one at my art director. And I was stuck. This was a product 're-launch', a marketing ploy for one last attempt to resurrect a moribund line. Who, in their right minds, still bought packet soups? Why should they? Packet soups were disgusting. Packet soups belonged to the space age, the era of drip-dry shirts and string vests and Atlas-rockets—when science was cool, convenience was king and the idea that food should be delicious was a long, long way in the future.

This was the other side of advertising; the other side to Commes des Garçons suits and Zagato-bodied Aston Martin DB4s and working in 'a young profession full of bright, energetic people in fashionable West End offices' (as the careers man had put it). This was the difficult, dusty end of FMCG (Fast Moving Consumer Goods) that we all tried to avoid but got lumbered with now and again. Anyone could sell cars or trainers or airlines or fashion, but deadbeat, state-of-the-arc products like biscuits and white bread and powdered milk were not so easy, with their small budgets and pissed-off, passed-over brand managers who hated advertising people (for their energy, brightness and fashionable West End offices). And I didn't like it.

Lift Girl seemed to be calling my bluff. She hadn't been down to see me for ages, and had made no effort to talk to me in the pub—which annoyed me, despite the fact that, in my current frame of mind, I did not want to see her. I glimpsed her periodically, of course, for instance when the whole agency crammed into the big downstairs conference room for our monthly meetings. She would arrive late, every eye— every male eye, anyway—upon her, as she threaded her way through the chairs, sitting briefly in a lap here, balancing herself now and again on a shoulder, or with a hand on an inside thigh, there. I remembered what perfect hands they were; warm and soft without being dry or clammy. A snippet of gossip had reached me recently: a senior client had had to be tactfully warned off calling her out of office hours—not the first time it had happened. She seemed to have the same effect on men, whether they were sixty-five year-old company chairmen or motorcycle couriers.

As flying was the one activity sufficiently engrossing to force all other worries from my mind, it did not help that I had not got into the air since well before Christmas. As wet and windy February turned into windy and wet March, the TV news had twice been filled with scenes of snow ploughs and cars skidding in snowdrifts and freezing fog. (There was even an item about an enterprising Yorkshire farmer who had fitted a Thruster with skis to drop hay off to his sheep). But none of these invigorating conditions seemed to get as far as London, which remained cold, wet and resolutely overcast.

It was a phase that I knew would pass. But until it did, I wished that none of it seemed to matter so much.

Memphis Belle came out. As we emerged from the cinema, Richard said (in the authoritative way that he had): 'The Memphis Belle was based at Barsham Green.' I was fairly sure that he had no grounds whatever for such an assertion, but it got us talking about flying bases, Norfolk and the Second World War, and it raised the question as to what Barsham's role *had* been. I had once asked Sean this, and the short answer had been 'Liberators. It was a Liberator base.' As I didn't know what Liberators were, I was not much the wiser and with no source for further information the subject slipped my mind.

However, you could not fly in Norfolk for long without noticing what an absurd number of airfields—or one-time airfields—there were. Even on a journey as short as my regular hop to Priory Farm, I passed within view of six. There were so many, and they all looked so similar (three tarmac runways and buildings grouped in much the same places) that on cross-countries it was difficult not to get them mixed up. Priory Farm was sandwiched between two so close that they were almost touching—Old Buckenham and Tibenham. When I spread out my 1:250,000 chart of East Anglia to consider the matter properly, I noticed that literally *dozens* of village names were picked out in the larger, pale grey type which denoted airfields (or disused airfields): Bircham Newton, Docking, Sculthorpe, North Creake, Langham, Little Snoring, West Raynham, Great Massingham, Foulsham, Oulton, Coltishall, Swannington, Ludham, Wendling, Marham, North Pickenham, Swanton Morley, Shipdham, Barsham Green, Watton, Bodney, Downham Market, Methwold, Feltwell, East Wretham, Snetterton Heath, Attlebridge, Horsham St Faith, Rackheath, Deopham Green, Hethel, Seething, Old Buckenham, Tibenham, Harwick, Fersfield, Thorpe Abbotts ...

Poking about one lunchtime, in one of the specialist bookshops full of car maintenance manuals close to the office, I came across a book about wartime airfields and 'airfield trails'. It had occurred to me that checking out some of these bases might be a good way to get my mind off Lift Girl, prepare myself for the approaching flying season, clock up some hours at the controls and add a few sorely-needed entries to the 'AERODROMES VISITED' section at the front of my log book.

The strategic, logistical and practical requirements of mounting bombing campaigns against Occupied Europe, and of attempting to prevent their efforts to return the compliment, was something I had never considered. Norfolk was flat and close to Germany: in 1939, it had five airfields; by the end of the war it had thirty-seven. Most of these were constructed within six months and rushed into service in early 1940, with a second flurry of activity, to provide bases for the American 'Mighty Eighth', in 1943.

From these airfields, the great air campaigns of the war were waged. These included the routine: 'gardening' runs to lay mines in the North Sea and the nightly onslaughts on 'Happy Valley'—the industrial areas of the Ruhr—by Bomber Command, and later, the American daylight missions down 'bomber alley' into Central Germany. But they also included more specific tasks: the thousand-bomber 'Millennium' raids of the summer of 1942, the four-month Battle of Berlin at the end of

1943, propaganda leaflet drops, spy drop-offs and pick-ups, the bombing of Berchtesgaden (Hitler's mountain retreat), sorties to destroy V1 and V2 rockets and drops for Patton's tanks following the Normandy Landings. Even Douglas Bader's artificial leg was dropped by a Blenheim from Horsham St Faith.

Over a couple of evenings in London, I plotted a route to take in the airfields with the most interesting histories. My first destination was Shipdham, an American base which I knew from *Pooleys* was still an active airfield and was a mere seven minutes flying time from Barsham. It seemed a good start, as almost the full length (nearly a kilometre) of one of its original tarmac runways was still in use.

As I joined the circuit from the north-east and made my approach to land, I was surprised how run-down it looked. Little of the site seemed to be devoted to flying. It was a muggy Friday morning, the day before the first May bank holiday weekend, and the fields around were green with young barley. On the west side there was a big concrete and asbestos barn and farmyard with metal cattle pens, to the east an industrial estate. There were no signs of life. I swept round to make my approach (the wind was straight down the runway) and prepared for my first landing on tarmac. Sean had warned me: 'Remember, Ants, it's harder to land on tarmac. She'll bounce and bounce if you don't get it right. In fact, we might let a bit of air out of the tyres.' As I came over the threshold, the vastness of the runway felt simultaneously reassuring and absurd. It was so wide that I felt myself disappearing into the blackness. I held off like mad when I was a few inches above the surface of the runway and after floating for a moment, the tyres made contact with a satisfying squeak (just like in films) and I was rolling smoothly up the asphalt.

The tarmac was much split and patched, but it still felt far smoother than grass. Either side of the wide (though now faint) central white lines were thousands of thick black smudges where bigger and heavier machines had landed in the past. As I taxied in, I cut the engine in good time—but she still rolled for thirty yards, so that, eventually, I had to stick my foot out to act as a makeshift brake.

Any trepidation I might have felt about visiting such an illustrious flying site was dispelled by my surroundings. There was an old petrol pump and a couple of oil drums and a shabby, closed-up building which must have been a hangar. The 'tower' consisted of an old greenhouse on some scaffolding, reached by a ladder. The big windsock, frayed to half its proper length, was so sun-bleached and grey with mildew that it was hard to pick it out against the surrounding fields. To stretch my legs I walked a little way down the perimeter track to the farm. Abandoned low-loaders and rusting farm implements lay among clumps of brambles, heaps of rotting muck and round bales. The heavy, thundery air was full of bovine smells.

The clubhouse, a low shack behind the hangar in the shelter of a belt of *leylandiis*, was locked and deserted. In front there was a small black marble memorial:

8TH AIR FORCE B-24 LIBERATORS*
44TH BOMB GROUP (H)
FLYING EIGHT BALL GROUP (AGGRESSOR BEWARE)
READY THEN—READY NOW—READY TOMORROW
344 COMBAT MISSIONS
153 AIRCRAFT LOST IN ACTION
330 ENEMY AIRCRAFT DESTROYED

I peered in through the windows. Amongst the usual flying notices were framed pictures of planes and bomber crews and faded, much photocopied, newspaper cuttings. In the sweltering, midday glare, with the whine of flies and the fluttering of wagtails in the guttering, tales of high-altitude bombing and crews returning with frostbite, freezing gun and turret mechanisms, and oxygen masks rubbed with salt to prevent icing, seemed very remote.

Taking off, the Thrasher accelerated down the tarmac like a

---

* The B-24 Liberator was the less glamorous sibling of the other standard American four-engined bomber, the B-17 Flying Fortress.

Mustang. The tail came up immediately, and I must have been airborne within thirty metres. My next stop was Thorpe Abbotts, about seventeen minutes flying time on 150°. I had chosen the destination because the control tower had been restored as a memorial museum to the American 100th Bomb Group which served there, the jinxed 'Bloody Hundredth', which lost more planes and crews than any other unit during the war. I was over Old Buckenham at 1,500 feet (where, my books told me, James Stewart and Walter Matthau had served), with Tibenham in easy view to the left and Fersfield to the right (rooftop-level Mosquito mission to destroy the Gestapo HQ in Copenhagen), when there was a loud whumph, and oil spluttered across the windscreen, completely obscuring my forward vision.

Strangely, the engine kept going, and after a few seconds I realised that the liquid could not be oil but was, in fact, water. I had flown into a shower. I was not sure whether the Thruster was supposed to fly in the rain. The propeller started to make a fizzing sound, and the tips became visible as they traced a circle of tiny splashes. My forward visibility became filtered through sweeping white curtains of rain, billowing majestically as they passed beneath me. The propeller wash chased the water off the windscreen like a dryer in a car-wash until, as suddenly as I had entered it (and feeling quite intrepid) I emerged the other side.

The main runway at Thorpe Abbotts had gone, but a length of peritrack remained. I landed at the far end and taxied up as near to the restored tower as possible. It was quarter to five as I climbed over the fence from the barley field, surprising the straggle of people drifting back from the tower to the car park by the road. The museum shut at 5pm, but the amiable curators, who had seen me land from the tower, allowed me an extra quarter of an hour.

It was odd, stepping into an immaculate little war museum, from a farmer's field. Two exhibits stood out from the photographs and maps and flying knick-knacks: the certificates of membership of 'Ye Luckye Bastardes Club', awarded to those who survived a full tour of duty; and a giant three-bladed propeller, reclaimed from a crashed Flying

Fortress. I tried to lift it, but it was as if it were bolted to the floor: its three steel blades, each thicker than my thigh, were all bent back like ring-pulls.

After the museum had closed, I sat in the Thruster, reading the guide as the sun finally broke through the overcast sky and everything acquired shadow, colour and definition. There was an eyewitness account of a Luftwaffe fighter attack on the rear formation of a five mile armada of bombers during a daylight raid on a factory deep in south-eastern Germany in 1943:

> …the sight was fantastic and surpassed fiction … emergency hatches, exit doors, prematurely opened parachutes, bodies and assorted fragments of B-17s and Hun fighters sailed past us in the slipstream. I watched two fighters explode not far beneath, disappearing in sheets of orange flame, B-17s dropping out in every state of distress, from engines on fire to control surfaces shot away, friendly and enemy parachutes floating down and numerous funeral pyres of smoke, from fallen fighters, marking our trail on the green carpet far below … After we had been under constant attack for a solid hour, it appeared certain that the 100th Group was faced with annihilation … and it was only 11.20 hours with the target-time still 35 minutes away …

Feeling like Gregory Peck at the beginning of *Twelve O'Clock High*, I tried to imagine the scene fifty years ago: the noise and commotion as thirty or more Flying Fortresses—120 engines and propellers—prepared to depart and get into formation with equal numbers of planes from dozens of other airfields. The barley rustled and the skylarks twittered.* Had it really happened?

By the time I put the plane away on Sunday evening I had landed at

---

* From the diary of navigator Captain Harry Crosby, on crash-landing back at Thorpe Abbotts after a nightmare mission to Bremen: 'We are stopped. No-one gets out. We just sit … silence. At first. Then, as always, in the English countryside, we hear the birds …'

twelve airfields and over-flown numerous others,* and knew another Norfolk to the sleepy brick-and-flint villages with their round church towers and 'Please drive carefully' signs.

The more I learned, the greater the affinity I felt with those airmen. They were the same age (well, five years younger). Their flying was dogged by bad weather; the winters of the early 1940s were notoriously wet and cold, with murky visibility and fog a constant problem. (The difference being that, instead of going to the pub and feeling pissed off, the bomber crews were told that if the fog remained on their return, they could bale out.) The pilots were continually muddled because there were so many airfields and because Norfolk all looked the same.†
Even the drainage problems we were having with the waterlogged strip at Salsingham replicated those faced by the construction companies on the heavy Norfolk clay fifty years before. Seething and Shipdham never solved the problem, remaining, in wet weather, a muddy quagmire.

At Barsham, like a lot of Norfolk airfields, the different squadrons came and went like summer dew. It was not, needless to say, the base from which the Memphis Belle flew her last mission. (That was Bassingbourn, near Cambridge.) And although many different aircraft types did pass through—Blenheims, Spitfires, Mosquitoes, American Bostons, Mitchells and Venturas—almost the only one that did not was the B-24 Liberator.

---

* Many had returned to farmland and would have been impossible to find had I not had aviation charts to show me where to look. Hethel was the headquarters of Lotus cars, with the runway part of a test track. Horsham St Faith was Norwich International Airport, Attlebridge a Bernard Matthews turkey farm, Snetterton a motor racing circuit, Watton a prison. Others were still active military airbases and looked very intimidating from the air: RAF Marham and RAF West Raynham to the west; RAF Colthishall to the east.

† 'Airfields and towns and churches and hedges, more airfields and ponds and brooks, and cows. More airfields and roads and train tracks and radio towers ...' American bomber pilot Bert Stiles, *Portrait of a Guy Thinking about an Island*, 1943.

My tactics appeared to be working. Lift Girl had started to appear mysteriously wherever I went, in corridors, the pub, the lift, hovering endlessly near enough to my office for easy invitation. On each occasion I successfully contrived to be just going into a meeting, on the phone or immersed in conversation with someone else. If she wished to see or speak to me, she was going to have to make a committed effort. If I could get her to do that, I had decided, the balance would be redressed, and we could start again. On Day 217, I finally received a phone call. 'Are you sulking? Why are you avoiding me?'

'Avoiding you? Why should I avoid you?'

'Are you going to take me for a drink?'

I was so pleased I had to go for a short walk round Soho Square.

Finally, I did it. On 19 May 1991, nine months after Dan, I got my wings. I became a stick and rudder man. I earned the right to call myself an aviator. I passed my GFT.

I remember nothing of the test. It was not like going solo. The achievement carried none of the landmark 'I can fly' glory that followed learning to land; just a sense of quiet relief. I had badgered Sean into two earlier attempts, and he had calmly allowed me to make a fool of myself. The first time had been in April, before my weekend exploring the airfields, when I had not flown since before Christmas. My mind had been preoccupied with work matters and I felt a sudden fit of insecurity and petulant shame that I was trailing so far behind the others, still without my licence. I felt nervous, I could scarcely remember how to fly, it was a gusty day and I had no control of the plane. I was also unsettled by Sean's unfamiliar demeanour, issuing quiet instructions, interspersed with long, judgmental silences. I came out of my turns 30° too soon or too late. I couldn't hold a steady course. I miscalculated my reciprocal bearing in the circuit, cutting a quaint rhomboid downwind leg. I ballooned so badly on landing that Sean had to wordlessly grab the stick.

The second time, a Sunday evening in May, I had hung around the airfield the whole weekend waiting for a heavy, hazy murk to clear. Sean said we should wait for a more suitable day, but that would have meant yet another wasted weekend and I insisted we try. By the time I had taken off and climbed to a thousand feet, the ground was scarcely discernible. Ten minutes into this murk, with hardly any forward visibility and no horizon, I was so disorientated that all I could do was tensely scan one instrument after another, trying to keep her vaguely straight and level. We did a few turns and then Sean said, 'Could you tell me what airfield that is, please?' Looking in the direction of his pointed finger I could dimly make out the runways of a disused aerodrome beneath us, the main runway now given over to regularly placed, blister-shaped corrugated-iron pig pens. I realised that I didn't even know what direction we had been heading in for the last ten minutes. Raking the map, ransacking my memory from the weekend before, trying to maintain my course, I hazarded: 'Er ... Attlebridge. No. Oulton?' knowing miserably, as I said the words, that I had failed myself again.

'Could you take us home please,' said Sean quietly. I could not, of course, until he told me which heading to take. It was too ignominious. I was close to tears with fury and self-pity and self-loathing. Sean had not finished, however. When Barsham came into view he told me to land and taxi over to the hangar. We got out, still in silence, and he walked round the plane.

'What's this?'

He was indicating some sort of widget that connected the elevator wire to the elevator. I told him it was a clip of some sort. He thoughtfully nodded his head and chewed his lips. 'It's called a turnbuckle. What would you measure using the Bettsometer spring tension test?' He had made his point.

When the time was right, two weeks later, it was, in fact, Sean who suggested I do my test. There were no questions about turnbuckles. He even chatted in a normal, friendly way as the test proceeded.

I attribute my lack of elation to the fact that, for once, I was fully prepared. With no bluffing, busking or fudging, there could, of course, be none of the satisfaction derived from such short cuts.

Passing my GFT meant I could now come and go from the airfield as I pleased. It meant that I did not need Sean to sign me in or out. It meant that when I went flying with Richard, I could sit in the left-hand seat. But it meant something else far more important than all of these things.

Passengers.

A Ride for a Ride

The plane hit short of the runway with a violent impact, bounced down again, veered left for 1,500 feet, and made a 180° turn before slamming to a stop. The main landing gear broke off, the No.1 engine caught fire, part of the left wing sheared off, and the remainder was in flames. The Hajji, being unfamiliar with planes, apparently took this for a normal landing.

Country Life column, *Punch*.

Flying is a sexual symbol; flying dreams are held to be about sex. Therefore it is understandable that a pilot's professional and sexual worries intertwine. Ironically, many pilots find that flying has a deleterious effect upon their sexual performance.

David Beatty, *The Naked Pilot, The Human Factor in Aircraft Accidents*, 1995.

The Thruster had been procured as a sex aid, and it was time for it to deliver. At no stage did I doubt or question its pulling power. Flying, famously, attracted women. (Had not Cecil Lewis boasted of sleeping with more than 500 women? Did not Gabriel Voisin shag for France? Was it not 'Smithy'—Sir Charles Kingsford Smith, the trans-Pacific pioneer—whose policy of trading women's favours for a half-hour flight was the origin of the term 'a ride for a ride'?) And while the Thruster might not be a Gulfstream or a Lear jet, it promised a sporting wind-in-the-hair-and-the-wires experience.

A flying weekend promised to be a neutral, out-of-town date, in beautiful countryside, where there was enough time for proper, relaxed exposure to each other. Richard and I could each ask girls we liked, plus a couple of mates, thereby relieving the pressure of keeping our guests entertained. (There would be no danger of our friends moving in and outshining us if a girl we fancied showed them any interest because it was we, after all, who were the flyers.) The weekend had an activity and a centre to it to give us all something to do. Richard and I could feel relaxed because we were in each other's company. We had the flying to keep our minds off continual thoughts of sex and distract us from being too keen. And there were, if we cared to search for them, any number of additional psychological or psycho-sexual dynamics working in our favour. By getting into the cockpit, any girl was placing herself in a position where she was 100 per cent dependent on us—all in all, not a bad position to be in.

Recent events, of course, had moved this general plan on a little—and the significance was not wasted on me. Could it really be chance that, just as I finally qualified as a pilot, I had encountered the girl of my dreams? There was a powerful sense of the disparate threads of my life coming together, and there was no doubt that, in the back of my mind, I had decided that if I could only get Lift Girl to come flying then everything would be all right. We were now openly flirting and teasing each other again in a well-worked routine, though there never seemed any chance, with her boyfriend in the background, to get access to her alone, outside work. I did not want to risk a repeat of the kiss fiasco. So, for the time being, we had settled on a middle ground: she regaled me with anecdotes of her boyfriend's inadequacies; I knifed him with faint praise. Eventually, fortified by a couple of pints as we left the pub after work on midsummer night, I floated the idea of a flying weekend. We had got separated from the others and it felt like an intimate moment. 'Sounds cool,' she said. 'In your plane?'

'Uh-huh.'

Her face lit up. 'When?'

'Weekend after next?'

Then her face clouded, with a slight, adorable frown. 'So long as there's no ulterior motive here.'

'Please', I said. 'Can't you accept that someone wants you as a friend?'

Her parting kiss was on my lips, not on my cheek.

Looking back, I can see that there were any number of reasons why the flying weekend was doomed. Events unfolded, I can see now, with an almost tidal predictability. My one obsessive preoccupation was the weather, so much so that for the ten days before I telephoned Weathercall twice daily for forecasts. When I learnt that a long, slow-moving ridge of high pressure was scheduled, I was so ecstatic that Richard's announcement that he could no longer make the weekend hardly seemed to matter. Summer arrived that week. Restaurant tables spilled onto pavements, cars had their roofs down, everyone wore sunglasses and linen, and generally spirits soared. In a fit of spontaneous exuberance, when a cool(ish) commercials director called Ged whom I had known a bit since college said that he had always wanted to go up in a microlight, I asked him and his girlfriend Suzy (whom I mildly fancied) along.

I drove Lift Girl up after work on Friday night and we assembled at the pleasant B&B in Barsham Green which Richard and I occasionally used in preference to Salsingham during the winter months (it had seemed prudent to leave Salsingham out of the equation for this trip). We were settled in the pub with a pint when Ged arrived—alone. He and Suzy had split up, he announced—at his behest if his unconcerned demeanour were anything to go by. It was a shame, he said, but there it was. He seemed in excellent spirits, as he shared a cigarette with Lift Girl.

At the airfield next morning, things could hardly have looked more promising. The cloudless, windless sky was powder blue. Ged moseyed contentedly around the hangar, inspecting the aircraft, while I prepared the Thruster. Lift Girl was flying the first leg with me, to Seething, where Ged would meet us by car for lunch. While she zipped herself into Richard's absurdly overlarge ozee suit, I prepared my flight plan. Then I strapped her in and started the engine. It seemed to be running a bit roughly, but I ignored it as I taxied out onto the grass of the airfield. However, it soon became clear that something was seriously the matter. Although she sounded all right at low revs, when I opened the throttle, she started missing and popping as if she were only running on one cylinder.

Back at the hangar, Sean listened and pronounced that the points were probably sticky or dirty. He fetched a box to stand on, and started undoing bolts, occasionally straining and grunting as the box wobbled or he struggled with an extra tight or awkwardly-placed nut. For twenty minutes, he removed covers and prized off plates, revealing intimate and complex mechanisms which looked, to my squeamish eyes, far too private and pristine to be exposed like this to the outside world. Ged and Lift Girl sat on the grass in the sunshine, chatting. In due course, we were joined by Sean's next student, who, in the way that microlighters do, accepted the delay without complaint and sat down to chat and make helpful suggestions. (He, too, seemed particularly interested in Lift Girl's view.) Sean replaced the points, checked some other things and re-assembled the engine. We took her out, started her up and everything seemed to be fine.

'See you later, Ants,' shouted Sean.

I strapped Lift Girl in again and we taxied off once more. I had crossed the tarmac fairing and we had taxied almost to the take-off point when once again the engine started to falter and break down. As it did so, a wave of pure, vicious hate for the Thruster passed through me, unlike anything I could ever remember having felt before. Sean would not be back for at least an hour, and I suddenly saw the rest of the weekend I had set so much store by passing before my eyes.

'Tell you what,' said Ged. 'Why don't we pop into town, have a look round, get some papers, and come back in a couple of hours?' It was the only solution, though somehow Ged was beginning to get on my nerves.

'Good idea.'

I helped Ged put the roof of his TVR down, and they disappeared. I humoured myself by giving the left-hand wheel of the Thruster a series of brutal kicks until I noticed Keith watching me from the club-house window, missed my aim, and brought my shin agonisingly up against the sharp edge of the undercarriage leaf-springs.

There seems little point expanding this dismal chapter further than necessary. Sean eventually returned from his lesson to hear my tale of woe. 'Tuh. Bloody Rotaxes,' he sympathised. 'Still. Like the girlfriend, Ants. Where the Hell d'you find them?' After a leisurely cup of coffee, some chatting and fiddling around in his office, he had only just re-commenced work on the engine by the time Ged and Lift Girl arrived back around lunchtime. Laughing and teasing each other happily, they suggested a pub for lunch. I knew that Sean was teaching again in the afternoon, and that unless I stayed he would just drift on to other things, so with a leaden heart I sent them on their way, saying I would call later. By the time we met at a pub, in the evening, the engine still wasn't working properly. There would be no flying tomorrow. My final recollection of the day, before I fell asleep, was the creak of a floorboard in the corridor outside my door, a hushed murmuring of voices, followed by the click of Lift Girl's bedroom door.

After that, my emotional life became officially intolerable. I strove to maintain outward composure, but inwardly my world collapsed. The point, focus and aim of my life had gone: the reason I'd got the Thruster; the reason I'd learned to fly; the reason I'd moved jobs. Lift Girl's ready and immediate capitulation to the dubious charms of Ged, after my painfully sustained, expertly choreographed campaign, not to mention my prodigious life and career sacrifices on her behalf, maddened me. Every minor irritation at work prompted me to curse myself for working for a company I had not the least desire to be working for, and took my thoughts directly to the reason for my doing so.

It would be wrong to say that I thought about nothing but Lift Girl. Sometimes my mind turned to the egregrious Ged, to indulge in minute and destructive comparisons between him and myself, as I wished I were better looking, richer, cleverer, more successful. (Why wasn't I directing commercials, rather than writing them?) Now and again, they moved to the boyfriend I had invested so much skill and energy undermining. What had happened to him, I wondered? Where was he in all this? What, I wondered, did *he* have that I did not? At other times again, I found myself scrutinising Rob, the person at the agency who was alleged to have had a fling with Lift Girl before me. (Before *me*! As if I had even managed that!) Apart from these distractions, most of the time—say 99.98 per cent of every day—I thought about Lift Girl.

Her family lived near Newquay in Cornwall, and soon anything even vaguely associated with Cornish life served as an instant and powerful reminder of her and, by extension, my own deficiencies. This began with obvious things: pasties, surfers, clotted cream, lighthouses, vanilla ice-cream, RNLI collecting boxes, serpentine ash trays, books by Bernard or Patricia Cornwell; but had soon extended to include practically anything, from art galleries and paintings, to fishmongers, the countryside or any surfing or boarding-linked style or fashion accessory. Even watching the weather forecast, I could not stop myself looking to see what it was going to be like in Cornwall.

To make matters worse, I was now working on a project alongside her. As one of her penchants was a willingness to discuss sex (in the most intimate detail) with anyone who cared to join in—and few men did not—work became a form of exquisite torture as I became the recipient of information which raised feelings of possessiveness, jealousy and frustration.

Unable to think what else to do, feeling trapped and with low hopes (I had won no awards this year), I put 'my book out'—adspeak for letting it be known that I was in the market for a new job.

My next attempt to take up a passenger had to be postponed because the Thruster's annual 'Permit to Fly' had expired and Sean had forgotten—or, as he put it, we had failed to remind him—to do the necessary work to renew it in time. For our third attempt, in mid-July, we had arranged for two old college mates, Tom and Bob, to come up for the weekend. I was grateful at the prospect of all-male company.

Saturday dawned overcast but settled, and after breakfast it was decided that we should do a re-run of my earlier planned trip to Seething for lunch. I would fly the first leg with Bob. Richard and Tom would meet us there for lunch by car, and we would switch for the return journey.

It was my first experience, if you discounted my short taxi-run with Lift Girl, of flying with anyone apart from Sean, Ken, or Richard—in short, 'family'—and it was more of a strain than I had bargained for. Bob appeared to have vastly greater faith in my ability to fly him safely, competently and unthinkingly than I did myself, and proved the point by talking incessantly. I had forgotten about this characteristic of his. From the moment the intercom was connected, he maintained an unremitting stream of nonsense: inane commentary, vacuous observation, and incessant fatuous questions about minutiae of performance and costs of upkeep. The effort of fielding this barrage while simultaneously appearing relaxed and friendly, listening to the engine note, searching for landable fields, checking my heading and keeping an eye out for other aircraft began to tell. By the time we reached Seething I felt exhausted.

While we waited for the others to arrive—my first direct evidence of the superiority of air over road travel—we had the unexpected bonus of seeing a crash. We were having a cup of coffee outside the clubhouse, when a pricey-looking twin-engined plane landed and taxied in. In the cockpit with the pilot were two women. We watched as he swept off his headphones, ran his hands through his hair, fixed his wraparounds so that everything was just so when he got out. The women were lapping it up. Alas, Maverick failed to pay enough attention as he taxied briskly past a row of planes in front of the clubhouse. He was going a little too fast—all part of the show, no doubt—and his left wing tip clipped the tip of another plane's wing as he was swinging round to park. It was enough. That plane swung round so that its wing, in turn, caught the next in the line, leaving a four-inch dent in the wings of all three aircraft. It was a joy to behold. His coolness turned to a flush of horror, as angry figures started pouring out of the clubhouse.

After lunch, the time came for Richard and Tom to depart. As they taxied away to the main runway, I noticed, with a tingle of anxious excitement, that in the quarter of an hour since Richard had plotted his flight log, the windsock had wheeled round 180°. Satisfaction at my own airmanship for spotting this was eclipsed by a nagging fear that Richard had not. He was now 400 yards away, far too far for me to be able to attract his attention. Surely he would notice? He stopped to do his final checks, at what was now the wrong end of the runway. When he did a 360° turn, the final pre-take-off check, it became certain he hadn't noticed. I watched, nervous but fascinated, to see what would happen.

Fortunately, Seething's runway was tarmac and over 800 metres long, constructed to get fully-laden Flying Fortresses off the ground. The Thruster would normally have been away within fifty metres and at 500 feet or more by the time it passed the end of the runway. Richard and Bob made it, but not by much. The Thruster left the ground, sank back down again, lifted off again and crunched back down three times before she finally struggled into the air. I mentioned it to Richard, as we put the Thruster away at the end of the day. 'Long take-off run?' he said. 'Don't think so, Ants. No more than usual.'

164

'Lazy bones. I don't believe it. You're still in bed.'

'Who's that?' I murmured sleepily, fumbling with the receiver. I wasn't remotely sleepy. It was Saturday morning and, as it happened, I had been asleep, but one syllable of those soft, whirring tones and I was wide awake.

'What are you doing?'

'What do you think I'm doing at quarter to ten in bed on a Saturday morning?'

'Don't know. I'm sure boys get up to all kinds of things I wouldn't want to know about when they are in bed by themselves.'

'What makes you think I'm by myself?'

'Aren't you?' A sudden change in her voice. Then the seductive whir once more. 'I think you are.'

And we were off again. She was so maddeningly expert at timing her moments. The trouble is, it was irresistible and seemed so enjoyable when it was happening.

And so Lift Girl continued to play me, as Richard put it, 'like a fat salmon'.

It was fun, I told myself. In reality, of course, it was hell.

By July, the Thruster had moved to Salsingham. Dan had called a couple of weeks before to say that the last traces of the April flooding had finally drained away, the field had dried out and the runway had been cut for a first crop of hay. Sean christened 'Salsingham Airfield' with the first landing and pronounced it the narrowest and trickiest strip, with the most awkward approaches, that he had ever encountered. Dan said that he had done some circuits and that it took a 'bit of getting used to'.

Certainly the transformation from the muddy quagmire of January was complete. The field was now a swaying stand of ripening barley, through the middle of which a green turf stripe cut gently uphill towards the far hedge, disappearing over a hump about a third of the way along. My initial impression was of the narrowness: at fifteen feet or so, it was scarcely wider than the Thruster's wingspan. 'Where's the windsock?' I asked Dan, and he pointed out, at the far end, a minute silhouette, dangling stiffly from a telegraph pole. It looked absurdly small, but was, apparently, the standard eight-foot model. Tucked into an overgrown corner at the downhill end, amongst the elders and foxgloves and brambles and nettles, was a neat, steel-framed hangar with sliding doors. On the soft ground in front of it was a mat of thickening grass as a manoeuvring area.

Richard and I decided it would be prudent to do a few initial practices with only 'one up'. I went first. Taking off in the uphill 250° direction, over open fields, was straightforward enough, though it felt strange to have hedges and trees appearing quite so soon beneath the wheels. It gave the impression of having taken off from nowhere.

As I curved round to the right (getting a stunning view of the house on its low hill above the lake), any idea of landing on such a tiny strip of grass, even in emergency, seemed absurd. After the lavish chopping-board-flat acres that were Barsham Green, fields like Priory Farm had seemed fringe. Now Priory Farm seemed like JFK. It was not so much the length or narrowness that I found disconcerting, as the lack of clear approaches. There was no wide perimeter track; no open, surrounding countryside (at least not from the north-east) over which to pace my descent, or, if necessary, overshoot.

At my first attempt, approaching along the river, I found myself still at 500 feet at the point when I should have had my wheels touching down. The next time round I nearly crashed into the canopies of the Douglas firs around Lester's trout pond, I was concentrating so hard on being low enough to make the end of the runway. The approach from this direction was choppy and turbulent at around 500 feet, perhaps because of the combination of the trees and sinky air over the water. But with a few more attempts I found that, if I concentrated only on the strip itself, without allowing myself to be distracted by the cluttered local topography, after a few attempts I could do it. Once down, the upward slope of the ground acted as a handy brake.

From the opposite direction, the south-west end, the approaches were clearer, in that they consisted of wide, flat fields, but the downhill landing was more tricky. It required holding off over falling ground. Touch the wheels down too late, and I found I was travelling too fast at the point where the hump fell away to the hollow and I could find myself airborne again with less than a third of the runway remaining—and that still on a considerable decline. Moreover, should an overshoot become necessary, the tall firs ahead meant veering in a full-powered climbing turn either right over woods and the lake, or left over the trout pond and some copses and telephone wires across rough, rising ground. Either situation was hardly ideal in the event of an engine failure.

However, at the end of the afternoon, there was a feeling of having finally flown the nest as (remembering to turn the prop to horizontal first, to prevent it catching on the door lintel) we pushed the Thruster into the hangar, padlocked the door, hid the key in the branch of the elder and went up to the house for tea.

In August, I finally took my first girl flying. I was up at Salsingham alone and the Watsons were away. Mel was another advertising account manager, from my previous company, beautiful rather than pretty, in an icy, high-cheekboned way. She had come up more by her request than mine, driving over to meet me one Sunday afternoon. I installed her in the passenger seat, tucking away loose clothing, adjusting the safety harness, tightening her helmet strap, checking her feet were clear of the controls (suppressing, as best I could, a flash of resentment that she was not Lift Girl). I showed her what she could grab hold of if she felt frightened and, more importantly, what she could not—me, the stick, the throttle—and was generally every inch the responsible airman instilling confidence in his passenger.

After a sultry start, it had cleared to a fine evening with 'no weather'.

She wanted to fly over and look at Blickling Hall, a big brick National Trust house north-west of Aylsham, which she had once visited. I knew the house well—it was one of my familiar navigation way-points—and as it was barely a twenty-minute flight away, I did not bother to draw a line on my map or make a flight log. (The truth was that, a few weeks before, Lester had spotted me preparing for an equally short cross-country flight: his look, as he took in my detailed notes of distance, wind drift, fuel consumption and way-points, had been one of such incredulity, and I had felt so ashamed and ridiculous, that I had still not recovered.) I decided that if I followed a north-easterly heading for long enough I could not fail to spot it.

After we set off, Mel said nothing for several minutes. When she finally did speak, it was in an unsettling, soft, hypnotised monotone. I noticed that she was grabbing her side of the A-frame like a maniac, with both hands. By this time we were well away from the airfield, so I tried chatting to her to calm her down. She was intrigued by some crop circles, so I flew round them a few times so she could to have a good look. After fifteen minutes, I realised that I had been paying more attention to Mel than to my route, and we had veered considerably off course. I made a guess at a corrected heading, but after another ten minutes there was no sign of Blickling, or evidence of any identifiable landmarks at all. I regretted not having marked proper way-points and timings on my map. After another ten minutes, with still no glimmer of anything recognisable, not even the coast, I began to be seriously concerned. Where could I be? And what on earth should I do? Mel was beginning to ask awkward questions. 'Shouldn't we be able to see it by now? I thought you said it was a fifteen minute flight.' Her zombie voice was freaking me out.

Finally, I spotted an airfield at about three o'clock. I scanned the map for clues. The area where we were supposed to be was almost the only part of Norfolk where there were not scores of airfields. I vaguely hoped the name might be painted somewhere in white letters two feet high, as it was at some airfields, but I was out of luck. The only option, humiliating as it was, seemed to be to land, establish where we were, then proceed accordingly. I thought that, if I was skilful, this ought to be possible without alerting Mel to the situation.

'Look. An airfield. Where's that?' she said after a few moments.

'That's Oulton. Lovely little strip. We might drop in, in fact, as I could do with a pee.'

I landed on the wide, weatherbeaten strip of tarmac, the first third of what had evidently once been a massive wartime runway. Near the tower, two men were standing beside an immaculate bi-plane, passing the time of day. 'I should stay here, if you want,' I said, parking well away from them and rapidly unbuckling my straps once the engine was off. 'Won't be a minute.'

I walked briskly up to the two by the plane.

'Hi. What's the story of this place then?' I asked, hoping the response would tell me all I needed. One of the men, wearing a tweed cap, looked at me.

'This place? Lancasters. 115 squadron. Then a Mosquito base. Original control tower, one of the few ...'

I did not want to appear rude, but out of the corner of my eye I could see Mel beginning to unbuckle herself from the Thruster.

'What's the best way back to Barsham Green?' I tried.

'Easy,' the second of the two answered. 'Just follow the old railway line out of Fakenham. Glancing surreptitiously at my map-board, that meant I could be at Foulsham, Little Snoring or, at a pinch, North Creake. The most promising option, Langham, I knew it could not be, because I had been there, and it was near the coast. Almost certainly it must therefore be Foulsham. Which meant I was at least 45° off course. How the Hell had that happened?

'D'you know where you are?' The second man, chewing a match, was regarding me closely.

My doubt must have shown on my face. He gave a happy smirk.

'He doesn't know where he bloody is. Tell me, young man, where do you *think* you are?'

'I know where I am,' I said with what I hoped was bored disdain. 'This is Foulsham—'

'Foulsham!' He brought his hand down on the surface of the wing and gave a lumpen-headed cackle. 'Foulsham. He thinks he's at Foulsham. And where have you come from? Barsham-way, you say? What happened?' he said, raising his eyes to the clear blue heavens and sniffing the still evening air. 'Were you *blown* off course?' He dissolved into giggles again.

It turned out that I was at Little Snoring. Unfortunately, Mel caught the end of this exchange, though she later told me that she had already made up her mind to return to Salsingham by taxi.

My flight home—alone—felt quite different from my other flights of the last few weeks. I felt calm and relaxed and carefree and contented, and in control in a way I could hardly remember. I was thankful to be alone, undistracted and free to appreciate the landscape and the sheer pleasantness of a summer evening. I had forgotten how pleasurable flying could be: it had not felt so good since the day I was complimented on my landings. I resolved that from now on I would only fly by myself or with Richard, unless there happened to be someone present and waiting at a time when I was in the mood, the conditions were right and they were *burning* to come up. I had been disappointed and, I suppose, a bit hurt that, from their reactions, neither Bob nor Mel had been *that* moved—or, at least, moved in the way that I wanted them to be—by their flying experience.

In retrospect, this was a more significant decision than I realised. At the time, however, I was content simply to bimble along (as Sean would have put it), savouring the luminous glow of a cloudless August evening. The trees and hedgerows cast long shadows to the left, and, after fifteen minutes, I had flown over four village cricket matches. I felt I ought to be paying more attention to my route, following earlier events, but the light was so warm and friendly, and the visibility so good, and the engine running so well, that it was impossible to feel nervous.

At the same moment that I recognised East Dereham water tower, I realised that I could also see Salsingham. The house was at least eight miles away, but by a felicitous quirk of architecture and orientation, I noticed, it alone was picked out from the rest of the level and (now) darkening landscape. The south-western (lake) front squarely caught the setting sun, igniting the weathered brick to a fiery, almost luminous orange. It was my first view of what would become a familiar beacon after a long day's flying.

For the rest of that year and the next, Richard and I occupied ourselves with steadily more ambitious excursions—though now we only made the journey to Norfolk if high pressure was unequivocally scheduled. When someone told us about the impossibly steep and treacherous Nayland Airfield in Suffolk, it naturally became imperative to land there. We ventured further afield (one weekend we made it as far as Enstone Airfield, north of Oxford). We discovered farm strips not mentioned on the charts or in the flight guides and encountered some of the local characters of aviation.

There was Henry Labouchere, who restored vintage aeroplanes at Langham. I had heard about Henry. On his round-the-world trips, he pegged his washing out to dry on the wing wires of his Tiger Moth before take-off, and he flew to Holkham Beach to walk his dog. Finding him at work in his hangar when we arrived at Langham one Sunday morning, I asked him how he knew the sand was firm enough to land on. His response was to glance at his watch: 'Tell you what. You chaps got a minute? Useful thing to know.' And then and there, he ushered us into one of the elegant, high-winged, vintage planes that was parked on the grass outside the hangar—'Bit more room than your bus. Need more than a bikini bottom and a fold-up toothbrush at my age'—and he flew us up to Holkham Bay and demonstrated how to do a low, fast pass, plonking the wheels down firmly on the sand without attempting to land, then going round again for another low pass to inspect how deep the marks were. If they were shallow, it was safe; if they were deep, it was not.

There was the Gérard Depardieu lookalike who lived in a shed alongside his landing strip which was by a railway line in Lincolnshire. When he saw us circling and circling, he came up, dangling from the frayed canvas cradle of his foot-launched machine to guide us in to his junk-yard.

Our mutual loathing of time-wasting meant that Richard and I soon developed into a highly effective flying partnership. I would pick the route, prepare the plane and do all checking, planning and telephoning; Richard did the maths—plotting our track, calculating the windrift, working out the fuel. We were soon so fast and skilled at what we were already good at, and so hopeless in the areas that we were not, that it became unthinkable to fly alone. Once airborne, two pairs of eyes halved the strain of cross-countries. And from initial mistrust and a tendency to back-seat-fly, we soon had more faith in each other than we had in ourselves. We became forgiving—even welcoming—of each other's mistakes. Richard made light of it when, after I had arranged a fuel stop at Towcester Airfield, we discovered it was now a housing estate—necessitating a rough precautionary landing in stubble near a motorway service station to refuel. I said nothing when Richard over-ran into some barbed wire at a private strip near the M1. When Richard landed in a Nature Reserve (one could almost hear the crunch of plovers' eggs), I shared the fine. When I, under the impression that it contained dead batteries, rubbish and junk, chucked away a bag containing the phone recharger, mobile and rechargeable batteries, he did likewise.

Towards the end of the following September (which was particularly fine) I flew down to my parents in Somerset, where my father, touchingly, showed a great deal less reluctance to come up with me than most of my friends. (I repaid his confidence with five balloons and a go-around—the sun was in my eyes.) The weather, needless to say, promptly turned, and for a month every shower and gale that I watched from my office window in Soho made me think guiltily of the Thruster, tied down outside in the corner of a farmer's field. Eventually, the Salsingham syndicate had to invest in a trailer to get her back to Norfolk.

By her fourth winter, the appearance of the Thruster was what might be described as 'worn in'. The red and blue fabric of the upper surface of the wing and tailplane was faded by the sun. Flecks of oil from the exhaust streaked the tailplane and upper starboard side of her wing. Her sagging leaf-spring undercarriage suggested more heavy landings than anyone admitted to.

Recalling them now, these seem some of my happiest flying memories and in all material aspects, this should have been a near-perfect phase of my life. I was twenty-seven. I was single. I had a convertible BMW with leather upholstery and a fine sound-system. A timely call from a headhunter had finally allowed me to make my escape from Lift Girl, to a top-flight agency. With my career now back on track, I was working on famous accounts and, for the first time in my life, I had enough money that when I signed credit card counterfoils I hardly bothered to check the totals. Yet I wasn't happy.

I might have removed myself from the physical presence of Lift Girl, but this did not, as I had hoped, remove her from my thoughts. The information that she had dumped Ged, leaving him (I gathered with satisfaction) near suicidal, might have been briefly consoling, but it hardly assisted my own situation. My heart still surged ludicrously every time I glimpsed a red VW Polo of the type she drove (and of which there appeared to be around 10,000 in central London). I found myself indulging in sub-stalker activities, contriving detours that would take me down the street where she lived.

Flying remained the one activity capable of banishing her completely from my thoughts. Yet even here, for all my mounting experience, I could not help feeling that I had not sampled all that it had to offer. With over 100 hours in my log book—if I included dual and pilot-in-command time—I still did not feel, in any larger sense, an *aviator*. Our flying trips seldom took us further than a day's range from Salsingham. I had yet to fly over *real* scenery like Scotland, Wales or Cornwall (somehow the Chilterns, Wiltshire Downs, Cotswolds and Mendips no longer seemed to count). And, though regarded by my friends as a flying expert, I certainly didn't feel one at airfields. Although Richard was always happy to accompany me, it was invariably I who was the instigator of our trips and I began to wonder why I was happy to devote so much time to a hobby which gave me butterflies (not to mention nausea and loose bowels), which left me exhausted, headachey and frequently miles from my intended destination, which brought in regular and substantial bills, and which consumed hours—sometimes days—of planning to make journeys that could have been undertaken in an hour or two by car.

I bought books about planes, but though they always seemed momentarily interesting in the shop, once I got home I seldom opened them again. Looking at pictures of planes, I soon realised, didn't have much to do with flying. I liked reading the steady stream of fighter pilots' obituaries that appeared in the broadsheet press* and, for a time, I collected and avidly read every flying story I could lay my hands on. But, like the obituaries, the overwhelming majority seemed to be by or about heroes and record-breakers—fighter aces, bomber legends, test pilots, mail route pioneers, top guns, astronauts—and this only increased my sense of alienation. The same went for flying movies which I mechanically videoed and sometimes watched. Full of hope, I went to several air shows and although they too were initially exciting, I always came away bored and slightly disappointed (with the mandatory stiff neck and a headache). They appeared to be about

---

*They all said much the same:

'… qualified Brooklands flying school … delivered airmail in primitive aircraft over the inhospitable Arctic wastes of the Northwest Territories … frostbite, fuel shortages and forced landings par for the course … vast expanses of sea to be patrolled on the Murmansk run … corkscrew spiral climb earned nickname 'Twister' … Bar to his DFC … pushing successive marks of the Spitfire to the limits … found return to the London Stock Exchange a trifle staid.'

many things—noise, speed, power, danger, the chance of explosions—
but, oddly, not really about flying or what it felt like to fly. I realised that
it was doing it, not watching it, that I liked.

I had even taken to reading *Flightline*. Flicking through its pages
the following April, I noticed, as usual, the incessant references to the
Round Britain rally—plainly the event of the microlighting calendar.
There was even a tear-off application form. Something like *that*, I
mused reflectively, as I began and immediately gave up on an
impenetrable article on 'induced drag', would certainly kick my flying
into a new realm. A moment later, I turned back to the form. Why
not?

With a resolve I could not remember having felt before, I opened my
diary, put a line through the third week of July, then posted the
completed application.

Epaulette Country

Members of the board were amazed that the microlight pilot could have found himself in such a predicament ... It seemed incomprehensible that he was not conscious of the extent of his unusual ascent ... during the 15 minutes or so it would have taken him to reach 11,000 feet ... Moreover, it was equally mystifying how he could have passed within 100 feet of a large passenger jet without in any way being aware of its presence.

Report of the Board of Enquiry submitted to the Civil Aviation
Authority following a 'near miss' nine miles north of
Liverpool Airport, 10th February 2000.

The note from Richard was decisive, peremptory, formal, impersonal, unexplained and entirely out of the blue. Characteristically lacking in frills and signed using his Christian and surname, the printed letter read as if it were addressed to a remote business supplier (cc Lester Watson and Dan Watson). 'Dear Antony, I have decided to give up flying. In due course, when the Thruster is replaced or sold, I would be glad of the repayment of my quarter share. In the meantime ...' There was no reason or explanation. And he had made no mention of his decision when I had spoken to him on the phone the day before. I had dialled his number before I finished reading.

'Well?' I asked.

'I don't know, Ants,' he said, with a reflectiveness absent from his letter. 'It's not a snap decision. I've just decided I've had enough.'

Richard had recently got married—a development as sudden and dramatically announced as all the larger decisions of his life—and I could see that a hobby as self-indulgently time- and cash-consuming as a Norfolk-based microlight might well be incompatible with such adjusted circumstances. However, I suspected that there was more to it than this; specifically a trip we had taken the previous summer.

On this occasion we had planned a combined flying and walking trip to the Peak District over an extended August weekend, and after a flying summer interrupted by weddings and other activities, there was no question that, flying-wise, we had been out of our depth. On the way up, we had arranged to 'drop in' on some friends who lived in Grantham. I flew the first leg from Norfolk to Langar Airfield in Rutland, to meet Richard by car. (On long-distance trips, we had regretfully concluded, we required more kit than could be carried with both of us aboard the Thruster.) When I arrived, our friends said they had spoken to a local farmer, and there was a big field we could land in almost backing onto their house. I took off from Langar Airfield with one of our friends to guide me to the designated field. We duly landed; but what had appeared to be a soft, inviting-looking seed bed from the air turned out, on the ground, to be lumps of dried-out rock-hard clay. Accordingly, we decided next morning that Richard should take off without refuelling and make the short hop back to Langar, where we would load the plane properly.

In the morning Richard was in one of his brusquely impatient moods. Without even the pretence of a pre-flight check, or getting into his flying clothes, he sat down heavily in the pilot's seat, gave the fuel bulb a couple of pumps, then began buckling himself in. I was giving the engine a couple of gentle pulls over with the chokes on to prime it, when, with a brisk stir of the stick and a 'Right, let's get on, then—' he flicked the main ignition toggle to ON and she burst into life. Through the windscreen, I noticed he did not have the flight-board. 'Where's your map?' I shouted.

'Thought you said the airfield was only a mile or two away?'

'Yes, but still. You want a map, don't you? Hang on.'

I went to the car and was rummaging among all the kit when I heard the engine note rise to a scream. Dust and grit whipped and rattled against the paintwork, and, turning round, I was just in time to see the Thruster speeding away down the field.

He took off safely enough into the slight northerly breeze, and I decided to watch him until he turned onto his westerly heading for Langar before getting into the car to follow. Except he never did. At 800 feet, at 1,000—in fact, as long as I watched—he neither turned nor showed any sign of turning. I waited, as the Thruster grew smaller and smaller, and the noise of the engine gradually faded to be replaced by the birds. I watched until the black dot was so tiny I lost it and could not find it again. Then, wearily, I switched on the mobile and settled down to wait. It was a little over an hour before it rang.

'Antony, is that you?' Richard's tone was businesslike.

'Morning, Richard.'

'I can't talk for long, Antony. Unfortunately I have run out of fuel. I am at RAF Symington.' His voice went faint. 'How do I spell that?—' Louder again: 'S-Y-M-I-N-G-T-O-N. Got that, Antony? Just off the A46 going north. Oh ... and ...er ... you'll need to bring some money and a means of identification for me. Unfortunately the Thruster has been impounded. I am temporarily under arrest. A fine is payable for my release. Your name will be left on the gate.'

The air base was a large one; clean, cold, new, patrolled by military police with dogs. There were no khaki Bedford trucks or homely Nissen huts; just the businesslike accretions of a science park. As I was taken from the guard room to Control, I could see in the distance what looked like giant molehills—hardened bunkers containing jet fighters. Once I had vouched for Richard's identity and written a cheque to the Ministry of Defence for £22 as a release fee, the Thruster, which had been removed to a hangar, was found to have a flat left tyre. We were ordered to remain in the Land-Rover while an overalled fitter, with some difficulty, attached her to an aircraft tow tractor and manoeuvred her to an enormous service bay. There the pressure pumps were deemed too powerful for the Thruster's tyres, so another fitter was despatched to fetch a foot pump from his car boot. It ought to have been funny, but the RAF did not think so. And at no stage did Richard and I have the chance to speak to each other privately. My final view, as I was driven away under guard, was of a perplexed Richard trying to fathom the gestures of an overalled figure wearing headphones and waving coloured ping-pong bats (the tower was not geared for non-radio aircraft). Though Richard made it without further incident to Netherthorpe Airfield, near Sheffield, on the eastern edge of the Pennines, I think the incident unsettled him. I arrived, in due course, and we set out for what should have been a perfect trip together: an evening flight over the High Peak to Ladybower Reservoir (where the Dambusters practised), down through Dove Dale to Darley Moor and back via Chatsworth.

In fact the flight was a nightmare. Our lack of recent hours in the cockpit meant we were tense, unconfident and out of practice. We unsettled each other by continually imagining that the engine note had changed. The rising ground of the Peak moorland beneath us meant that we were continually having to open the throttle to maintain height above it, with the result that, by our final leg, we were panicking that we were about to run out of fuel.*

For the return trip south, as I had flown the Thruster most of the way up to Derbyshire, I flew just the first leg; then it was agreed that Richard would fly back to Norfolk. I could not have been more thankful to get out of the cockpit and hand over, my flying done. Whether it was my imagination, or whether there was actually something wrong, I do not know. But the engine had seemed to sound just a little rougher than normal, to be vibrating slightly more, to be delivering slightly less than full power. There was no logic to my feeling, nothing I could put my finger on. But it was there and it would not go away. And for whatever reason,

---

* One of the quirks of the Thruster was that the only fuel gauge was a window running round the cylindrical tank. As the tank was below and behind the pilot and passenger, once the level sank to below a third, it was virtually impossible to tell whether you had fuel in hand, or whether the engine might stop at any second.

whether through my vibes or his intuition, I knew that Richard felt it too. And nothing—nothing—saps the joy of flying more completely.

I could only guess that that was how Richard had felt. En route back to Salsingham he had to make one landing stop-over to top up with fuel from the spare jerry cans he was carrying. This had been arranged at a private landing strip at a motel near Holbeach. By the time I got to Salsingham, he was pulling the plane round to put it away. He seemed more serious than was usual at the end of a flying day (when the relief and satisfaction tend to promote a feeling of buoyant, if tired, wellbeing). As I went to help pull the plane back into the hangar, I noticed that the tail-wheel spring, the sturdy twelve-inch strip of spring steel onto which the little tail-wheel was bolted, was bent. But it was not just slightly bent. It was freakishly turned back on itself, 45° or more out of its normal position. It could not have been like that earlier or I would certainly have noticed.

'What the hell happened here?'

'Where?'

'Here. Look at the tail-wheel: it's fucked. It's taken an almighty pasting.'

'Where? What?' Richard peered at it noncommittally. 'That's what it's always like.' But there was an emptiness to his voice I had never heard before.

We tried to straighten the spring, but it was so stiff that even our combined efforts could only get it halfway back to its normal position, a measure of just what a blow or succession of blows it must have received. I imagined the wild, terrific bounces and balloons which must have seized the machine to do such dramatic damage—how out of control, panic-stricken or just plain desperate to be back on the ground you would have to be to persist with a landing going so badly wrong, rather than opening the throttle to go round for another go. I wondered whether it had happened at Holbeach, or just a few minutes earlier at Salsingham. He was lucky to be in one piece.

It was years later that Richard told me what had really happened that day.

He told me how, with the fuel level so low he could no longer see it, and believing himself to be on the point of running out, he had misjudged his final approach at Holbeach. His landing was so disastrous, he said, that the bent tail-wheel—had he noticed it—would have seemed almost incidental alongside the other structural damage he feared he had done. Over a cup of tea at the airfield, he tried to calm his racing pulse, which, he said, was pounding away at about 180 bpm from the moment he stepped out of the plane until the moment he stepped back into it for his final leg. As soon as he was airborne again, he noticed that the air speed indicator was not working. This meant that he could not be certain of his speed through the air or, consequently, how near he was to stalling. Accordingly, he kept the nose down and the throttle well up until he arrived overhead at Salsingham, where, to be on the safe side, he made his final approach at about twice the normal speed, freaking himself out for a second time. Once down, he discovered that the reason the ASI had not been working was because the Pitot tube—the air speed indicator 'intake' high up on the nose—was hopelessly bent from his earlier landing. He had only just finished bending it straight again, he said, when I arrived. As we clicked the padlock shut on the hangar door that evening, he said, he had just one thought in his head: 'Thank God I never have to set foot in that machine again.' And, though I only realised it when he pointed it out, he never did.

The Rally instructions described it as 'as much a test of navigation, logistics, airmanship and resourcefulness as pilot skill'. 'Resourcefulness', I presumed, was a euphemism for cheating, since some seven pages of accompanying blurb consisted almost entirely of rules and caveats designed to counter the elaborate and ingenious mechanisms that competitors had devised in previous years. These ranged from unsubstantiated claims and faked punched cards, to historic photos (visited airfields had to be photographed on a continuous roll of film), secondary teams in cars, hidden GPSs and spare fuel cans.

The rally, it transpired, was not the race around the coast that I had imagined at all. In principle, it was a contemporary version of the *Daily Mail* 'English Circuit' race of 1911. That, the third of the three great *Daily Mail*-sponsored aviation challenges (the first being the cross-Channel prize and the second the London-to-Manchester race the following year) took place over three days in July, with a mandatory nightly stop-over at three designated locations: one in the north, one in the south and one in the west. But where the early pioneers knew from the start where those places were—Edinburgh, Brighton and Bristol— we would not be given this information until the day. Between departing from these (8am earliest) and arriving at the next (7pm latest), the aim was to visit as many as possible of around eighty other nominated airfields, each of which was worth a set of points graded according to distance, remoteness and general awkwardness. The competitor who made it to the Finish—romantically situated on the vast, smooth tidal reach known as Pilling Sands, ten miles south of Lancaster—with the most points, won.

My first thought, when the envelope of rally bumph had arrived, was that it was no longer relevant. Richard's decision had effectively spelled the end of my rally hopes—and perhaps even my flying. Without him, I felt lonely and exposed. It had taken us years to get used to each other in the cockpit: the thought of doing it all again with someone else, at short notice and under pressure, didn't bear thinking about. Because Richard was my flying partner, and the Thruster carried only two, I had never flown with either Dan or Lester. And I had no desire to do the rally alone.

After two months of inactive procrastination—and no flying— however, I decided that perhaps this was a feeble and weak-minded attitude. What better way to kick-start a relationship with a new flying partner than under race conditions? I had no doubt that both Dan and Lester would be up for it. I decided to try Dan first, as the thought of flying with Lester still intimidated me: he snapped up the idea.

Dan was three years younger than me, and was, essentially, Lester on beta-blockers (or maybe Rohypnol): a younger, cooler, lazier, more laid-back, less worldly, more charming version of his father. His father's independence of mind was there, but it was subsumed beneath an unambitious and appreciative relish for the sensual pleasures of life— food, music, clothes (many of which he made himself), sex (he and his girlfriend routinely did nothing else for weekends), an appreciation of landscape, and a general savouring of the moment. Whatever he did, be it walking down to pick some damsons from the walled garden, replacing the bearing on the bracket of the windsock, or skinning, gutting and preparing a meal from a rabbit he had shot, he contentedly immersed himself in it as if it were, at that moment, what he wanted to be doing more than anything else. Sometimes he would appear from the woods with strange and frightening-looking fungi and puffballs which he would proceed to cook. His celebrated dinners would be followed by mugs of magic mushroom tea (served with cinnamon and honey) prepared from a large bag he filled from secret dells each autumn.

His life was conducted to a background score of ambient music, with or without drumbeat according to the energy level he required. His first action on coming into any room or getting into a car was to regulate the music to his taste. When I complained that all ambient albums had identical titles (things like Odyssey in Aphasia, or Astral Beach), identical covers (computer-generated psychedelic imagery), identical track names (SL2 (Rainbow Dub) or Altern 8 (Elysium mix)), and identical hours of nondescript electronic swirling, he was appalled and mixed me several tapes, drawing up the cassette sleeves in his splattery-nibbed Gerald Scarfe-style handwriting.

Like Lester, he drank only very moderately and I always felt an alcoholic in his company. Though he loved cooking, he had a minute appetite and ate only when he was hungry, not by fixed habit or routine. He was immune to time, timetables or scheduling of any kind and he made my habit-prompted hunger and need for alcohol seem the last word in artificial and joyless living. Needless to say, his aura of all-the-time-in-the-world calm was as maddening as it was charming. There was never a reason to end a telephone conversation. A short stop at a motorway service station might be extended almost indefinitely as, lost like a child amongst the aisles, he agonised between whether Tangy Cheese Doritos or Cheese and Onion Pringles better suited his forthcoming sensory requirements. For him it was the doing of anything that was the complete pleasure, never the end result. I had no idea what he was like in the cockpit (other than he was 'a good little pilot') any more than he knew what I was like, but I had watched him preparing his cross-country flights as calmly and methodically as he did everything.

And so, urgently, preparations began. With only a fortnight to go, I still had not read the detail of the bumph; when I did so, the blizzard of documentation that was demanded appalled me: licences, medical certificates, permit to fly, personal information sheets, entry forms, indemnity forms, third party insurance, log books stamped with proof of experience, up-to-date maps.* I called Sean to warn him of the dramatic promotion of our flying ambitions. He agreed to do an emergency overhaul and, thoroughly entering into the spirit, suggested we invest in a three-bladed propeller and aerofoil wing-struts.

Getting hold of these items was not as straightforward as it sounded, as it involved dealing with Thruster Air Services Ltd. Calls to Thruster were invariably met with the same response: the phone was answered by an absurdly sexy French female voice, sounding like Emmanuelle Beart in *Bitter Moon*, who put you through to one of the staff, all of whom were called John. John was unfailingly helpful, friendly, courteous, well-informed and attentive to your enquiry— though for some reason immediate action was impossible. However, he explained, this was not a problem because, fortunately, whatever it

---

* 'When the weight of the paperwork equals the weight of the aeroplane, you are ready to fly'—flying adage.

was that you needed was going to be possible tomorrow. Leave it to them, John would say, and they would be back in touch shortly. A week or two might pass without hearing anything, and you would call up for a progress report. Emmanuelle Beart's silky tones would be followed by the ever-charming John who—courteous and friendly as ever—would have no recollection of any previous conversation, or record of action required. No problem, he would say; just leave it with him. And so on. The first time this happened, I was left wondering if I had actually made my original call, or just imagined the whole thing, but after several repetitions, and when Richard—and even Dan—reported similar experiences, it became clear that Thruster operated in a parallel universe; a universe with deceptively similar rules to our own. (In fact, the 'factory'—a farmyard south of Oxford—rather resembled a *Dr Who* set.) It was decided that Dan—coming from a very similar universe himself—was the person most temperamentally suited to the successful execution of the task; he eventually collected the propeller and wing struts and, with them poking out of the open sunroof of his Scirocco, drove them through pouring rain back to Salsingham.

I went to get the maps one lunchtime. At £12 each, it took twenty-four sheets to cover the whole of the country at the larger 1:250,000 scale; three to cover it at 1:500,000 scale. I got three of the large scale, to cover the area where the rally started and finished around Manchester and Blackpool, the Lake District, because come what may I was determined to fly over it, and East Anglia, because mine had been lost; plus three smaller scale 1:500,000 maps to cover the whole country.

The race began on the third Thursday in July, and I drove up to Norfolk on the Tuesday afternoon, my head full of logistics. The schedule for the following day was tight, and dependent upon a range of interlocking variables. I had to plan my flight, prepare and pack the plane, drop by at Barsham Green for Sean to stamp my log book, give me the Permit to Fly and get some oil, then get to the start of the rally (near Manchester). At precisely eight o'clock, according to the bumph, maps would be pinned up in the aero club bar revealing the names of the designated rally airfields. By that time, hopefully, Dan would have arrived by car and planning in earnest could begin. Then a not-too-late night in a B&B, to be up and ready for the 9 am briefing the next morning, followed by departure at 1 pm. It was tight, but I felt the next phase of my flying was about to begin. As I turned onto the M11 the overcast sky began to break up, revealing a red sky. Pilot's Delight, I thought—a good omen.

'Lester?' called Rhona, severely. 'Lester? Where are you? There are endless people coming up the drive. Is this something you've arranged?'

It was about quarter past six, and I was sitting in the kitchen talking to Rhona while she was plucking a heap of pigeons, when a car came up the drive. It was followed by another. Then another and another.

'Wonder who they can be,' frowned Lester. 'They must be here for something.' A steady stream of cars was now assembling in front of the house. I watched through the window as Lester went out to investigate. A few moments later he was back. 'It's the Choral Society—we're singing *Elijah*. I'd forgotten. I'd better unlock the front door.' He turned to me. 'Could you help me put out some chairs in the hall?'

Over the next twenty minutes between 200 and 300 people arrived. Lester could not find the music immediately, but soon the sound of striking chords and voices tuning up indicated that this deficiency had been remedied. I made my way, with a jug of Rhona's lemonade (unsettlingly held together with Sellotape), out onto the lawn on the lake side of the house. The sun, huge and orange, was sinking over the lake. I put the jug gingerly on the low balustrade in front of the ha-ha, and spread my maps on the lawn. From the house came the muffled sounds of Mendelssohn's oratorio:

Baal, we cry to thee,
Baal, we cry to thee,
Hear and an--swer us!

I was extremely nervous about the day ahead. Salsingham to Manchester would be by far the longest solo cross-country flight that I had undertaken. The first intimation of the magnitude of the task ahead had come a day or two earlier when I had attempted to look up Barton Aerodrome, the start of the rally, in *Pooleys*. It was not there. After Barra ('three firm sand strips below high-water mark' on the foreshore of Traigh Mhor) and Barrow (Walney Island), there was only Bedford (Castle Mill). Barton, it seemed, did not exist. Initially, I was unfazed. Barton, I reasoned, was probably a farm strip in a secluded valley in the lea of the Pennines so small that it did not warrant inclusion in an official publication like *Pooleys*. This, it had to be remembered, was microlighting. However, on re-consulting my 1:500,000 chart, I noticed, right in the middle of the sea of grey denoting the built-up area of Salford, the ominous legend 'Manchester/Barton'. Barton came under *Manchester*. *Manchester Airport*. The airfield was in the middle of a city. Looking up Manchester in *Pooleys*, I found fourteen pages—if you included all the Intentionally Blanks*—of maps and instructions and entry and exit lanes and special rules devoted to getting in and out of the Manchester area. Barton, it was true, was no longer Manchester's main airport, but it still had ten grass runways and was contained within the same area of forbidding shading denoting controlled air space. Of the white, open, unregulated sky that I was used to, there was none.

Be not a-fraid,
Saith God the Lord.
Be not a-fraid!

---

* A bizarre feature of flying publications.

188

I had refused to panic. But after re-consulting the rally notes, it had seemed prudent to call the Rally Secretary and confirm that this could not be where the rally started.

'Yes, that's right. You're in Manchester Airport TMA,' said the Rally Secretary crisply. 'So keep a look out for 737s on finals. Make for Crewe at the southern end of the low level corridor and follow the middle of the three north-bound railway lines out of the junction. Don't fly above 1,250 feet QNH. Continue on 340° True even after the railway deviates left. After Northwich, look for a couple of large lakes at 11 o'clock and 2 o'clock. Fly over the east end of the one at 11 o'clock and look for the disused airfield at Stretton, bisected by the M56. Continue on 340° True until you get near Warrington. Turn right where you pass a river and the Manchester Ship Canal. Follow the canal until you see another motorway on your left, climb to exactly 1,500 feet and you'll see Barton next to the motorway, just before you get to a bridge carrying the M60. Join the circuit overhead and let down on the dead side to 800 feet. The signal square will tell you which strip is in use. All circuits to the north, so 27 is right-hand, 09 is left-hand. Likewise 32, 24 and 20 are right-hand, and 02, 06 and 14 are left-hand. Just keep inside corridor without screwing up, as it's taken us years to get it, and don't bugger about in circuit, as there'll be a lot of microlights in the air.'

'Right,' I had said.

Thy help is near,
Thy help is near,
Thy help is near.

Now, fortifying myself with a draught of lemonade, I marked a line on my 1:500,000 series chart between Salsingham and a point just north of Crewe (from where, I presumed, I could pick up the Rally Secretary's instructions). The Barton approach, it promptly became clear, was but a detail of the problems that lay in front of me.

The first hazard to be negotiated, squarely guarding my exit from

East Anglia, was massive RAF Marham. A long haul over the Fens followed, free of intimidating air traffic graphics, but equally free of any recognisable landmarks as clues for navigation. Skirting the Wash, which was a 'Danger Area' (live firing), no sooner had I passed it than my way was blocked by the overlapping Military Air Traffic Zones of several Lincolnshire RAF bases: Barkston Heath, Cranwell, Coningsby and Waddington. Thereafter fields for emergency landings began to disappear as I passed into the built-up area of the industrialised South Midlands north of Nottingham and climbed to cross the Pennines. More concerning, this was where my flight path entered a dense six-inch-wide band of shading, shaded shading, and shaded, shaded shading which roughly linked Liverpool, Birmingham and London. Here all standard features of the map were virtually obliterated beneath a cat's cradle of criss-crossing lines, meaningless ciphers and overlapping shaded areas. What this meant, in a nutshell, was Epauletted Officialdom. But it was an area I had no option but to traverse, if I were to reach (if I ever found it) the famous Low Level Corridor to Barton.

My nerves meant I slept badly, at first too hot, half-awake, endlessly seeking out cooler recesses of the bed; later messily hauling mounds of bedding hither and thither to try and warm up extremities left exposed. Phrases of *Elijah* punctuated my shallow dreams, conducted by men wearing white shirts with epaulettes. Around five, after lying awake for ages, I decided to get up and start to prepare the plane. In the still of the early morning, every squawk of the floorboards sounded deafening. The retrievers' tails thumped the linoleum as I let myself into the kitchen to make a cup of coffee. Outside, as I made my way down the grassy track to the hangar, my feet left a trail of footprints in the dew. There was a little temporary difficulty when I fumbled the key in the elder, and it fell down a rabbit-hole (did Santos Dumont and

Blériot contend with such problems, I wondered?), but after twenty minutes prodding with a stick, I retrieved it and the hangar doors were screeching open.

Sean had done us proud. The new aerofoil wing struts were in place, and the three-bladed prop. Together they looked very business-like. 'She flies completely differently now,' he had said over the phone. 'You won't believe it. Climbs faster. Smoother running. Different aeroplane.' New rubber wires connected the electrical leads, the fuel lines were new and on the seat he had left a small tool kit containing spare plugs and a selection of spanners. The pod looked immaculate— not a dead fly to be seen—and the windscreen positively glinted. It even looked as if he had given the tyres a polish.

I had been over the Fens for about half an hour before I began to relax, wriggling in my seat to get comfortable and un-snag the seat harness. I had safely negotiated a pair of Tornadoes at RAF Marham, over flying the base (as instructed) at 3,000 feet. At that height my wings had been slicing the cloud base. Soon it would be time to start looking for my first landing point: the private strip at the transport café outside Holbeach where Richard had met his Waterloo. Navigating over Fenland was never easy. The map looked as if someone had tested a blue Biro by drawing brisk SW–NE lines on it with a six-inch ruler. From the air the Hundred Foot Drain looked exactly like the Sixteen Foot Drain which looked exactly like the Middle Level Main Drain, the Twenty Foot Drain, the South Forty Foot Drain and so on. And all the smaller, unnamed but ramrod straight channels carving up each individual fen combined to make the whole area uniform and freakish. As Richard had once pointed out, navigating across the Fens was a case of being lost all the time, except for the brief moments when you knew where you were.

Harold, the owner of the Anglia café, to whom I had spoken an hour earlier, was well-known for his friendliness to visiting pilots. 'We're just south of Holbeach. After Sutton Bridge, follow the A17 and we're on the roundabout where it joins the B1515,' he had said. 'It's a big transport café. Red and white flags, a pink plastic elephant'—private strips tended to have more character than licensed airfields—'Pop your head round the door when you get here and we'll give you a cup of tea.' So when I spotted a big iron bridge which was plainly Sutton Bridge, I followed the main road the nine miles or so on to Holbeach. There I could see nothing remotely resembling the spectacle he had described. Over the phone it had all sounded so obvious that I had not troubled too much with the details. Yet now there seemed to be nothing except endless fields under row after row of polythene cloches.

I circled pensively for fifteen minutes or so, during which the procession of my thoughts might loosely be summarised as follows:

1. Sutton Bridge. Excellent. Making good time—ten minutes ahead of schedule, in fact, by the time I've landed—maybe time for Harold's cup of tea after all. Just find the roundabout where the A17 joins the B1515. That must be it there, which means the landing field should be about ...

2. Strange ... should have thought it would be about there, just to the south. A big transport café with flags, lorry park, pink plastic elephant and runway ought to stand out well enough.

3. Why can't these old gits give proper instructions?

4. It *isn't* the roundabout. It's the wrong fucking roundabout. Get a grip. It *must* be the roundabout. There can only be one main roundabout outside a hicksville like Holbeach. If this is Holbeach, then it's the rounda ... Christ. It *isn't Holbeach*. Then where the ...

5. Was that an engine miss? Was it? Bloody was. And, Jesus, I can't even see how much fuel there is left ...

6. Get a grip. Get some height. Check your heading. See? There's plenty of fuel. OK, you can't find the Anglia Café. So, what was the alternative plan? Head five miles south to Fenland. Off you go then ...

And so, grousing bitterly, I headed off to the south. Why the Hell was it me ferrying the Thruster to Barton anyway? Why did I always land the donkey jobs? It was all very well for Dan, sailing up the motorway to pumping music, munching crisps in heated comfort.

After ten minutes of level Fenland with not a building to be seen, the tension began to seep back. I did not have the fuel for dicking around like this. I started to look out for a suitable place to land: the next decent-sized field of grass would have to do—I would have to chance getting hold of fuel, even if it cost getting to the race in time. Most of the fields contained beet or cabbages or standing corn, but fortunately it looked as if there was one up ahead of grass. Certainly it was large ... and level ... there didn't seem to be any power lines ... in fact it wasn't bad at all. Almost good enough, in fact, to be an airfi—*an airfield! It was an airfield.* There was no doubt about it. A smooth, wonderful, verdant, gorgeous, inviting airfield; green and flat and mown and friendly, with a neat little clubhouse, and hangar, and rows of cute little Cessnas parked into wind.

Fenland, presumably—and Fenland it was, spelt out in five foot-high white letters on the roof of the clubhouse. I looked at my watch. Twenty past twelve. Not too far behind schedule, either. I joined the circuit behind a Cessna and followed it in. A few minutes later, I was sipping a Coke and tucking into a cheeseburger and chips in the comfortable clubhouse, reflecting how very much better it was to be at a proper airfield, rather than some grotty transport café.

It is surprising how long even the most disciplined flying stop-over takes. By the time I had signed in, re-fuelled, paid my landing fee and for the fuel, had lunch, extricated myself from a lecture about the amazing accuracy of his GPS from a man with a beard,* planned my next leg, repacked the plane, and was taxiing out to take off, it was well

* In the early 90s, before Global Positioning Systems—GPSs—had become

after two. My next leg was to Hucknall, Rolls-Royce's test-site, pressed up amongst the housing estates of the north-west side of Nottingham and inside the dreaded shaded area of the air chart. In fact the flight was uneventful, but a direct headwind meant it took longer than expected. By the time I flung myself onto the turf of that historic site, I was so tired that I promptly fell asleep. When I woke, chilly and disorientated, it was getting on for six. I refuelled the plane from the jerry cans and set my heading of 283° across the Pennines to Crewe.

My first scheduled landmark (one that I had circled on my map to look out for) was the M1. And, gratifyingly, a few minutes after take-off, there it was. It was always satisfying, having calculated a heading to allow for wind drift, to find the features on the ground corresponding with those on the map—nothing gave a greater sensation of being in control. My timing was alright. The weather was hazy, but OK. I began, over the roar of the engine, a lusty rendition of the overture that was now irretrievably stuck in my head.

There came a fiery chariot,
With fiery, fiery horses ...

I continued singing for ten minutes: until, with some surprise, I crossed the M1 again. The singing ceased abruptly.

It *had* to be the M1. There was no mistake this time. It had six lanes, blue motorway signs, and there was one of those ugly concrete bridges unique to the M1. I scrutinised the map: there was not a hint of any other major road this side of the Pennines. Short of flying in a circle, there was no way I could be crossing another motorway. I scoured the map for features which might offer up a clue. There was supposed to be a big reservoir up ahead at Carsington; it was there on the map, a huge great smudge of blue. I peered into the murk ahead.

universal in flying, this was a regular hazard at flying clubs. As they become more widely incorporated into cars and mobile phones, it presumably will become so in everyday life as well.

The glare of the lowering sun was making the haze impenetrable. There was nothing there.

Jesus, I thought. The compass must have broken. I had never had much faith in the Thruster's compass. It had that unmistakable look of cheapness and cut corners. I wondered what sort of things might affect it. Could I be flying over magnetic rock or a force-field from power lines? There were certainly power lines below me.

As usual, when I was preoccupied, my heading went to pot. The compass, supposedly reading 283°, bounced around, oscillating between 260° and 300° as I wagged the stick to and fro, gazing out of the cockpit. Suddenly a reflective silver gleam appeared through the haze up ahead, about five miles north of my course—water. My doubts about the compass were confirmed. My heading might not have been perfect, but it was not that bad. The instrument could obviously no longer be relied upon. Probably we would be able to get a new one at the start of the rally; that kind of thing was bound to be available. Still, it was disquieting to discover that one of my principal instruments was faulty. I altered course 45° and prepared to head north to the lake. As I was turning, another lake loomed out of the haze directly in front of me. Carsington Reservoir! My course had been perfect. I switched back to 283° and the singing resumed. I was actually going to cross the water at the precise point where my pen had bisected it on the map.

My exhibition, of course, was an almost text book example of how not to navigate. I had the supreme arrogance to accuse my compass, attributing greater faith to momentary, overwrought emotion to the most reliable of all instruments tried and proven over centuries. I had not waited for my timed way points to come up before leaping to conclusions and I had committed the cardinal error of reading from map-to-ground instead of vice-versa, selecting prominent features on the chart—motorways, reservoirs—then raking the landscape for similar, and wrong, matches. The first 'M1' was probably just a section of dual carriageway (roads are notoriously hard to classify from 1,000 feet, which is why air charts give prominence to railways). The gleam of water to the north could have been anything.

I did not trouble myself with these aspects, however. Instead, my flush of self-satisfied pride and lusty rendition of *Elijah* lasted until the water of Carsington was left far behind. A pleasing thought had struck me. It was that the greatest aerial endeavour of the original pioneers, after Blériot had crossed the Channel, and for which the *Daily Mail* had offered no less a prize than £10,000, was to the first person to fly, within twenty-four hours, from London to Manchester. In short, *that was a measure of the kind of trip I was undertaking.* I would even (assuming I got there) do it with just the maximum two permitted stopovers. True, I had not started from London; but Salsingham must be almost as far. And true, conditions were a good deal more favourable than the blustery April day that Palhau and Grahame-White battled it out in their Farman biplanes. Nevertheless, it was food for thought. And I was about to enter the Round Britain, the *third* great *Daily Mail* challenge offered to those early pioneers. It was all very satisfying.

The ground was rising rapidly. The flat, open fields of moor and marshland of Nottinghamshire had given way to tiny squares of dry-stone-walled limestone escarpment, pockmarked with sink-holes and rocky outcrops. I decided it was time to switch from the 1:500,000 scale chart on my map-board to the larger scale 1:250,000 chart, the better to face the precision-flying rigours of the approaching 'low level corridor'. This required the removal of the outgoing chart from the clips and elastic straps of the map-board to reveal the large-scale map underneath.

Aeronautical charts are two foot six inches square and handling them in flight is like trying to fold a sheet in a gale. As I had to hold the stick with my right hand, the task also had to be performed one-handed, and with my gloved left hand too. When I let go of the throttle, I also discovered that the throttle friction nut had worked loose, so the lever would not hold its position and the engine revs gradually tailed off, forcing me every few seconds to let go of the map, shove the nose down and re-set the throttle. I had just succeeded in freeing the outgoing chart the first time this happened: in my haste to re-set the throttle, the chart slipped out of my grasp. An eddy of air caught the folded sheet, flicked it open then wrapped it tightly round me, obscuring all vision.

Getting a purchase through a ski glove, on the shiny, plastic-coated surface of a chart, with the airflow pressing it round me, was like trying to pick off a fridge magnet with an oven glove. For several seconds, I flew blind, until I managed to sweep the map clear. It immediately flew up to the roof of the cockpit, flapping and crackling. I would have left it there, but one corner was flicking annoyingly at my neck. My attempts to grab it only sent it sliding behind my seat, out of reach, where I could feel the wind worrying and sucking at it. Unbuckling my safety harness so that I could reach further back, I very nearly fell out of the plane as, at that moment, the slipstream finally caught the chart and it left the cockpit. I deliberated, as I watched my £12 investment fluttering downwards, whether to follow it down and pick it up, but a rapid assessment of the terrain beneath put paid to the idea. Perhaps we'd be able to get another at the start of the rally.

The bleak topography of the western Pennines had now scaled down to cosy grass vales containing rocky streams, enclosed by stone walls. As the high ground fell away, these melded into the brick crescents, roundabouts and out-of-town shopping warehouses to the north of Kidsgrove and Alsager. Moments later I was crossing the M6 and, hard as it was to distinguish anything with the hazy sun directly ahead, I could just make out three railway lines emerging from the north of Crewe. I throttled back to 5,300 rpm, began a gentle descent from 2,000 feet, and swung onto 355° to pick up the central line, as instructed.

My new heading had the happy effect of switching my view from an eye-watering squint to a handsome, side-lit view, bathed in the yellow glow of a summer evening. The area was flat, industrial, bisected by rivers, waterways and power lines, but there were enough uncluttered fields for comfort. Behind me were the chimneys of Stoke. Over to my right beyond the M6 I could see the dish of a huge radio telescope.

It had to be Jodrell Bank: one of those Northern landmarks, like the Liver Building, or the Humber Bridge, that I knew about but had never seen. The industrial landscape was equally exciting: the brick smokestacks, factories and warehouses (everywhere red brick); the meshes of power lines and the canals. I spotted a microlight a mile ahead and a little below me. As I watched, another, a flexwing, came speeding up behind me, and, with a cheery wave, buzzed past.

The last eight miles passed in a happy blur. I had the Rally Secretary's instructions on my map-board and they could not have been more straightforward; each feature appearing clearly and on time. It was more relaxing, though, just to follow the other machines and enjoy the strangely beautiful landscape of canals and reservoirs and motorways. Barton, when it appeared, was a big square of green hemmed by motorways and flyovers. The five mown strips were like light green spokes. They had white lines down the middle, which I had not seen on grass before.

The air was swarming with microlights. The two in front of me opted to land on 27, the widest and longest strip. The windsock, however, indicated that the wind had veered 50°, so the correct strip, to land into wind, was 32. As if to prove my theory, below me I watched a little biplane, a Pitts Special, taxi out into position on 32 to run through its pre-take-off checks. I felt quite smug as I swung round, lined myself up and slid neatly down in front of it. Only the Pitts and myself had selected the correct runway, showing independence of mind and awareness of local conditions. That, I reflected, as I taxied in and allowed a marshal to direct me to where I should park, was what this game was about: airmanship.

The clubhouse, prefab like a Seventies classroom, was a hive of activity. Forty or fifty people, singly, in pairs or in fours, were perched around small tables, or sitting or kneeling on the floor, or spilling out on to tables outside in the area of lawn enclosed by a white picket fence. Kit was everywhere: flight bags, clipboards, exercise books, note pads, maps, rulers, protractors, calculators, mobiles, cigarettes. On one side of the room, a barman, streaming perspiration, was dispensing pints of Boddingtons and taking orders for burgers. On the opposite side, people were urgently studying three 1:500,000 air charts, taped together to form a single map of the British Isles, which, from the interest it was generating, had only just been put up. On it were marked the eighty or so designated airfields from which points could be collected over the next three days.*

The busy atmosphere and sense that everyone knew each other contributed to a familiar feeling of alienation. Partly this was because, so far, my efforts to make friends had not met with much success. On arrival, seeing that the microlight next to me was the machine that had powered past me fifteen minutes earlier, I had gone to say hello. It was a flexwing, and though they all looked much the same to me, I could tell that this was a fancy affair. The stubby wing, huge engine and chunky, aerofoil wheel spats over its fat tyres had a businesslike air about them. I had been admiring the twin stainless steel exhausts, four-bladed propeller and heavy-duty, high-tech fittings when the owner finished speaking into his mobile and came over. He was in his twenties or early thirties and wore a purple and green flying suit.

'Nice,' I said.

'The best,' he said, with the faintest perceptible nod.

'You must have beaten me by twenty minutes.'

'Bit more than that, I think. Please don't touch anything.'

I knew for a fact that he could not have landed more than ten minutes before, and had exaggerated the time out of friendliness. If this were a

---

* Highest-scoring airfields: Castletown, John O'Groats (1,000 points); Oban (700); Glenforsa, Mull (700); Lamb Holm, Orkney (600); Land's End (1,000); Dunkeswell, Devon (550); Haverfordwest, Pembrokeshire (500); Sandown, Isle of Wight (500). Also of note: Barsham Green (400); Priory Farm (400); Sutton Meadows (300); Nayland (350).

taste of things to come, it did not bode well. A few planes away there was a Thruster—the only other one I could see amongst the assembly of offbeat aircraft present—so I had wandered over in search of a friendlier reception. The owner was a nervy man called Trevor. The world seemed to be against Trevor. He said he had just been made redundant and could not really afford to do the race, but having paid his entry fee felt it would be a waste not to come. He had entered last year, he said, but had crashed on arrival and been warned off for dangerous flying.

I had wandered on round the arrivals area. One or two latecomers were still trickling in by air or trailer, but most machines had already been put away for the night. They were tied down, many with a neat dome tent alongside, into which everything had been tidied away. There was no doubt that the trikes were funkier, and looked more serious from a competitive point of view. The three-axis machines had an amateur and more eccentric look about them. No two planes were the same.

Making my way over to the clubhouse, there had been rows and rows of planes and helicopters; Barton was plainly a wealthy flying club. I had reported my arrival to the Rally Secretary, a big man with a beard, ordered a pint of Boddingtons and felt immediately and hideously southern. Until that moment I had not noticed what a large proportion of those present, or certainly those with the loudest voices and the most confident manner, were northern. I was smoking a cigarette and trying to look inconspicuous when Trevor came over to join me. He looked, if anything, more depressed than before. I offered him a drink, but he held up a glass of fizzy lemonade. His burger and chips had arrived and I was looking on hungrily when the Rally Secretary came up and clamped a meaty hand on his shoulder. 'You. Yours is the blue Thruster, isn't it?' Trevor twisted his head round nervously. 'Air traffic supervisor wants a word with you. Outside. Now.'

'What … what's wrong?' said Trevor. The blood had drained from his face. But the Secretary was already on his way to the door. Trevor looked as if he might burst into tears as he got up. 'I don't understand. What's wrong now? …' I ate one of his chips reflectively. Poor Trevor. I wondered what he had done this time. Probably he had infringed the

Low Level Corridor and Manchester TMC had complained, or he had flown over the houses and industrial area south-east of the airfield on his final approach. It was bad luck, especially with his confidence at such a low ebb. I was flooded with a sense of warm satisfaction. I could hold my own with these people, after all. Yes, it was bad luck on poor old Trevor. But on the other hand, if he could not handle the rigours of competitive aviation, then, frankly, he had no business to be here. It might sound harsh, but it was safer for all of us.

I cast my eye over the competitors. There were leather-faced men in their sixties or older, pale twenty-somethings with boyish haircuts, clean-cut professionals with briefcases and Psions, rednecks with beards and baseball caps, one of whom, as he passed wafted a homebuilder's whiff of wood dust, roll-ups, body odour, two-stroke oil and axle grease. The first impression, depressingly—not helped, probably, by the classroom setting, studious air, and rulers and protractors—was of a schoolmasters' convention. There were several team entries, by the pairs of matching printed tee-shirts: 'Men Working Overhead', 'Sedbridge Scrap Metal', 'Tavington Old Boys'; and a number of father-and-son teams, plus a few solo entrants working quietly by themselves, one of whom sat impassively smoking a double corona. There were a few women. These were divided into supportive wives—wearing make-up—and competitors, wearing combats and body-warmers festooned with pockets and zips.

Efficiency levels and planning techniques varied. Maps every-where were being folded and refolded as the designated airfields were marked up. (One person used little self-adhesive red circles, of the 'picture sold' kind.) Lines were drawn with marker pens then, moments later, rubbed out using cloths moistened from bottles of blue fluid. Pencils were chewed then put back behind ears.

Comments drifted out from the different huddles. "Ad bad experiences there,' (jabbing at the eastern Grampians with his ruler). 'Specially wi' westerly wind: very choppy.' Another, shoving a Metfax under his partner's nose, 'Don' wanna frighten yer, but take a look a' tha.' 'Look,' said another impatiently. 'We'll 'ave groundspeed o' 40 if we go that way, groundspeed o' 80 if we go that way.' Then, increasingly exasperated. 'We're not goin' to *'ave* tailwind goin' that way tomorrer. It's goin to be a bloody Westerly tomorrer.' 'Vis won't be as good Friday. We should do 'igh ground tomorrer.' The weather seemed to be coming from the north, so the consensus seemed to be to head in that direction first.

After ten minutes Trevor returned. I was curious to hear what his misdemeanour had been. As he picked his way towards me, stepping over the maps and figures hunched on the floor, he didn't look too shaken up. Indeed, for a worrier he looked calmer and happier than I had seen him so far. 'How did it go?' I asked.

'It's not me they want to see after all,' he said cheerfully. 'It's you.' He jerked his thumb. 'They're waiting outside. Now.'

At first I thought he was joking. What could I have done? My approach had been perfect. I had followed the Low Level Corridor instructions to the letter. Even my landing had been a peach. What could it possibly be?

'You made a Pitts abort take off after final checks, apparently. Pilot's livid—on the Club committee too. Talking about a formal complaint. You could be disqualified.' There was no doubt, Trevor's spirit had magically restored.

Shit. The Pitts. I might have known.

'I thought incoming planes always had priority over planes on the ground,' I said. Trevor responded by jerking his thumb towards the door.

'Better tell them that. Phew, they really had me going for a second, there. I should have known I hadn't done anything. They thought I was the only Thruster in the race. Took us a while to realise there was you, too. God, some bastard's eaten half my food.' He took a swig of lemonade. He was a new man.

Outside, the Rally Secretary, looking vexed and careworn, was perched against the white paling of the clubhouse fence, with another man, plainly from the Aero Club, wearing, ominously, a white shirt with epaulettes.

They were berating a figure in a baseball cap. '... What d'yer think t'low level corridor's for? Ya daft bastard.'

'I couldn't find it.'

'Couldn't *find* it?' said the Rally Secretary. 'Couldn't *find* it? T'isn't painted on bloody ground, yer know. Know 'ow long it's tekken us to get tha' corridor? An 'ow quick we'll lose it if you keep messin' wi' it?' He made a mark on his clipboard. 'Do it again an' yer out. Got it?'

They turned to me.

We were within easy earshot of the tables outside the clubhouse, now crammed with empty glasses and ketchup-smeared plates. Everyone had fallen quiet to enjoy the show.

'You the Thruster?' said the Club Secretary, not unpleasantly. I nodded and Epaulettes cut in:

'Yer caused Pitts Special to abort tek-off after final checks. Yer cut straight across'im on 32, when runway in use was clearly marked as 27. Pilot's on Club committee an' 'e's furious. Talkin' bout makin formal complaint t'CAA.'

'But the wind had changed. I was only landing into wind.'

'Yer land on runway indicated in t'signals area,' said the man angrily. An' signals area indicated bloody 27.'

I had forgotten all about the signals area. The signals area is the patch of grass all airfields have in front of the control tower where, amongst other things, there is a huge white-painted metal 'T' on a turntable. The T is swung round to indicate the runway in use: take-offs and landings being parallel with the shaft and towards the cross-arm. The Rally Secretary, I noticed, said nothing during this exchange, leaving the talking to Epaulettes. Plainly he—Epaulettes—was the man from the aero club, at whose behest the microlighters were allowed to use the airfield. 'Yer don' just land wherever yer app'n to feel like landin'. What d'yer think signals area's for? Christ, *microlights!*'The Rally Secretary winced. Conversation had stopped at all the nearby tables. I remembered something Lester had once told me about not giving in to air traffic controllers too easily.

'But if that wasn't the runway in use, why was the Pitts about to take off from it?'

'E was an experienced local pilot who 'ad radioed tower that 'e wished to use alternative runway because there were microlights all overt' place on 27. Did yer even check the signals area?' he demanded, surmising my weakest link.

'I thought an aircraft in the air, especially one on final descent, always had priority over an aircraft on the ground, anyway?' I persisted.

'Not when pilot's member of club committee, they don't—ya daft bastard. Next time, bloody get it right.'

I bought another pint and wished Dan would arrive. Trevor had departed to get an early night, and by now the clubroom was a hive of planning as everyone plotted their routes.

'Was that you getting it back there?' A good-looking man in his thirties sat down next to me. He sounded like a Londoner.

'Fraid so,' I said. 'Didn't take long, did it?'

'Don't worry about him. Hates microlights.' He offered me a cigarette. 'First time?' I nodded.

'What did you do?'

'Wrong runway.'

'Is that all? Jesus. You'll do worse than that before Sunday. If it's any consolation, couple of years ago I got arrested. Re-routed a BA turbo-prop.' He chuckled. 'Apparently I was right in its flight path. Scottish Air Traffic went mad. I was chased by a Police chopper. Licence confiscated. Criminal proceedings. For a time it looked as if I might go to jail. Luckily I was doing the flight for charity, so the magistrates took pity.'

'And Bryan, last year—' a man in a baseball cap had joined us. 'Remember Bryan? He only flew into that danger area near Sandtoft during a live firing exercise.' He raised his eyes and shook his head. 'Live ammunition, up to 50,000 feet.'

I felt my spirits beginning to return. 'What? He flew through the middle? While they were firing?'

'Through? No, not through. Not through at all.' He chuckled again. 'He landed. In the middle of the exercise. The artillery commander frantically ordered a cease-fire and cancelled the exercise, thinking Bryan was in trouble. Then, watching through his binoculars, he saw Bryan get out his sandwiches... Before they could get to him, Bryan had taken off again. Army went mad.'

Dan finally arrived, with news that he had booked a B&B en route. It was nearly eleven and the bar had thinned out as people headed for their hotel rooms or tents.

As I too got up to leave, I asked my new friend what he did.

'Me?' he said. 'I'm a flying instructor.'

It was nearly twelve, the sun was gradually burning through the heavy white haze and the day was rapidly warming up. The nine o'clock briefing had lasted until shortly before eleven, discharging everyone into the heat with two hours to get to the grid for the start. The briefing had been a matter-of-fact affair. After welcoming us to the 'Tenth and Greatest' Round Britain Rally, the Rally Secretary had revealed the locations of the three mandatory overnight stops: Kirkbride, north of the Lake District; my friend Fenland; and Compton Abbas, on top of the rolling Cranbourne Chase in Dorset. He had congratulated last year's winner, which turned out, depressingly, to be the owner of the flash microlight from last night. Then he had recapped the rules, warned us that there would be random spot checks for GPSs or the carrying of spare containers of fuel, and read out a list of warnings of air shows and military exercises. Finally the Safety Officer had solemnly warned us about the dangers of flying in overloaded machines. 'At least two of you will crash for this reason,' he prophesied. 'The combination of flying on the limit of your weight, in warm, muggy air, is a recipe for an accident. Make sure you've got plenty of runway and hold your plane down to build speed after take-off.'

Since then an hour seemed to have passed with no appreciable progress. Dan, having dumped all our gear from the car into a large heap on the grass beside the Thruster, immersed himself in the task of fixing his Sony Discman into the cockpit and wiring it to the headsets. Only now did he stand up, straightening his back, and pronounce the quality of the sound system satisfactory. I, meanwhile, after sticking our competition numbers onto the pod and wings (we were number sixteen, out of over eighty), had been at a loose end. In a moment of inspiration, I deposited one of the spare bolts from our tool kit on the grass underneath the engine of last year's winners. This had the happy result, when the bolt was discovered, of instigating a frenzied engine-stripping session to ascertain where it had come from. Apart from this, and some desultory and unproductive telephoning to airfields where we might pick up fuel, I had not done much.

We now had just an hour to get to the grid, having settled a route, arranged refuelling stops and necessary permissions, sorted and packed the plane, removed the car to a safe area, and tested and run-up the Thruster. As we stood back to assess the situation, it was hard to see how it could be done. Into a two-inch gap behind the seats, a five inch gap beneath them and an area the size of a beach bucket in front of the rudder pedals, we had to fit:

Document bag: *Rally Entrant*
Competitor's pack—licences, log books,
medical certificates, Permit to Fly,
third party insurance
2 x 1:500,000 maps
3 x 1:250,000 maps
2 map boards
Rucksack
Ruler (calibrated in nautical miles)
Protractor
Flight calculator
Calculator
4 (empty) 1-gallon petrol cans
1 4-litre can 2-stroke oil
Funnel+ Mrs Watson's stocking
3 dog tie-downs plus 3 lengths nylon rope
Pooleys *Flight Guide*
Lockyear's *Farm 'Strips' and Private Airfields*

Toolkit
Two-man tent
2 sleeping bags
Headsets and intercom system
Roll loo paper
Stove
2 foam rubber cushions (for seats)
2 feather cushions (ditto)
2 ozee suits
2 incredibly thick jumpers
2 beanie hats
2 pairs skiing gloves
2 log books
Carrier bag: *spare elastic bands, batteries, marker pens, chinagraph pencils, pencil sharpener, clothes pegs, velcro, elastic, needle and thread, rag, aftershave (for cleaning pencil marks off map board)*

Carrier bag essential sustenance—
Marlboro Lights, Snickers, Cokes, Red Bulls
Leatherman tool
Collins Road Atlas
2 cameras
Mobile phone plus 2 spare batteries
Mobile charger

Large bag assorted camera accessories and films
Small bottle after-shave
(to clean marker pen off maps)
Roll gaffer tape
Roll parcel tape
Ball string
Roll green garden wire

DAN
Silk scarf
Shades (mirrored Oakleys)
Psion Organiser
Change underwear
Washing kit
(*toothbrush and toothpaste*)
CDs:
Cosmic Cubes—Volume II
Shamanic Tribes on Acid—303 to Infinity
Hallucinogen—Lone Deranger
Dreadzone—360 Degrees
Union Jack—There Will Be No Armageddon
Jam and Spoon—Tripomatic Fairytales 2001
Trancemaster Volume 6—Aural Brainfood
Aura—Butterfly, Chrysalis and Caterpillar
Real Life—Journey of Carcharadon
Shpongle—Are you Shpongled?
Astralasia—7 point star
Afro-Celt Sound System—Sounds Magic
Eat Static—Abduction
Children of the Bong—Interface Reality
Irresistible Force—It's Tomorrow Already
Terra Ferma—Turtle Crossing
Platipus Records—Volume I
The Orb—U.F. Orb
Dragonfly Records—A Voyage into Trance
Green Nuns of the Revolution—Rock Bitch Mafia
The Starseeds—Parallel Life
Mashed Mellow Grooves
Mashing Up Creation
Way Out West—Way Out West

ANTONY
Cashmere scarf
Shades (safety-pinned Ray-Bans)
Filofax
Change underwear
Washing kit
(*toothbrush and toothpaste*)
Aspirin-codeine tablets
Strepsils
Lipsalve
Savlon
TCP
Thermometer
Band Aids
Bandage
Otrivine decongestant
Lemsip
Anthisan cream
Dental floss
Milk of Magnesia
Immodium
Contact lens kit
Insect repellant
Condoms
Kendal Mint Cake
Dextrosols
Ear plugs
Travel wash
Cotton buds
Soap

For a few minutes we just stared in silence. 'Well, we only need one map-board,' said Dan, finally. 'And why don't we lose those bulky air charts. The road atlas would do perfectly well.' I had invested nearly £80 on the maps; this was not an option.

'Then we can certainly reduce them,' he said, taking hold of the Scottish 1:500,000 chart and, with the Leatherman, briskly slicing the half north of John o'Groats off. Such moments defy logic, but I could not help being irritated.

'The CDs,' I said. 'They've got to go.'

'This,' Dan was weighing my Filofax in his hand, 'weighs about a stone. And what's in here?' he said, picking up my washbag. 'Why have you got all this stuff? Jesus, you're a hypochondriac.'

'*Fifty minutes to start,*' echoed the Tannoy of Rally Control. '*Any competitor who has still not removed their car to the parking area please do so at once. Competitors should be moving to grid positions.*'

We were getting nowhere and desperate measures were called for. Already some competitors were pushing their machines past us towards the starting grid. (The seasoned pros, I noticed, carried almost nothing: just a slim map-board and the clothes they stood up in.) In the end we put all our clothes in a heap; we would have to wear them. In the rucksack we put all the navigational and other indispensable equipment (mobile and money) that would fit. The rest—the documents, tent, sleeping bags, stove, my Filofax and washbag, and most of the CDs—we shoved in the car boot. For overnight accommodation we would have to chance it. Dan had a cousin who lived across the Solway Firth in Scotland, so if we made tonight's overnight stop at Kirkbride, we would stay with him. This left every square inch of cockpit space rammed—and by the time the tie-downs, rope, funnel and empty petrol cans had been gaffer-taped to the boom and spars, the Thruster resembled, more than anything else, a giant kitchen tidy. This left a densely-packed rucksack, hard and heavy as a case of wine.

'*Final call to any competitors not yet in grid position...* called the Tannoy.

At 12.55, we struggled to push the laden Thruster to the start. (Engine starting was not permitted until planes were on the grid.) We had made the elementary mistake of putting on our jumpers and ozee suits, to get them out of the way. Now, with the baking July sun at its midday height, we were soon slippery with sweat and gasping with thirst. Dan was flying the first leg, so he strapped himself in while I primed the engine.

'Ignition on.'

'Clear prop,' I called and hauled on the starter cord. There was no response. This wasn't especially surprising after a night outside. But after four more pulls my eyes were stinging from the sweat and I was finding it hard to keep a grip on the starter cord, my hands were so slippery. I leant against the wing to catch my breath and the marshal motioned the flexwing behind us on the grid to move in front. Engines were backfiring and bursting into life all around us now, issuing clouds of blue, black or white smoke as they did so. The flexwings, with their electric starters, purred into action at the twist of a gloved hand. Fortunately for us, with the fifth pull the Thruster's engine finally woke up, washing me with a life-saving blast of cool air. With my gloves in my teeth, trying to lengthen my harness straps so that they would reach round my bulky clothes and the cushions, the marshal motioned us forward. Dan opened the throttle, I heaved the rucksack up into my lap, and we crawled forward down the runway.

The Round Britain

Sometimes, certainly, a motor will fail in awkward circumstances—say when a pilot is over wooded or precipitous country. But with the airman, always, it is a point of honour that he should see the humorous side of things …

The Aeroplane, Claude Grahame-White and Harry Harper, 1914.

The take-off run seemed to last forever. After 300 yards we finally clawed our way off the ground like a bomber and Dan turned onto our westerly heading of 276°. It took fifteen minutes, rather than the usual three, to reach our cruising height of 1,000 feet, by which time Barton was left far behind and flexwings were streaking past. At the last minute we had opted for an easy first hop to the nearest nominated airfield, Ince Blundell, thirty miles west of Barton. From there, we would head north to our northern overnight stop at Kirkbride. Navigation was straightforward, as it seemed that nearly every other competitor had decided to do the same, and we were soon part of a flotilla of screaming midgets.

Dan radiated calm control as pilot. Having trimmed her to climb and set his course, he hardly touched the controls again; the compass needle remained steady and motionless, the slip ball remained dead centre. The flight, for the most part over a semi-urban brownfield wasteland, was notable only for its acute discomfort: twice I nearly dropped the rucksack while attempting to attach it to the cockpit A-frame with a karabiner. In half an hour we were joining the downwind leg of the circuit at Ince and one thing became obvious: we would not be getting fuel there. It was an airfield in the most literal sense. There were no Portakabins or hangars. The only building was a small boarded-up clapperboard hut, like a village cricket pavilion, with what looked like a 'Pay and Display' machine outside it. The flexwing pilots were not even bothering to get out, as they landed, taxied up to punch their cards on the machine, then accelerated off again. Dan put us down with a perfect three-pointer. As he did so, there was a click and a rattle from behind us, something bounced into the air, then started dragging along the turf.

'What's that?' I said, craning my neck to try and see what had happened.

'That,' said Dan, 'was our tail-wheel.'

He was right. As we came to a juddering halt, I saw that where our tail-wheel used to be there was just a sharp, sheared stub of metal, catching roots and vegetation as it dragged in the turf. The wheel itself was out on the runway; sheared clean away.

We stared numbly at what remained of our landing gear. How could this have happened? This, of all things. Engine failure we were prepared for, even expected; blocked fuel lines, fouled plugs, electrical problems were all par for the course for the field pilot. A worn or broken elastic on the rudder controls, lost Pitot, a puncture, even a cracked tail-frame assembly or a chipped propeller would have been understandable; they had happened before and we could deal with them if they happened again. But a sheared tail-wheel! How could we have predicted that? It was a disaster. Richard's last flight, plus five years of unconfessed heavy landings, had come back to haunt us. And chosen this of all moments to do it.

It was 1.36 pm. By seven o'clock we had to check into Kirkbride, north of the Lake District, or be disqualified. A single pilot in a flexwing, landing immediately after us, noted our predicament with glee as he stamped his card and departed. As the drone of his engine receded, the silence and the sultry white glare of the midday sun closed oppressively over us. It was hard to see a way out. We could not go on without a tail-wheel, because the tail-wheel was an integral part of the rudder and tail-plane assembly. To land without it would risk tearing apart essential parts of the control system of the aircraft.

Our race was over, and at the first hurdle. No, worse: *before* the first hurdle. There was not even anyone we could turn to for assistance: the airfield was deserted. I could not believe it. All the preparations, the paperwork, the log book stamping, the medical and insurance forms, the expense, the new maps and equipment, my daring flight up yesterday, the week off work, the fine weather—all a waste of time. It might have helped if I could at least have blamed Dan for a bad landing. But it had been perfect.

I was so dejected that I wandered off by myself. The unpalatable facts spoke for themselves: before we could go on, we had somehow to repair the tail-wheel. The sheared spring was plainly irreparable, so this meant getting a new one from somewhere: presumably delivered from Thruster. That would take at least a day, so, whatever happened, there was no way we could reach Kirkbride by seven. We were therefore out of the race. The first task, accordingly, after contacting Thruster, tedious as it might be, was to arrange overnight accommodation and a taxi. I walked back to the plane to give Dan the benefit of my conclusions.

He was finishing a conversation into his mobile.

'Forty-five minutes? Okay, quick as you can. We're in a race, you see. OK, bye.' He turned to me.

'The mobile welding unit is eleven miles away. It'll be the best part of an hour by time they find us—that's if we're lucky. The first thing to do is get this broken spring off.'

I was about to launch into a list of reasons why all such activity was pointless. Dan had plainly not grasped the seriousness of our situation. However, as it had not occurred to me that the spring could be repaired, or that such a thing as a mobile welding unit existed, or that, by contacting Talking Pages, such a unit could already be on its way, I decided it might sound defeatist to point out that we had no suitable tools.

213

The tiny clinker-built clubhouse, more a garden shed really, was padlocked and barred, and with the departure of the last microlight the place was once again deserted. The only other building in sight was a Dutch barn several fields away. There were a couple of apparently abandoned cars, so to fill the time I wandered over to them. One, an old Nissan, turned out to be occupied. It contained a fat, purple-faced man, and a white-faced woman. They were sitting in silence, listening to the radio, the windows hermetically sealed. Spotters, or lovers, I supposed. Knowing I was wasting my time, I walked up to the window and said 'Excuse me'. The man lowered the window three quarters of an inch. I explained our predicament, while he nearly, but not quite, nodded at each statement. When I finished, he carried on nodding.

'What you doing 'bout it?'

He spoke slowly, as if he had nothing to do except while away the long afternoon. As I had already explained that I was urgently trying to locate tools, his languid enquiry was aggravating, but nevertheless I battled on. He pursed his fat lips, then ran a thick tongue round his mouth

'Well, if you can't help, I'd better get on,' I said, turning away. I had gone about six paces before he spoke..

'There's a Thruster at the end of the field,' he said.

At first I wasn't sure I had heard correctly.

'What?'

'I said: there's a crashed Thruster up at enda field. Came down last month. Tail-wheel oughta be OK. You could 'ave that.'

And he was right.

At the end of the field, tucked in behind a corrugated iron shack I had not even noticed, was a bent Thruster. Badly bent, as it happened, but the tail-wheel was fine—rather better than ours, as it happened: in place of our trolley wheel it had a proper pneumatic tyre. The fitting was slightly different, but near enough. As I was examining it the Nissan pulled up. With a heave, out stepped one of the largest men I had ever seen, his black trousers winched practically up to his armpits by marine braces. Opening his boot, he produced from beneath a

214

broken deck chair, a set of pram wheels, and assorted nuts, bolts and the sort of miscellaneous ironmongery you find at the bottom of tool boxes, a large box of spanners.

'Yer in luck,' he said. 'Bloke said 'e was collecting it yesterday. Dunno why he 'asn't. Ah'm Big George.'

I looked at my watch. It was five past two.

By the time the welding unit arrived, we had the sheared tail-fitting off the Thruster, which was propped on a pair of jerry cans, and the new wheel was being tightened into place. Before Big George's dubious gaze I scrawled a note to the owner of the Thruster, outlining our circumstances, thanking him in advance, and promising to return the tail-wheel the following week when the race was over.

"E won't thank yer for it,' he said. 'Funny sort. Aggressive-like. Why don't yer top up yer tank?'

He nodded at the brimful tank on the wrecked machine. Two-stroke mixture, too. It would be absurd to throw away such an opportunity. The Ince–Barton flight had only been forty minutes, but two-up and fully laden we had already consumed nearly a third of a tank. Surely it couldn't do any harm? While Dan and the welding team repaired our broken wheel, I siphoned the fuel out of the tank into our own.

Our one hope now was to make for Kirkbride as directly as possible. The nearest marked airfield on the way was Cark, south of the Lake District, where we would have to take our chances to get fuel as best we could. By the time we were ready to depart, at quarter past three, quite a farewell party had gathered. There was Big George and his wife, a couple of tractor drivers from the surrounding fields, the welder and his mate, and three kids who had appeared from nowhere. As we zipped ourselves into our flying suits, a rapidly-moving cloud of dust came into view, approaching down the track to the airfield: a car towing a microlight trailer.

'Oho,' said Big George. 'Ah'd git goin' if I were you.'

Even as I hauled on the starter cord, I knew what, inevitably, was going to happen. She wouldn't fire, in that stroppy, bloody-minded way the Rotax had sometimes when she was still warm. After twenty pulls, wearily, we unzipped our suits and prepared to meet the new arrival. He was looking at us suspiciously before he was even out of the car; a small, thickset figure with hostile eyes.

'Hi,' I said. 'We've a bit of a confession. We've got your tailwheel.'

His face flushed. 'I was warned this would happen. I'm just in time. You were about to fuck off, too. Well you can take it right off and give it back. Now.' His countenance whitened, his left hand unconsciously sliding his right sleeve up his arm. Our farewell party had melted away.

I grovelled. I explained about the race. I explained that we only needed the tail-wheel for a couple of days. I showed him the note that I had left in the cockpit. I appealed to him, as a fellow Thruster pilot.

'Yeah, yeah,' came the sarcastic response. He was ducking under the wing, sharp eyes darting over other parts of his machine. 'Wonder what else you've taken.'

I waited for him to spot the fuel. Suddenly his tank looked yawningly, cavernously, empty and I couldn't seem to look anywhere else. I had not mentioned about the fuel in the note. However, finally, grudgingly, he said that we could have the tail-wheel—but on one condition only: we were to help him dismantle his machine and put it on his trailer. For the twentieth time I checked my watch. 3.40pm. It was touch and go whether it would be quicker to give him back his tail-wheel and replace our own. Resignedly we started undoing his bolts.

It was nearly half past four by the time we took off. As I taxied out I had a vague feeling that we had forgotten something, but could not think what. 'The card,' I remembered, just as we left the ground. 'We didn't punch our card.' I traced a hedge-skimming circuit round and taxied up to the Pay and Display machine. Dan did the honours, and at last we were off.

We crossed the housing estates and pylons of Southport, the Ribble

Estuary, then climbed to 4,000 feet to clear RAF Warton. A precautionary call to Warton had warned us that a Jaguar fighter was practising '50-second circuits'. Now, far below, and surprisingly hard to spot against the grey landscape, we could see the sleek black shape. Blackpool Tower on the coast was soon visible over on our left, the only recognisable feature of what seemed to be a long ribbon of depressing concrete. The ribbon ended in the wide tidal flats called Pilling Sands—the Finish. I wondered what the next three days held in store? Would we make it?

By five o'clock we had left Lancaster behind and in the far distance ahead we could make out the grey headland on which was situated our next airfield, Cark, with the Lake District beyond. The only hitch was that between us lay the wide expanse of Morecambe Bay. I couldn't remember why Morecambe Bay sounded familiar. Something, I dimly recalled, to do with quicksand. Whatever the reason, we had a decision to take. Wise policy dictated that with a two-stroke engine with a well-proven unreliability record, we did not cut several miles across open water. The safe course was to hug the coast round the bay at least as far as Silverdale before striking west to Grange-over-Sands and Cark. This, however, was at least twice as far, and galling, when the Cark peninsula was so plainly visible ahead.

'What d'you reckon? It's a risk,' I asked. Dan said nothing, a device I had begun to notice he often employed when faced with queries he either did not know the answer to, or did not want to think about. I was about to repeat myself when he replied.

'If there weren't any risks, Tony, it wouldn't be an adventure.'

It was a catchphrase we had picked up from a documentary where two people flew a pair of Thrusters up the east coast of Australia.

'The engine doesn't know it's over water,' I replied.

I headed out to sea. It was ten past five.

In these periods we tended to go quiet. The tide was out, but coming in fast. As I headed towards the Kent Channel, the main channel dividing Warton Sands on the east coast of the bay from Cartmel Wharf, the wide sandbank which extended for several miles south of the Cartmel peninsula*, we were busy with our own thoughts, probably along similar lines. Until we were halfway across the bay, I was gauging how far I could glide back to the mainland from 2,000 feet if the engine stopped. Initially, it was to one of the good-sized fields east of the railway line. Thereafter, it moved to a soft but messy spot in the marshes between the railway line and the coast. As we approached the middle of the bay it became a wretched decision as to where was the firmest part of the sand and mud channels. Over the Kent Channel itself, it was a case of the best procedure for landing in quicksand.

What, I wondered, was the proper technique? Like Lester in the Med, three-point, nose-high? And get the belts undone PDQ as there would not be much time before the pod was sucked under. Involuntarily, I noted the position of the wing wires and struts, so that I could avoid them as I scrambled in the water and sand. Escaping from a high-winged plane was much more difficult than a low-winged machine, of course. How fast would the sand pull us down? That was the question. If we got out and up onto the wing, surely that must help? But how much time would it buy us? Assuming rescue was possible from such a situation, of course: the water surely was not deep enough for a boat. A hovercraft or amphibious vehicle of some kind? But who would have one of those? I felt hopelessly unversed in such things. All that I knew about quicksands was contained in the description I had once read in *The Moonstone*† and B-movie vignettes of people slipping into quicksand which I had recently been trying to rip off for a Pot Noodle commercial.

I had concluded that helicopter rescue was the only option, and was

---

* This easy, nodding familiarity with details of British local topography should not be taken out of context: I had a map in front of me.

† 'At the turn of the tide, something goes on in the unknown deeps below, which sets the whole face of the quicksand shivering and trembling in a manner most remarkable to see, and which has given to it, among the people in our parts, the name of The Shivering Sand. A great bank, half a mile out, nigh the mouth of the

surreptitiously scanning the map for the nearest Air-Sea Rescue bases, when I realised we were well past the channel, and Humphrey Head Point was fast approaching to our right. A moment later the wide east-west tarmac runway of Cark Airfield was visible, and the atmosphere in the cockpit switched to one of businesslike efficiency. The strip was remote and deserted, with no buildings of any kind. We noted that the nearest road was a lane entering the airfield at the south-west corner. The closest petrol station was three quarters of a mile to the north, up a lane, on the outskirts of Flookburgh. I flew a low pass over the runway to check the surface—tall weeds sprouted along most of its length, but there didn't appear to be any pot-holes—then I touched down in a smooth two-pointer. 'Nice landing, Tony,' said Dan.

As I backtracked down the runway towards the road, an old yellow dump truck at the gate of an adjacent field at the far end started its engine in a cloud of smoke: the driver had stopped to watch us land. I opened the throttle and we skimmed down the runway to catch him, Dan out of his seat and rummaging in the nose for the empty cans. At our wild waving, the driver paused. We looked at our watches. It was 5.27 pm. 'Wonder what time petrol stations shut in this part of the world,' said Dan.

As the dump truck and Dan disappeared, calm descended. It was disorientating the way flying switched so suddenly from hectic activity

bay, breaks the force of the main ocean coming in from the offing. Winter and summer, when the tide floes over the quicksand, the sea seems to leave the waves behind it on the bank, and rolls its waters in smoothly with a heave, and covers the sand in silence. A lonesome and a horrid retreat, I can tell you! No boat ever ventures into this bay. No children from our fishing village, called Cobb's Hole, ever come here to play. The very birds of the air, as it seems to me, give the Shivering Sands a wide berth …'

to calm. It took a while for the mind to catch up. All I had to do before Dan returned was measure out the right amount of oil to mix into the petrol. The new 'Plasticans' he had with him, I knew, contained a gallon each. To our usual 20-litre jerry cans we added 400 ml of oil, or two 'sections' on the calibrated window of the plastic oil carton. How much did that mean I had to allow for each Plastican? I lit a cigarette. The calculation now seemed less straightforward than I had supposed. How many gallons was 20 litres? Or rather, how many litres were there to a gallon?

How the Hell was one supposed to know this kind of thing? Was it ten? That seemed a bit much. *Make a rough estimate of your answer to avoid silly mistakes* I remembered Mr Millington, my maths teacher, endlessly repeating as a child. Think now. A jerry can was a lot bigger than a Plastican; it probably contained, say, three or four times as much? But somehow three or four gallons seemed rather an unlikely amount. *Five!* It must be five: that would be logical. So. If there were five gallons in a jerry can, and we added 400 millilitres of oil to that, how much did I need to add to four gallons? It was like one of those depressing exam questions that I had so gratefully left behind at fifteen. Where was the calculator? I rummaged around for five minutes extracting the bag wedged in the nose, and retrieving our tiny solar powered machined. Now, what to calculate?

I sniffed the warm early evening air. The sun was beginning to sink. Dan would be appalled if he returned to find I had not sorted the oil out while he was gone, and rightly so. It was absurd: it couldn't be that hard. I started again: if we put 400 ml of oil in a jerry can of five gallons, how much oil did I need for 2 gallons? Put like that it sounded easier to work out. But were there five gallons in a jerry can? I was beginning to have my doubts. I could hear Mr Millington. 'You are a moron, Woodward: a King Size moron. What are you?' I found a piece of paper. This was about solving equations, about finding the missing piece of information, I was pretty sure. But exactly what was the equation? Maybe it was fractions? Making the units match, that was the key: the litres to gallons problem again. There was no way round it. I needed to know how many litres there were in a gallon. Maybe we should just fill up the tank, then guestimate and add a bit extra for good measure? The important thing was to have enough oil, after all. A bit much would not do any harm.

Finally, it struck me what an idiot I was being. Richard. He was a mathematician. He worked for a bank. This kind of thing was meat and drink to him. I found the mobile and called his office. He consulted his *Economist* diary and announced that there were 4.55 litres in a gallon. (See? Not bad.) I heard the distant hum of voices in an open plan office; it all sounded very remote from my lonely headland. Therefore I needed to add 91 ml of oil to each Plastican. Or 182 ml for both—near-as-dammit one calibrated section of the oil carton, or half the amount I usually added to a full jerry can. Richard said that, if that were all, he would go back to work now. At that moment the chug of the dumper truck behind me indicated that Dan had persuaded the driver to drop him back. 'Oil's sorted,' I said.

'Should think so. We need about 200 ml, as the Plasticans are five litres.'

'How do you know that?'

'Says on the side.'

The two cans brought the fuel up to rather less than two thirds full: about an hour's safe flying at our weight, or fifty-five nautical miles at our standard cruising ground speed, assuming no wind—exactly the distance in a straight line from Cark to Kirkbride. Forty of these were over unlandable country. The only safe routes, skirting the high peaks to the west along the coast, or up the Lune Valley along the course of the M6, would add at least fifteen miles to our journey, so were therefore untenable. There was also the question of time. It was now ten past six. There did not *appear* to be much wind, a light south-easterly if anything, but there was no knowing what it would be like at 4,500 feet, or what strange things might happen in the mountains. (Neither of us had flown over mountains before, and were only dimly aware of 'wave effect', 'hill lift', 'rotor effect', 'anabatic winds' and the nameless other exotic upland currents not to be found in Norfolk. In Norfolk, where ninety-nine per cent of our flying experience had been gained, the highest point above sea level was 210 feet.) In short, the margin for error was zero. 'If there weren't any risks, it wouldn't be an adventure,' I said.

'The engine doesn't know it's over mountains.'

Flying over the Lake District on a summer evening had been a private dream for some time. In fact, for the last eighteen months, it would be fair to say it represented pretty much the summit of my aviation ambitions. Yet, now that I was poised to do it, it was not at all how I imagined. The high ground that loomed before us bore no resemblance to the russet-coloured uplands in my mind, with their rounded, grassy summits, limestone walls, tinkling streams, and glassy tarns. The mountains rose dark and forbidding: big grey-blue lumps pressing up against a cold, murky grey cloud base. They rose fast, too. Cark was virtually at sea level and now, though we had been climbing at full power since take-off, and the altimeter was reading 2,000 feet, we seemed only to be losing height.

After skirting Grizedale Forest and clipping Windermere (where a rogue sunbeam picked out a luminous scene of painted landing jetties and white sailing boats against the peat-brown water), the famous landmarks began to appear in swift succession. Scafell Pike over to the west beyond the Langdale horse-shoe. Much nearer, just to our right, Helvellyn appeared, our first proper 'three thousander'. As steep ridges were followed by deeper dales, one moment we were 100 feet above the ground, the next, 1,000, inducing a vertiginous, mildly nauseous sensation. It felt as if there should have been some accompanying up-and-down motion, like on a rollercoaster, yet there was none. I grabbed the A-frame bar with my right hand.

The hitherto soft air now started to become distinctly choppy. We were prepared for this, knowing that air currents got mixed or messed up as they blew across ranges of hills, creating turbulence or setting up a wave motion, but the reality was still unsettling. Suddenly our passage seemed pitted with potholes. The altimeter would bounce and waver, Dan would open the throttle to maximum, but it would make no difference: we would be sucked downwards, as if to an airway far below. A few moments later we would hit a patch of lift—'hit' being the operative word, as, usually, it felt hard and rough—and it was as if a giant hand had come quietly up beneath us and shoved us up a few hundred feet.

At 3,000 feet Dan throttled back to our level cruising revs of 5,600 rpm to try and eke out the fuel. We maintained a climbing attitude as we still had to go almost over the summit of Skiddaw before we were clear of the high ground (at 3,055 feet, one of the five highest peaks in the range). At 3,400 feet, we were nudging the cloud base. As we encountered another 200-foot patch of sink, followed moments later by an equivalent bump of lift, it was becoming touch and go whether there would be room for us to clear it. Our chatting had long ago dried up. We clipped the east side of Keswick and approached the steep climb up Lonscale Fell, over the crags of Little Man to Skiddaw itself. There was no longer any grass or vegetation beneath us at all, just jagged crags of broken shale and frost-shattered volcanic spikes, falling away to the slate scree hundreds of feet below. And it was at that moment, just as we were suspended over those crags, that the engine missed.

Just one, single, simple, solitary, clean, clear, unmissable miss.

A 'miss' on a two-stroke petrol engine is when one power stroke of one piston in one cylinder does not take place. At the split second when the correct mixture of compressed air and petrol vapour should be igniting to send the piston shooting off down the cylinder and powering the propeller a bit further round, for some reason it doesn't. On a regular, smoothly running engine, the sound is as if it has missed a beat. It can happen for a number of reasons: because the sparking plug is fouled with oil; because a piece of grit or an air bubble in the fuel line momentarily interrupts petrol reaching the cylinder; because, similarly, something interferes with the air-flow from the carburettor; because, due to a faulty connection or electrical problem, insufficient charge reaches the sparking plug.

The overwhelming, overbearing, million pound question is: will it do it again? Was it a one-off? Or is it a forewarning that the engine is about to fail altogether? From the air there is frustratingly little that you can do. You can reach behind the seat to pump the rubber fuel bulb in the hope that, if the cause were an air lock or a bubble in the fuel line, that might shift it. You can try opening and closing the throttle (though this takes considerable courage) to see if it is a speck of dirt in the fuel which an uneven fuel flow might dislodge. You can hope it was a freak fouling of one of the plugs which has cleared itself naturally. Ideally, you land so that you can test and rectify the problem in less trying circumstances. Apart from that, the only readily accessible option is to cross your fingers, hold your breath, rake the terrain beneath for the least awful place to come down, and pray.

That was what we did. At least, that was what I did. I caught my breath and held it, while inside my ski-glove my knuckles turned white. A pair of walkers waved to us from the top of Skiddaw. Bastards, I thought, waving back. Why couldn't I be standing safely on a lump of rock?

The engine, however, continued to run. As it did, very cautiously I released my breath and gently, with infinite care, no presumption and without prejudice, took another. Still there was no repetition, nor even any rough running. We were over Skiddaw now, past the vicious crags, and, while there was still nowhere to land, the terrain was getting less brutal. Still the engine ran. Had I imagined it? Had my imagination gone into overdrive because we happened to be somewhere unlandable? Surely not? No, it missed all right. Whatever else happened to be on one's mind while flying, the one thing you never stopped monitoring, subconsciously, every nanosecond, was the engine. Every time even the tiniest aspect of the mixed chord which was piston roar, gearbox whine and propeller swish changed, you not just heard it, but analysed it like sonar. I was sure I could not have been mistaken.

On the other hand, I did not wish to appear the jumpy kitten who was hearing things. 'Er ... did you ... er ... Did you hear anything then. Just back there?' I said with what nonchalance I could summon.

'I surely did Tony,' said Dan. And I noticed his chin was set and his right arm was braced against the bucking stick which, for Dan, was about as tense as things got.

And, then, as things can suddenly turn bad in flying, so, equally fast, they can come good. Almost before I had realised it, the mountains were behind us and, with them, the clouds too. The ground began falling away fast to big green fields, every one a landing strip. Dan throttled back and we began to descend. With the glow of evening sunshine and the warmer air, there came a thawing of tension. The 1753-foot radio mast to the right appeared on cue to confirm that we were exactly on course, with the big television mast visible over on the far right. A forest of steel radio masts clearly visible on a far headland extending into the Solway Firth suggested that Kirkbride, which was much nearer, ought to be well within view. And suddenly, there it was, right in front of us.*

It was 6.52 pm. The next eight minutes seemed interminable. Our speed appeared to have slackened off completely, leaving us hovering over the flat basin of the Solway. As we inched nearer, we could see numerous flexwing microlights clustered on the grass. Two more appeared in the air from our right. The minute hand on my watch was vertical as our wheels touched down and we tore up the peri-track to a

---

* It's odd the way this happens. Flying across country, you appear to be over much the same scenery for ages. Then suddenly some feature—say a radio mast or a ruined abbey—becomes identifiable, and immediately everything else 'clicks' into place in such a blindingly obvious way that you cannot believe you could not see them before.

black hut, where I handed our punch card to a woman in a baseball cap. 'Cutting it fine,' she said, turning to a fat fellow next to her. 'OK, that's it for today.'

We had done it. Against all odds. We were still in the race. We had shown resourcefulness, initiative, seamless teamwork, and all the other qualities specified by the rally instructions. I confessed the doubts I had felt when I saw the broken tail-wheel. Dan admitted he had nearly freaked out when the engine missed. We called Sean to consult him about the engine. 'Typical,' was the response. 'Typical, typical, typical. Yup, that's icing alright.' It sounded a most unlikely diagnosis in mid-July. 'It's this humid weather, I'm afraid. Been having trouble with it myself this afternoon. Not much you can do, except put up with it. It'll normally clear itself.' I had heard of engine icing, of course, but, without bothering to ascertain the full details had written it off as a hazard attached to flying in cold weather. It came as a surprise to learn that a muggy summer's day presented the perfect conditions— and that, in fact, it was only when the temperature of the air was well *below* freezing that engine icing could *not* occur.*

The question arose as to our plans for the evening. 'Seems to me, Tony,' said Dan, 'that our options are simple. We can camp here— which we can't, because we haven't got a tent'—the other competitors' tents were sprouting like mushrooms on the grass alongside their machines—'or we can hire a taxi and find a local B&B, with all the messing about that that involves. Or'—he paused for emphasis—'We can flit across the Solway Firth to Scotland, a flight of ten minutes, check ourselves into a farmhouse bed, have a hot bath, a slap-up home-cooked dinner, and get back here in time for the start at eight tomorrow morning.' He inspected the fuel level in the tank. 'There's even enough gas left to get us there. What's it to be?'

* See Glossary.

'I'm not sure,' grumbled the Rally Secretary suspiciously, when we called to clear our plan with him. He plainly suspected cheating, but could not put his finger on how we were doing it. 'No one's requested this before. Why is it necessary?' Eventually he was persuaded: we did not seem to be breaking any rules. 'Just make sure you're back before the start tomorrow,' he said sternly. 'Or you're out. No concessions.'

Fifteen minutes later, Dan put us softly down in Scotland, on the smooth, light green sward of a field of freshly cut silage, indicated by a big figure by an old Land-Rover, waving. We were joined on our landing run by two wildly barking sheepdogs, racing alongside, nipping at the wheels. It was ten miles south of Lockerbie.

At 6.30 am the next morning, when Dan's cousin Arthur banged on our bedroom door, things were not quite so rosy. We had proceeded straight from the landing field, via the petrol station, to the pub to celebrate. From the pub we had proceeded to the farmhouse, where Arthur's wife had put an enormous steak and kidney pie in the oven. Rather than preparing for the next day, we had sat up late drinking whisky. Consequently, over breakfast, it was a struggle to collect our wits. There were long silences filled only with the sounds of chewing and slurping as (between anxious glances at our watches) we bolted the sausages, burnt our mouths on the fried tomatoes and sipped at the scalding coffee Arthur's wife had put before us. 'If we're off the ground by quarter to eight we'll be fine,' said Dan, at twenty past seven. 'Just chuck everything together. We can sort ourselves out at Kirkbride.'

I was feeling bloated, bleary-eyed and liverish, still teasing morsels of sausage from between my teeth, as we got to the field. It was one of those dead still, muggy days where the white overcast sky seemed to deaden and absorb all sound. There was not a murmur or a rustle from the belt of oaks that ran down the south side of the field and the steam from the cooling towers of Chapel Cross power station five miles to the east trickled vertically upwards. Dan hurriedly undid the tie-downs and gaffer-taped them to the airframe. Then he stuffed our overnight kit in the nose and stowed the oil in the footwell. I filled the tank until it spilled over, then crudely folded the map into position on my mapboard. Dan had flown last, so it was my turn in the left-hand seat. I did a hasty pre-flight. The wings and engine were soaking with dew. I heaved the tail round so that we were pointing in the right direction, pumped the fuel bulb, set the chokes, started the engine, and shook Arthur's meaty hand goodbye.

Although the field looked level enough, it was on a gentle incline. If I took off from where we were, it would be very slightly uphill. It was a big field, however, at least twice as long as we needed and the grass was very short. 'Worth taxiing to the far end?' I said, plugging the jack into the intercom and turning the ON/VOLUME dial too far, so Dan's voice came back deafening and with a screeching whistle of feedback. 'Go from here,' Dan answered, looking at his watch. 'Come on, let's get moving.'

I opened the throttle and we began to crawl forward up our runway.

Perhaps because I felt so full and heavy myself, perhaps because we were so loaded with fuel and spare oil (plus a second tail-wheel), perhaps because the engine was not warm enough to be giving full revs, perhaps because the gradient was steeper than we thought, perhaps because the surface of the field was not so smooth as it looked, perhaps because the air pressure was lower, perhaps because the new, heavier tail-wheel had marginally shifted our centre of gravity—for whatever reason, the Thruster felt weighted with lead.

I was not worried. The farm dogs kept up with us with no difficulty, barking and snapping at the wheels long after the tail came up. By the time we reached the point where Arthur and his wife were waiting with their cameras, three quarters of the way up the field, we were hardly off the ground. I gave a regal wave as we passed them, though it struck me that it was taking us a long time to gain height. When the low hedge along the road at the end of the field loomed, it looked touch and go whether we were going to clear it. I still was not worried, though. Once off the ground, with so much less drag, we could expect to climb rapidly. I checked the air speed indicator. It read about fifty knots; at full throttle not the speed for maximum rate of climb, but good and safe, and only at yesterday's briefing we had been warned to keep the nose down well after take-off, to let the speed build up. The trouble was, we were not climbing at all.

We squeaked over the hedge; literally squeaked. It was not one of those illusions where it just looked close, then you exaggerated it in the pub afterwards. As we came over, a car was passing along the road, towing a sailing boat on a trailer. I can still picture the driver's atonished face as we lunged over the hedge hardly above windscreen height. The tallest part of the boat's deck, where the mast attached, drew abreast of us as we crossed. If our wheels had not happened to straddle it, we would have hit it.

At a height of six or seven feet we crossed the opposite hedge into the field beyond. Normally, at our speed, the stick would have required a considerable pull to maintain a climbing attitude. Now, there didn't seem to be any firmness, any pressure, at all. The stick just felt mushy and loose. Worried that I was on the point of stalling, I kept the nose down, trusting that if we could pick up some more speed the reassuring pressure would come. Even as we screamed low across the next field I was not especially concerned; it was a muggy day, with no wind, and we were laden to the gunwhales. It was then that I saw the cables.

They were not pylons. They were the smaller ones, the branch lines—like telegraph wires, but for electricity—on tall, capped metal poles. About twenty feet high. They were directly in front of us, a field and a half away. I initiated a gentle right-hand turn. Very gentle, because I feared that the slower-moving inside wing might stall. I kept checking the air speed indicator. Its reading just did not seem to tally with what I was feeling through the stick. Fifty-five knots should have had us gripping the air like a Chinook: climbing like a lift when I pulled the stick back. We came round 90° only just in time, and ran alongside the wires for a hundred yards or more. Still we were not gaining height.

Things began to happen fast after that. I remember seeing, with a sense of helpless dread, that the wires did a right-angle turn 500 yards ahead. I initiated another gentle turn to the right, but we were travelling at nearly 60 knots now and we seemed to cover the distance like lightning. In the same moment, I realised that we were not turning quickly enough. We were going too fast. There wasn't enough room. *We weren't going to make it.* Things went into slow motion. The wires were exactly at cockpit height. We were just too low, just not flying well enough for me to risk yanking the stick back for a kangaroo hop over them; the chances of a wheel catching was too great. I did the only thing I could think of: shoved the nose down and tried to go underneath.

There was a blinding, cold blue flash as we hit the cables.

Ye Luckye Bastardes Club

A crash appeals to everybody.

American tycoon Patrick Turner on his new venture, a string of
restaurants themed around plane crashes. *Time Out*, 11 March 1998

There are no accidents and no fatal flaws in the machines; there
are only pilots with the wrong stuff.

Tom Wolfe, *The Right Stuff*

There are several kinds of crash you can have in a light aircraft. Most
dramatic, disastrous and rare—though probably the accident most
feared by those who know nothing of flying, but who watch the wings
of their 747 wobbling as they are about to take-off—is the full-blown,
catastrophic airframe failure. The engine falls off, the wings fold up,
the tail breaks off, or the machine simply disintegrates around you.
Survival, except by a freak of chance, is impossible; and this would be
pretty well the only time it would be worth carrying a parachute. In the
normal run of things, this kind of crash is not just incredibly unlikely, it
is impossible. It happens only following deliberate sabotage, terrorist
booby trap, wartime attack, mid-air collision, unapproved aerobatics or
chronic oversight in a pre-flight check.

A crash from a malfunctioning control system is almost equally rare.
On light aircraft, systems are so simple—far simpler than on a modern
car—and so well-proven, installed, tested and backed-up, that there is
no reason for them to fail unless they have received unauthorised

tampering. This is the reason that even the simplest or most trivial modifications to a light aircraft embroil the modifier in a blizzard of bureaucracy: all systems have to be rigorously tested before the Civil Aviation Authority will approve them.

No, as everyone knows, pilot error is the cause of the vast majority of crashes—negligence, incompetence, rotten judgment, human weakness. The top causes of fatal light aircraft accidents in the last fifteen years, ranked in order are:

1. Loss of control (including stall/spin).
2. Pressing on into bad weather or hitting high ground.
3. Low flying.
4. Mid-air collisions.
5. Hitting trees, masts, cables.
6. Runway too short (performance accidents).
7. Running out of fuel.
8. Alcohol.

In short, every one due to pilot error.

Now, when things go wrong in the air, the best possible insurance policy is height. Height gives you options. Height gives you the opportunity to pick a good place to land, and the time to recover and plan a descent. As crash situations go, flying at fifteen feet above the ground, when things go pear-shaped, the prognosis is poor.

Low, fast crashes are the kind that are not survived; the kind that happen at air shows. There is no time to recover control. No time to prepare a soft landing. Masses of energy to dissipate when you do make contact. Factor into this unsatisfactory equation high voltage electric cables, and short of a kamikaze dive into a fuel tanker or a Semtex factory, the circumstances are as unpromising as they come. The horror stories—of which there are many because it happens so frequently—are unending. I had heard of pilots who survived the impact of the crash only to be left dangling, until the sagging cables finally touched their machine to the ground, earthing the supply, and—PSZZZZZZST—the electric chair. There were pilots who scrambled from the wreckage, only to be caught by bare-ended live cables thrashing around; pilots who, soused in aviation spirit from ruptured fuel tanks, were trapped when the volatile, vapourising fuel ignited from sparks from the cables. One of the fitters in the hangar at Barsham had recently told me, with considerable relish, of someone who had crashed into electric cables and received multiple burns on his legs. Congratulating himself on getting off so lightly, bit by bit the burns turned gangrenous, where they had partly cooked his flesh. Both legs had to be amputated.

I remember thinking, as we cartwheeled through the air, 'This cannot be happening—not to *me*.' Other people got killed in plane crashes: people I heard about, but never knew. People for whom the drama of their end became a sort of social triangulation point. 'Oh— the person whose brother was killed in a plane crash?' What was *I* doing in this situation? It did not fit. It did not fit that I had taken up this activity. It had never fitted. I had known from the start that it was not my thing. Why did I never learn?

And now this. A wrap. Slow motion and all. This was what it had all been leading up to, was it? Well, well. And Dan, too. That was a thought: Dan. What if I were all right, but Dan got it? Or maybe I would not kill him. What then? A quad, perhaps? Or a coma? What about that? A 'do we switch him off' scenario?

I was going to have to go to Salsingham and tell Lester and Rhona that their son was no more. I could see it now.

'What happened? Who was flying?'

That was a point. Whose fault was it? Why were we in this predicament? What was the reason for us pirouetting through the air like this?

'Well, Lester, that's not really the point. The point, Rhona, is that the plane just would not climb. Maybe it was overweight. Maybe, if we had taken off in the other direction, there would have been no power lines. You know, if we had gone downhill—'

'Downhill? You took off *uphill*?'

'Well, it was hardly uphill really, and we both agreed it was fine, and we were in a tremendous hurry, you have to remember ...'

'You took off uphill? You were in a hurry? Who was flying?'

'Well, I was, as a matter of fact. But when the power lines appeared, it wasn't really a matter of who was at the controls. Just a case of right or left really. I chose right. Then—can you believe it?—the lines did a right-hand turn.'

'You chose right?'

'Yes, bad luck, I know, but one of those things. If Dan had been flying, I suppose it's possible that he might have turned left. But he might, equally, have chosen right.'

'But Dan wasn't flying. You were flying. You took off uphill. You were in a hurry. You turned right. You hit the power lines.'

That was what it boiled down to. What was happening was the consequence of my decisions and mine alone. If I had misgivings, I should have acted on them. Did I have misgivings? No, not really. It was just bad luck that the machine was climbing so slowly. Bad luck that the wires were there. Bad luck that I turned the wrong way. No, not bad luck—*the wrong decision*. The last of several *wrong decisions*. I was the pilot. It was *my fault*.

This was the gist of the thoughts that passed through my head in the moments immediately after making contact with the wires. I do not remember them being in any way hurried, though they must have passed through my head reasonably swiftly, as we were still twisting and somersaulting through the air when my line of inquiry shifted to: what the fuck did any of this matter, when I was about to be spread across the fields like fertiliser. *As* fertiliser, in fact. When was this going to stop? When were we going to hit something? More specifically, where was the pain going to come first? Which bit? What was it like to break your neck? Or back?

Finally we did hit something. Or the Thruster did. There was a massive, jolting crunch and thump. Followed by another. And another. Crunch. Thump. Thump, crunch. Let that be it, I thought. Please let that be the last one.

THUNK WHUMP THUMP BANG BANG THUNK CRUNCH.

And, finally, it was. The jarring lurches stopped. We were hanging upside down in our safety harnesses. My side of the inverted cockpit was up against a wall of earth and stones. There was silence apart from a trickling noise above me. A cool, thin liquid was running down my neck, into my hair and stinging my eyes. For a moment we both just hung there, upside down, neither moving or speaking. 'You OK?' I remember croaking. In response Dan came to life, and in a single rapid movement unclicked his harness and scrambled out. I followed him.

For a few minutes we stumbled around, dazed, disorientated and trying to comprehend what had happened. There was no sign of blood.

We were in a tip of some kind, on the edge of a quarry. Scrambling up to the top of a heap of dirt and rubble, I could see a vast hole, faced with blasted pink rock, now abandoned and filling with red water. Lorry-loads of hardcore, soil and quarry waste were everywhere, strewn with weeds and sprouting ragwort. The wings of the Thruster, in its final, inverted descent, had straddled two of these heaps, gently placing the pod—and us—in the gap between, in such a way as to completely break our fall. The waste heaps had saved our lives.

Sitting on top of a heap I pulled out my cigarettes. The packet was wet and slimy but they looked just about serviceable. As I put one in my mouth and began rummaging for my lighter, the true extent of our luck began to sink in. We were both not just all right, but without a scratch between us. We could walk and talk, sing and see and breathe. It really was a chance of chances. As I clicked the lighter and raised it towards my mouth, Dan knocked it out of my hand. 'Maybe not such a good idea, Tony.' For the first time I noticed that we were both drenched in fuel.

The poor old Thruster was no more than a heap of debris—and not a large one either. Collapsed on the ground, it had to be said, a £12,000 microlight aircraft did not amount to much. The wreckage resembled three or four cheap aluminium picnic chairs which, perhaps with a chainsaw, had been backed over by a cement mixer. It lay, because of the uneven ground, not quite on its back. What remained of the tail jutted up against the angle of one of the dirt heaps. The mashed pod lay upside down with its wheels in the air, leaving its scratched and grass-stained underside ignominiously exposed, like an inverted beetle. The fibreglass was caved-in and splintered. Fissure-cracks of stress snaked all across the curved windshield. The engine and propeller had buried themselves deep into the earth and rubble, with two of the three-blades sheared off around three inches from the shaft. Shards and splinters from the blades were strewn around.

Both wings were snapped back from the fuselage, the left much more severely than the right. Near the left wing tip, where the leading edge must have struck the power line, the nylon fabric of the wing covering was completely melted and charred, as was the metal of the aluminium frame beneath. Most dramatic, was the state of the main boom—the backbone of the Thruster. The heavy gauge 6" diameter alloy tube was sheared, or buckled to the point of shearing, in three places, folded back on itself like a collapsed music stand.

We tried to piece together what had happened. The severe burn near the tip of the port wing indicated where we had struck the cables, shorting two or more together and causing the flash. Our speed would have flicked us vertically upwards, maybe into a couple of cartwheels, from which we had evidently descended tail first; there could be no other explanation for the main boom being broken in three places. That had taken the brunt of our fall. Any remaining energy must have been absorbed in the final keel over, when the span of the wings caught the tops of two adjacent heaps, depositing the cockpit into the space between. The dear old Thrasher had absorbed every last bit of shock, reducing herself, in the process, to skip fodder. Even the altimeter glass was cracked: there was literally nothing left to take any strain—except us.

Our race was over this time, and no mistake. Yet I could not shake off the sense of urgency, that we should be on our way. Involuntarily I glanced at my watch. It was still not eight o'clock. We could still do it. My thoughts were interrupted by a puffing from behind one of the slag heaps and Arthur appeared. The ruddy complexion of the working farmer had been exchanged for a pallor of uniform grey-green. I had forgotten that our aerial antics had had an audience. He stared at us disbelievingly. 'You two are alive? You are alive?' After that he kept just pacing up and down, looking almost as dazed as we felt, shaking his head and repeating, 'Can't believe it. Can't believe it. You're alive.'

'Happens every time,' boomed the Rally Secretary, cheerfully. 'Didn't we warn you about tekken-off in warm weather? I don't know. We say it every year. Makes not a blind bit of difference. Thanks for letting us know. That'll teach you to go staying wi' friends. Better luck next time.' Perhaps because I was still a bit dazed, I did not ring off instantly, but kept the phone to my ear. I overheard him turn to his colleague to say that the Thruster was out of the race. There was a murmur and a chuckle. I caught a final phrase before the line went dead.

'Daft bastards,' the other voice said. 'Who are these people?'

Sean puffed out his cheeks and gave a low whistle. 'My God. I have to hand it to you boys, when you do a thing, you do it properly. *Look - at - That.*' He whistled. 'The poor old Thrasher. Well-and-Truly-Culled.' He picked about amongst the wreckage for a few moments, shaking his head and chuckling incredulously. 'Look at the boom. Look at the bloody boom. Broken in three places. Don't think I've ever seen a Thrasher quite so thoroughly culled. And the instruments. Even the glass. Oh, you boys. You do make me laugh.'

MIRACLE ESCAPE

A RALLY ROUND the UK almost ended in tragedy yesterday when a microlight plane crashed near a disused quarry north of Annan.

Antony Woodward, of Ashbury, London, and his passenger, who has not been named, were guests of Cummertrees man Arthur Banham.

They had been taking part in the prestigious Round Britain Rally and were making an overnight stop in the area.

However their event came to a premature end yesterday morning when their aircraft developed engine trouble soon after take off.

It struck a power cable and spun out of control, plummetting to the ground at Wintersheugh, on the Kinmount estate.

The plane, which was said to be extensively damaged, is valued at about £14,000.

Yet miraculously both pilot and passenger walked away with minor bumps and bruises.

"They were both very shocked by the incident but remarkably neither of them were badly injured," said Mr Banham.

"They have both set off back home with the remains of the wreckage."

A spokesman for the British Microlight Aviation Association said they would be carrying out a full investigation.

"We will be looking into the causes of this accident in due course and hopefully we can come up with some answers.

"It is a blessing that neither person involved was injured. These planes don't provide much protection and they could very easily have been killed."

Scottish Power spokesman Ken Stein said the incident had not damaged the power cables and as far as he was aware there had been no interruption to power.

When I returned the hired Transit to Scotland next day, Arthur gave me a copy of the local paper, the *Annandale Observer*. We were the cover story.

According to a friend in Lancashire, we also made an item on national radio news: along the lines of 'Londoners involved in Scottish air incident'. She said it was funny: it had made her think of me.

And that was the Round Britain.

A few weeks later a letter arrived bringing 'amended' results of the Tenth Great Round Britain Air Rally. It seemed that several teams had alighted on the same novel and enterprising method of cheating: 'accidentally' stamping the box on their score cards marked 'Insch' (north of Scotland: 350 points) when they arrived at Ince (scene of our tail-wheel drama: 50 points). In the tabulated final score column, the letters 'DNF' were entered against our names (as for eleven other entrants), signifying Did Not Finish. A chatty covering letter said that it had been the biggest and most successful rally yet. It congratulated the winners and criticised contestants for 'yet again' infringing air space at Edinburgh and the Manchester Low Level Corridor. 'Finally I know everyone will be happy to hear that Bill Tricks will soon be out of traction at Southgate General. Rustom Irani is making rapid progress at Oddstock. And David Wilson should be out of plaster by the time you read this. I know we all wish them well.'

Maybe we hadn't done so badly.

Sabres of Paradise 'Smoke Belch II' (Beatless Mix)

I am convinced that a judicious participation in aeroplaning provides a man with a very fine mental tonic ... I hear people very often talking about 'Brain Fag'. Business men, too, complain very often that they want a change and need 'bucking up'. I already foresee that in the future, flying will come to be regarded as one of the greatest health givers. It will not be long, in my opinion, before doctors tell ailing men to go in for a course of aviation.

Claude Grahame-White, *The Story of the Aeroplane*, 1911.

I finally made it into the *Accident Survey*. The reports had recently adopted a new user-friendly style, longer and more chatty than of old: 'Stephen King could make something of this accident, the pilot must wake up at night in a cold sweat. It is every pilot's nightmare ...' It went on to outline a slightly amended version of the (slightly amended) version of events that I had described in my Accident Report.

As it happened, I did have nightmares for a few weeks after the crash, and always about the same thing: the closing seconds. In one scenario I was ten feet off the ground, engine screaming, no pressure on the stick, as the electricity cables loomed and there I would remain, caught in the awful moment. In another, I managed to squeak under the wires, then got trapped in the quarry basin, circling demonically at seventy or eighty miles per hour, like a vast bluebottle, in a climbing turn that never quite got me clear of the rock face.

We never did discover why. Was the engine not giving full power because it was not warm enough? Dan thought it was not revving as highly as usual at full throttle. But that alone would not have explained it. The likely answer was that several minor factors contributed to make us too heavy, or marginally altered our centre of gravity. Probably we had been on our limit the day before, when we left Barton. Since when, we had added the new (considerably heavier) tail-wheel, plus a spare bottle or two of two-stroke oil in the nose. Combined with a brimful tank, the well-victualled crew, dew on the wings (everything makes a difference in a microlight), no wind and light muggy air, it might have been enough. It hardly mattered now. Had I turned left rather than right when I saw the wires, or had we taken off the other way, we would probably have clawed our way gradually up to cruising altitude and, as we burnt fuel and became lighter, remained blissfully unaware how near our limits we had been.

At no stage did Dan venture a word of criticism, accusation or blame. Nor did Lester or Rhona. Dan asked me why I had turned right when the power cables loomed because, he said, he would instinctively (from the left-hand seat) have turned left. Rhona gave me a hug and said it was nice to see us back in one piece. Lester, as close to emotion as I have ever seen him, said sympathetically, 'You can't be too careful when it comes to wires. You know, you might easily have been hurt. I remember once coming out of a dirt strip in Ol Molog ... '

There was no dramatic reappraisal of values, or sense of having sorted my priorities out. In my mind, I think that I had quietly decided that that was that, as far as flying went. I had got my licence. I had proved I could do it. I had flown over the Lakes, had a couple of crashes, at least got as far as entering the Round Britain Rally. How much more was there to be gained? It was the obvious time to hang up my goggles—had I worn goggles.

Back in London, I enjoyed some minor celebrity within my own circle of friends, and at work. 'Good old Tony,' was the gist. 'Heard what happened this time? Parked his plane in some pylons.' And soon, in the old Pavlovian way, I was playing up to it. There seemed no advantage to be gained by minimising the scale of the accident, so soon the fourteen-foot poles were, indeed, promoted to pylons and the 10,000-volt wires became 60,000-volt high-tension cables which, once severed, thrashed around, arc-ing showers of sparks. It was fun, having a real adventure to tell.

Privately, of course, it was not so funny. The banter had a slightly hollow feel; a ring of falseness and dishonesty: it was the same feeling that I remembered after our first accident—the one following Richard's engine failure over the standing corn. I followed the same strategy we had then: buried it—and went clubbing.

For a happy period, I subsumed worries of all kinds in a happy blur of dancing, sweating, snogging, and progressive house music. I forget now which of the various efficacious and engagingly-named pills ('Rhubarb-and-Custards', 'Dennis the Menaces', 'Pink Cadillacs', 'Yellow Cabs') transported me to a world blissfully free of electricity cables, iced carburettors, bad weather forecasts, men with epaulettes—not to mention packet soups, deadlines and blank layout pads. As the only drawback to these lost weekends appeared to be a mild aching the next day, plus a certain lowness of the spirits around the following Tuesday (I recall on one occasion bursting into tears when the paper cups at the water cooler ran out), I do not remember whether I considered the risks attached. If I did, no doubt they seemed incidental alongside piloting a well-fuelled aircraft into live electricity cables. For a time, I seemed to have found the solution to my problems.

As the evenings shortened however, the leaves began to turn and damp, hazy air once again proclaimed the onset of autumn, an odd feeling came over me. It was there when the late afternoon sun glinted orange in a plate-glass window, or in the clear, bright sunlight and washed brick-work that followed a heavy shower, or if a particularly well-formed cloud was visible from my office window. It was hard to pin down exactly what this was—a twinge of something: a restlessness or impatience; a feeling of *lacking* something. And after a few weeks, it became equally evident what was missing—flying.

The idea scared me sick, yet it was what I wanted to do. In fact, it was stronger than that—I didn't just want to go flying again, I *needed* to. And I finally realised what it was that my absurd pastime gave me. It had nothing to do with girls, or a love of the air, or the need to escape or feel free (though all these played their part). It was because my world had become so disconnected from reality; so phoney—its shallows ran so deep.

Any existence which allows you to live in Britain without owning a waterproof coat, and spend most of your waking moments propagating a relentlessly shiny, happy, vacuum-sealed, pre-tested, extra-safe, longer-lasting, double-protected, extra-strength, discreetly-perfumed world is likely, it could be argued, to have lost a measure of connection with the natural order of things. But it was not as if the actual world I inhabited was so different. Almost everything about my lifestyle, my job and my relationships was about convenience, comfort, style, safety, showing off: about fast fixes to keep the unpleasant realities of life at arm's length.

Taking a flight in the Thruster somehow seemed to put things back together in an honest way. The thrills and excitements came, but they came with a price—and the price was commitment, decisiveness, discipline, responsibility and courage: all the things I assiduously spent my life avoiding. Being forced to confront and overcome these, as flying made me do, was what made the afterglow so fulfilling. In a strange way, flying earthed and grounded me. It let me feel real again.

Flying was the antidote that I didn't know I needed. Initially it had baffled me why the first simulated flight computer games which had begun to appear, and which many people at work played (more or less continuously, in fact) held no appeal. I felt I ought to be interested, ought to want to have a go, but somehow I couldn't summon any enthusiasm. Now it was obvious. Computer games, however realistic, had nothing to do with the feelings and emotions of real flying.

It was the fact that I could never believe that I could do a thing until I had done it that gave me the drive, determination and commitment that Richard lacked. He was never as hooked on flying as me because he lacked the self-doubt. There was less of a gap between where he thought he was, and where he wanted to be. The thrill for him was less, and the downside correspondingly greater. He had no *need* to fly. Richard's trouble, as a pilot, was the opposite of mine: he had too little self-doubt; he didn't take enough care—and that was why he frightened himself. Self-doubt unquestionably made a safer pilot.

This torrent of self-discovery was all very well, but it hardly helped address the practical daily requirements of unrequited infatuation. As summer faded into autumn, I entered one of my cyclical lows. Clubbing no longer seemed the answer. I began to wonder whether advertising was really what I wanted to do. I developed a persistent cold. And as always, when I was depressed, my thoughts turned to Lift Girl. It was now well over two years since there had been anything which could, even in the most favourable light, be construed as promising sexual electricity, yet the embarrassing, impossible-to-admit truth was that I was as mad about her as ever. In no mood for socialising, and with no plane or prospect of any flying to distract my thoughts—and Richard married—I spent increasingly large amounts of time brooding alone.

This was how things stood in the last week of October, when a friend from home whom I had not seen for some time called to say he had rented a cottage for the weekend in Somerset. Glad for the diversion, but without particular enthusiasm, I accepted, driving down late on Friday night. The door was opened by Lift Girl.

It was one of those brutal, apparently unlikely chances that happen all the time in the small world that is real life. Lift Girl had arrived with a friend of my friend; I had met him once before and now recalled that she knew him.

I found it hard to enter into the spirit of the weekend. Having gone to bed early, and got up late, we all went to the pub for lunch, then set out for a walk. The weather was unsettled, one of those autumn afternoons, mild to the point of being warm, even hot, in moments of sunshine, where you could feel as well as smell the dampness in the air. For a time it had looked as if it might clear, but the time-lapse clouds, after scudding and swirling like pouring Guinness, closed up, snuffing out any rays and leaving a drab, lacklustre light, which certainly did not help my mood. Gloomily disconsolate, I separated myself from the others, walking well ahead.

Towards the end of the afternoon, the countryside began to take on a vaguely familiar feel, but it was a moment or two before I realised why: the path had strayed onto an airfield. It was a disused wartime aerodrome, and with a quickening of interest I had not felt for months, I walked down the section of peri-track now used as a runway, towards a heap of hardcore at one end, by an old caravan. This, too, had a vaguely familiar aspect—and suddenly I realised why: it was Marston Mallet, where Ken had taught me to land. Arriving from a different direction, by a different motorway, by night, I had failed to realise how close the cottage was. In the shelter of the heap of hardcore, the barn and the caravan, an old Cessna was tied down, plus another plane and three or four three-axis microlights. And there, under covers, tied to old tyres and blocks of concrete, was another unmistakable shape.

As I wandered around it, appraising it with a practised eye, my black mood was forgotten. I had not seen a Thruster since the crash. Absently I tugged the knots of the cords holding on the covers. What I thought I was doing, even as I heaved the tail onto my shoulder and pulled the machine out from its bay in the lee of a slag-heap, I do not know. I just wanted to see her clearly, I think, free of the clutter and the other machines. Automatically, after I set her down, I wandered round, twitching the ailerons, brushing dead leaves and twigs from the surface of the wing. I pulled off the plastic bag round the engine and flicked down the two carburettor chokes. I turned on the fuel-tap— the tank was three-quarters full—pumped the bulb, and pulled the starting cord a couple of times to turn the engine over. There was no-one around; and certainly no sign of Ken. Surely there couldn't be any harm? I returned the chokes to normal. 'I'll just run her for a minute or two,' I think I thought to myself. 'Just remind myself of the old sound,' and before I knew it, I had flicked on the main power switch and tugged the starting cord again. She fired on the first pull, and roared into life on the second. I ducked into the cockpit to adjust the throttle until she was running smoothly. Ken couldn't mind a quick spin—I'd tell him next time I saw him. Hadn't he actually said 'It's always here, Tony. Anytime'?

It was great to feel the pedals under my feet again, and have my hands back on the throttle and stick. I taxied briskly out across the fairing just as the others were coming up the runway. 'Going for a spin,' I yelled.

'Hang on,' someone shouted back. The group was obscured by the wing, so I could not see who it was. Then Lift Girl was clambering in.

'Right hand on the strut,' I commanded tersely over the roar of the engine, smacking it firmly with my hand. 'Left foot on the bar. Don't put any weight on the floor: you'll go through.'

I was speaking automatically. The rush of nervous adrenaline which always hits me just before flying had taken hold, boosted by the slightly different arrangement of the controls. Although familiar, they were all at slightly different settings to those I was used to; the seat seemed further forward, the throttle lever stiffer, the rpm gauge was above me in an overhead panel. All of which contributed to a slightly disorientated feeling. Towards Lift Girl I felt nothing; I was oblivious. For the first time in months, as I leant over to secure the harness straps over her shoulders and round her waist, my mind was fully engaged elsewhere. I was me again.

'Do up your collar.'

When I went to buckle my own harness, I found there was something bulky in my pocket. My Walkman. I was about to drop it on the ground to collect later when a thought occurred. It contained the 'Wings of a Dove' cloud-hopping mix Dan had made for me, beginning with The Orb's *Little Fluffy Clouds*. I unwound the phones—the in-your-ear type—pressed play and leant over Lift Girl to put them in her ears.

'They'll help with the noise as we haven't got headsets.'

Then I opened the throttle and we surged forward. Lift Girl cannot have weighed more than seven or eight stone and on the tarmac the tail came up instantly. I kept the stick forward, though, holding her down as long as possible. When I finally allowed the stick back, we pole-vaulted into the air. It could hardly have felt more different from the last time I had tried to take off. She gasped. As we banked over the rest of the party, who were waving from the ground, I felt calmer and happier than I had for months.

I was also flying superbly. The air was mild and smooth and the Thruster was responding precisely, which gave me extra confidence. I had already decided what I was going to do. It was slightly risky, and I had never done it before, but I knew the conditions were perfect; that if it worked, it would never work more dramatically than today. Putting the machine into a gentle climbing turn I managed, at my first attempt, to trim her well enough that she just wound gently upwards in a perfect spiral, without me having to touch the controls again. The cloud base was around 1,500 feet, perhaps a little more, but the air was still warm and I had seen, from those few rays earlier, that the cloud was not thick. The altimeter was winding smoothly clockwise. I checked the fuel. The level didn't seem to have altered at all and already we were at 1,400 feet. Soon the first wisps of water vapour were being sliced by the top of the wings. A moment later we were lost in fog.

The temperature dropped a couple of degrees. Lift Girl looked at me slightly nervously. I knew the cloud could not be more than, at most, a few hundred feet thick. Even so, we seemed lost in it for ever. I checked the altimeter to make sure we were still climbing and was just beginning to think that perhaps this had not been such a clever idea, when the vapour began to brighten dramatically. Suddenly it thinned to gossamer and, like a veil, was whipped from over us. Momentarily we were blinded by the brilliance.

At first, after the gloom of the cloud, the scene was so bright it made my retinas ache. But as the plane, still climbing in a perfect spiral, banked gently away from the low sun it gave our eyes a chance to accustom. She gasped again. I could feel it, even over the noise of the engine.

I do not know what I had been expecting. I suppose a flat layer of cloud, above which the sky would be clear and blue, perhaps streaked with pink from the low autumn sun: the standard window-seat view. The scene that greeted us was far more dramatic: a vast, enclosed stadium of water vapour of apocalyptic beauty. We had come through a particularly deep mass of cloud, bringing us out some 700-800 feet above the level of the general shelf, which was far from even. It was a boiling, volcanic landscape, like a John Martin painting, of exploding geysers and towering canyons in lurid, glowing acid-trip colours: reds and oranges and greys and blacks, as absurdly removed from the drab evening we had left behind as if it were a scene from Jack-and-the-Beanstalk.

Clouds erupted beneath and around us in every shape and colour: forbidding grey-black on their undersides, but with electric, luminescent, burnt-orange coronas where they blocked the sun on their western sides. Blue wisps of ragged *fracto-stratus* hung between them, like eddying tobacco smoke, the delicate threads flaring like cobwebs on a burning log where the sun caught them. To the east, hanging puffballs of cumulus glowed pastel pink. To the west their heaping cauliflower tops sliced the light into a biblical fan of rays. We couldn't have caught the light at a better moment.

As the initial assault on the senses passed, a wave of euphoria washed over me. Still unable to do anything but stare, I let the Thruster climb for another 200 or 300 feet, bringing us up to the level of a fireball of cumulus hanging directly in front of us. Then I cancelled the turn with a dab of opposite stick. I felt fingers burrowing round the back of my arm, then scooping round my biceps.

For some reason, I felt a sort of proprietorial pride. We were here entirely by my work. It was as if all this, the whole magnificent scene— cloud-design, lighting effects and, yes, you're too kind, colours too—

was my personal handiwork. I felt I was showing a favoured guest my private view. It was a most satisfactory sensation. Who would have thought a little old 'Thrasher' could deliver something like this? The hand gripping my arm shifted and squeezed. For the first time, my thoughts turned to my passenger.

It was a stroke of luck that, of all the people I might have had with me at that moment, Lift Girl was the one. Now, as I smiled at her, I noticed that she looked somehow different from the person I had always seen before: smaller and more vulnerable: a pretty girl, certainly, but no more than that. In that moment of confidence and control, perhaps, I saw that my 'love' was not really about her, or any real person at all; it was about me. She just happened to be the person upon whom I had chosen to foist my needs and hopes, and about whom, in reality, I knew next to nothing. I did not need her, or any other pretty girl, to prove that I was all right to the world.

Perhaps she sensed this shift, this new certainty and independence, and it made her uneasy. Certainly her face suddenly looked doubtful, confused and desperate for something, perhaps the love and attention she sought endlessly from men like me. I felt a new sensation towards her: of affection, warm and protective, unfettered by any need of reciprocity.

About a quarter of a mile away, a staircase of cloud flattened out into a smooth shelf. I skimmed along it, dragging the wheels in the cotton wool beneath. (The joy of flying in clouds is the sense of speed and movement that they confer, tediously absent in clear skies; all the thrills of low flying, but without the attendant risk of catching a wheel in a telephone wire.) The next twenty minutes were like a private fairground ride, as we brushed, skimmed, and dived through clouds luminescent with colour, repainted every few moments by the dying sun. We flew down ravines and tunnels of water vapour. I stood the plane on its wing tips in turns so steep that the rudder became an elevator (for an awful second I thought I had overdone it, and we were going to fall over into a roll). I flattened us into our seats with the gs. Lift Girl took out one of her earpieces and put it in my ear. It was the opening bars of *Sabres of Paradise*, the spine-tingling bit.* She kept looking at me with a gooey, transfixed expression, her eyes screwed up and her face orange in the sunlight.

As the sun began to disappear, and the sky cooled to a dim pink glow, I reduced the throttle to 2,000 rpm and put the nose down. In a single, confident side-slip I slewed down through the cloud to find myself perfectly placed at the end of the runway. When we came to a halt, Lift Girl sat silent and motionless. As I leant over to help undo her harness, her hand found its way inside my shirt, running gently up to rest on my shoulder blade. With her other hand she reached behind my neck, pulling me towards her and shutting her eyes.

I pressed her nose with an affectionate finger.

'You and I,' I said—and I really meant it—'should go and get some tea.'

---

* Not quite so spine-tingling, of course, since copywriters like me have used the track on every other bank and mobile phone ad.

Intentionally Blank

We are going to form a new society, 'The Society for the Extermination of Amateur Aerial Authors', the purpose of which will be to protect the public from a flood of bunk.

Entry, 19 August 1918, *Diary of an Unknown Aviator.*

The new Thruster arrived in the spring: Golf Mike Zulu Hotel Alpha. And very smart she was, too. We put more thought into the colour scheme this time: lime green and dark blue—blue pod, blue wings and tail; green ailerons, rudder and elevators. She bears none of the scars of novice airmanship that her forebear carried into her finest hour. She has a working fuel gauge just like on a car, an absurdly high-tech GPS with moving map which only Dan knows how to work, an exhaust gas temperature gauge (whatever that does), a vertical speed meter, dual-ignition, an electric fuel pump. There is even a cigarette lighter socket for charging the mobile. The extra instruments are mounted on a fancy T-shaped binnacle making her cockpit reminiscent of a helicopter's. She also has a radio, which has opened up a whole new area of confusion and complexity and with which we are gaining in confidence. (An early setback occurred when, inadvertently, I rested my map-board on the 'speak' button—located on top of the stick—and Bristol Airport plus all local air traffic on the frequency received an unsolicited rendition of Bohemian Rhapsody.)

Lester does not fly much now. He never formally gave up, of course, but he had to have a new hip. There was a period of almost a year while it bedded in, during which he could not fly, and, when he did return to the cockpit, he found the new, aerodynamically improved Thruster harder to land. He seemed reluctant to receive further instruction from Sean—mainly, Dan and I suspected, because he had not been told what to do by anyone for fifty years and had no plans to start now. When I intimated to him that I was thinking of writing a book about our flying adventures he looked baffled. 'But you haven't had any,' he said.

Dan and I still fly together. Every July or August, we book a week out of our diaries, pester every friend or acquaintance we can drum up in remote parts of the British Isles and, whatever the weather is doing, cross our fingers and set off. Last year we had to abandon the Thruster at the Cairngorm Glider Club and return south by train. After numerous attempts to fly her out, all thwarted by bad weather, we finally arrived to perfect conditions—to find (a classic microlighting moment) that an apron of wet cement had been laid outside the hangar door. It was eight months before we got another chance.

I don't see Lift Girl often. Once I had moved agencies, we no longer bumped into each other and frankly, we don't have much in common. Last time I saw her, she was still gorgeous, but I find it hard to understand what all the fuss was about.

Although I had worked out an explanation for what my personal motivation for flying might be, it did not seem to have much in common with anyone else's. I felt no closer, spiritually, to either the epaulette-friendly technophiles, the grand old men with moustaches, the gung-ho Biggles wannabes with their Breitling watches, sheepskin bomber jackets and Aviator sunglasses, the natural born tinkerers or the waggish beard-and-baseball cap brigade. Or, for that matter, the danced-the-skies-on-laughter-silvered-wings sentimen-talists either. I did not seem to think like they did, or be turned on by the same things. Reluctantly, I concluded, I was just someone with my own agenda.

Then I came across a couple of second-hand books (I was always hunting for books about amateur flying, especially from the 1930s, the so-called Golden Age): *England Have My Bones* and *Pilot's Summer*.

Both repeatedly referred to a book written in 1931 called *A Rabbit in the Air* by David Garnett. 'Get *A Rabbit in the Air*, if only for the last page and a half alone' said *Pilot Summer*. 'He's seized there on an immutable something about fine weather flying that is for ever crowding into the pilot's memory and yet about which he is wholly articulate.' When I finally got hold of a copy of what (I have since learned) is an acknowledged flying classic, this is what I read:

I may not ever have the aeroplane of which I dream, my own 'plane which will be stowed away in a lonely barn between a hay-tedder and a horse-rake. When I do own it I shall neglect it for weeks at a time, but then one morning when there are big white clouds and the spring air is soft, I shall walk across the fields and unlock the barn door and there the 'plane will be, waiting for me. As I edge round it, a brown hen will fly up cackling from her clutch of eggs in the cockpit and I shall chase her away angrily. There will be a thick layer of hay dust over everything, sparrows will have dropped straws from their nests and have made messes on the wings.

I shall prop open the double doors and lifting the machine by the tail push her out into the sunlight to look her over carefully. Then I shall swing out the wings and lock them, unhook and fold away the jury-struts and kick the chocks into place under the wheels. Then, after flooding the carburettor, turn the prop over once or twice to suck in, switch on, and seizing the propeller blade, give her one good swing.

As I jolt along, taxiing out into the sixteen acre field, I shall be all alone. There will be no one within sight, not one living thing to watch me and nothing in the sky except a lark or two. And then, when I've strapped myself in and turned into wind, I shall take-off alone and unobserved into the empty sky.

For a moment, I was so amazed that I had to re-read it. For what Garnett had described was—give or take a detail or two—*my* dream.

As I write, I have been flying for twelve years and two hundred and twenty-eight hours. That's nineteen hours a year—not much, you might think, over such a long period, but a fair amount if you allow, say, ten hours of driving, hanging around, tinkering, preparing, and general time-wasting to the power of three, for every hour airborne. I have had two engine failures, two engine 'troubles', dozens of precautionary landings and two crashes. I have landed at fifty-four* different club airfields, over fifty farm strips and made thirty-eight 'bush' landings on fields, roads, beaches, fields or tracks. I have thermalled over the cooling towers of power stations, slept under the Thruster's wing in fields in Devon and Rutland, flown the Pennine Way and Offa's Dyke, crossed the Firth of Forth from East Fortune to Fife Glenrothes (sixteen interminable minutes over sea) and been trapped in the Cairngorms by bad weather for nine months. I still have not crossed the Channel.

I carry in my head all sorts of strange details of natural or celestially-linked events that I never used to.† I know the British sky a bit, and have encountered some of its appealing local quirks: the westerly winds, for instance, that are forced into rising currents over the escarpment of the Lincoln Cliff; the haar that steals romantically (but treacherously) up the Spey valley in the evening; The Helm, Britain's only named wind, to be found up the western Pennines. I know that blousy, showery days of boiling clouds often settle down, as the sun sinks, to still evenings with electrifying cloud formations for a perfect pre-drink flight.

Yet I remain, fundamentally, as far from being a natural pilot as it is possible to be. At an aviation museum recently, when I managed

---

* Most beautiful strips in Britain: Broadford, Isle of Skye; Plockton, Kyle of Lochalsh; and North Connel, Oban—all on the west coast of Scotland in savage landscapes of foaming surf and mountains; Long Mountain, Welshpool, Montgomeryshire; Sutton Bank, North Yorkshire; Pilling Sands, Lancashire; Halesland Glider Station, Somerset; Compton Abbas on the Wiltshire Downs; Perranporth, above the cliffs of the north Cornish coast.

† Best sunsets; November to February. Best low clouds; April and September. Best misty mornings; September to November. Best chance of frost with blue sky; January to February.

fractionally to outscore my girlfriend on the 'Aircrew Aptitude Tester', it sent me into paroxysms of competitive jubilation, until she said, a little perplexed, 'But you've got a pilot's licence. I've never done it before.' I still have to say 'Never Eat Shredded Wheat' to work out where the points of the compass are, and I still have to think to work out which way a windsock indicates that the wind is blowing (it would help immeasurably if an arrow were printed down the side). Before every flight as Pilot-in-Command, I still feel like Blériot in the 'before' photograph. And I still marvel at the presumption of airline pilots who, at 25,000 feet, begin sentences, 'After we have landed, please ...' As if they can be so sure.

Yet, equally, as every summer ends, and the thumbed, dog-eared, filled out pages of my log book, have eaten a little further into the pristine white pages beneath, I always think 'that's flying cracked, then'. The Thruster's been put away until next week. Then, as the skies grow unsettled and blustery, next week becomes next month. Then the next month the one after that. By which time the nights are closing in and I have started doing winter things at the weekend like going to movies or walking in Wales. And as I turn to other things, all that snappy top-of-mind flying knowledge gently evaporates away, and the old 'Thrasher' in her hangar is almost forgotten. Christmas and the New Year come and go. Winter settles in, dim and damp. There is talk of holidays.

Then, after interminable rain and gloom, suddenly the forsythia bursts into yellow flowers, the chewing gum skies turn blue and it is April in a fortnight. The weekend is so warm everyone switches off their radiators, throws open their windows and (struck, apparently, by a simultaneous imperative) hurries to their local garden centre. Dan rings to say how about flying up to the coast and landing on the beach for a walk on Sunday? There's a flurry of activity. Where are my jerry cans? Where are the oil bottles and the funnel? Everything's all over the place. My flying bag is full of gym stuff; my gloves are with my cycling gear; someone's nicked my cashmere scarf; I've left my thick flying sweater at someone's house. My flight board is as it was left after my last flight: stopwatch stopped at forty-eight minutes and twelve seconds. The laminated flight plan is still covered with faded scribbles. The map, still folded in the position it was left in, has set hard around its folds. The marker pens have all dried out, the elastic bands have perished and snap with a 'phut' when I pluck them. My flying suit smells musty.

At the petrol station outside Salsingham, I fill up the jerry cans and suddenly I can't remember how much oil I'm supposed to put in. I begin to feel a bit nervous. So I start quizzing myself. What do I do on a crosswind landing? If I am following a railway line, do I keep to the right of it? Or keep it on the right? If I am heading for another aircraft head on, do I turn right? Or left? And before I know it I'm thinking: I can't remember a bloody thing. By the time we are at the hangar, it's late afternoon, and my pulse is up because I'm flying the first leg and I have to have a pee before we get the plane out.

The wing fabric looks dusty and there's some powdery corrosion on the aluminium spars and the exhaust is covered in rust spots and there are cobwebs across the engine which tear as we manoeuvre her out onto the wet grass and then she takes a bit of starting, but finally she does and the blast from the prop feels icy, but she seems to be running okay and I tell Dan I'll just do a quick circuit by myself to get my eye back in; so I do a couple of fast runs down the strip to warm her through and then I am all lined up, and I give the stick a final stir to make sure everything really is 'full-and-free', and check the instruments one last time; and then I take a deep breath, open the throttle to full and she surges forward and up comes her tail and suddenly the ride gets smoother and we are off the ground and beginning to climb and I am holding my breath waiting for the engine to stop, but for some reason it doesn't, and the controls feel all right, in fact they move smoothly and easily and the air is like velvet and the clouds have broken up, leaving everywhere bathed in luminous yellow light, and the grass looks absurdly green and mossy and the blue of the sky is washed with pink and the shadows are long and the impression is generally as if God has inadvertently sat on the colour contrast button of the remote control and I fizz along the river two feet above the water where clouds of gnats are playing, then I bank up over the wood at tree canopy level frightening the rooks and I spot a couple of hot air balloonists also out for the first time and I buzz in and around them and then I see some clouds to play in at 1,400 feet and up she climbs, and the sky is empty and I watch my shadow chasing me along the ground over the fields and water as the mist is beginning to gather between the hedgerows and everything is just fucking perfect.

Blue skies and fair winds, as we aviators say.

© Hulton Getty

Glossary and Definitions.

Aviation, as well as retaining its monopoly on the best crashes and the most wasted time of any motorised activity, also leads the field in acronyms, jargon and technical terms; even the Biggles books carried a glossary. The basic controls of the Thruster are the same as for all fixed-wing, three-axis aircraft, from Spitfires to 747s. This list expands on some terms mentioned in the text, defines the basic features common to most aircraft, and explains some concepts of flying, rules of the air, and colloquialisms peculiar to microlighting. Its accuracy should be relied upon under no circumstances whatsoever.

Accident Report—Mandatory form completed following a crash if anyone has been killed, injured or the plane is significantly damaged.

Ailerons—Flaps on the trailing edge of the main wing (often confused with *flaps*) which move in tandem, but (unlike flaps) in opposite directions, thereby 'rolling' the aircraft left when the stick is moved left, right when it is moved right. From the French for 'small wing'.

Air charts—Large-scale 1:250,000 or small-scale 1:500,000 Ordnance Survey maps simplified for the aviator to highlight high ground, power lines, masts, obvious permanent landmarks like rivers, lakes, reservoirs and railways (but not roads, which are harder to identify from the air) and overprinted with details of airfields and controlled air space. Immediately disorientating because prominent place-names refer to locations of airfields, not town centres. Updated annually.

Air speed—Speed of the plane through the air (seldom, because of the effect of wind, the same as its speed over the ground).

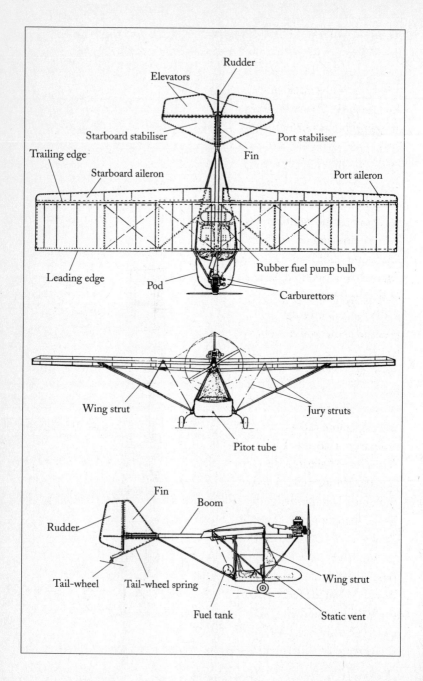

Air speed indicator (ASI)—Measures the speed of the plane through the air. Works by comparing the dynamic pressure of moving air entering through an intake called a *Pitot tube*, with the pressure of static air (measured in the *static vent)*.

Airmanship—'Airmanship is awaremanship'. Good airmanship consists of doing things like bellowing 'Clear Prop' to the deserted hedgerows before starting the engine, anticipating others' idiocies rather than blaming them after the crash, not running out of fuel when flying, not flying when drunk, etc.

Alcohol—Eight hours 'bottle to throttle' is the airman's rule, though if you really cane it the night before, and then go up high where the air pressure is lower, drunkenness (or its symptoms) may well reappear.

Altimeter—Altitude or height meter. Consists of a calibrated gauge attached to an aneroid barometer. As atmospheric pressure is constantly changing, the altimeter must always be 'zeroed' before take-off. On arrival at the destination airfield, the tower (if you have a radio) tells you the local pressure so that you can adjust the meter to give an accurate reading before landing.

Attitude—Not to do with the pilot's state of mind, but with the relative angle of the plane—specifically the wing—to the air-flow.

Avgas—Flying slang for aviation fuel or spirit, sold for general aviation at airfields: more refined, more expensive and slightly higher octane than ordinary unleaded or LRP from the pumps ('mogas').

Avionics—Aviation electronics: radios, GPSs, transponders and, in general, gizmos well beyond our scope.

Balloon—Undignified, ungainly bounce on landing. In fact, more of a bound than a bounce. Often, like buses, come in threes.

Bank—*Roll.* Efficient turning in the air depends on combining banking (controlled by *ailerons*) with *yaw* (controlled by the *rudder*).

Base leg—Third section (or side) of the *circuit*, after the third turn.

Bowser—Mobile fuel tanker at airfields. As in: 'What are the three most useless things in flying? The runway behind you, the height above you, and the fuel in the bowser.'

Certificate of Airworthiness or **C of A**—Mandatory, rigorous and extortionately expensive annual aeroplane MOT, for which a plane has to be stripped to the bone: the main reason, along with the price of instruction, why conventional private flying is so expensive. Microlights operate on a simpler, less demanding *Permit to Fly*.

Circuit—Around every airfield (or landing strip) there is an imaginary rectangular cube of air in which set procedures are followed by every arriving or departing aircraft, and around which every student pilot goes interminably during training. Circuits are described as 'left-hand' or 'right-hand' according to the direction you turn after take-off, and the four legs are known as 'crosswind', 'downwind', 'base', and 'final'. 'Circuit height' tends to be around 800 feet, though every airfield has its own specific rules and quirks (contained in the *flight guide*).

Circuits and bumps—Touching down and immediately taking off again for another circuit. This cuts out the time-consuming backtracking, taxiing, pre-take-off checking and general time-wasting otherwise involved in returning to the top of the runway. Designed to maximise take-off and landing practice for students.

Civil Aviation Authority or **CAA**—Epaulette Central, the supreme arbiter of safety and generator of unintelligible memoranda and acronyms in UK flying. Sometimes referred to as the 'Campaign Against Aviation'.

Clear prop—Warning bellowed by the pilot immediately before starting the engine of a propeller-driven aircraft.

Clouds—See *Visual Flight Rules*.

C or **Control**—Every licensed airfield has a 'control tower', whether it is an old caravan or a collapsed Portakabin. It is marked with a big black 'C' on a yellow background. In front of this is the *ground signals area*.

Control column—Otherwise known as *joy-stick* or *stick:* the modern *three-axis* control column working *ailerons* (side to side) and *elevators* (back and forth) was invented by Robert Esnault-Pelterie, and in place by the time Blériot crossed the Channel.

Controlled air space—Areas where specific rules apply and where set procedures have to be followed. With Control Zones, Control Areas, Airways, Corridors, Terminal Control Areas, Special Rules Zones, Special Rules Areas, Aerodrome Traffic Zones, Military Aerodrome Traffic

Zones, Restricted Areas, Mandatory Radio Reporting Areas, you can be sure, that if you are near an airfield, you are never far from doing something wrong. Experience teaches you that, for example, you do not need permission to enter or cross a Military Air Traffic Zone—useful information to have up your sleeve if you are being unnecessarily harried by a bored RAF air traffic controller.

Crossing the controls—Application of opposite stick and rudder (right stick with left rudder, say, or vice-versa; as opposed to the usual application of the two controls in harmony). Has the effect of making the plane *side-slip*—a useful method of losing height rapidly or (at a gentler level), countering a crosswind on landing.

Crosswind leg—First *leg* of the circuit, after take-off. See *Circuit*.

Cunim—*Cumulonimbus*, the big thundercloud with the anvil head. Beware.

Deadstick landing—'Engine off' landing; otherwise known as a 'glide approach' or 'without power' landing.

Direction Indicator (DI)—Fancy gyro-mounted compass that shows you your heading but, unlike the compass on a microlight, moves smoothly and slowly, without wobbling and jumping and bouncing. Found on planes, but not, alas, microlights.

Dope—Traditional aeroplane varnish, painted onto the linen fabric which is stretched over the wings and fuselage. As it dries, it shrinks the fabric to stretch it as tight as a drum. No hint of such timeless craftmanship on a Thruster.

Downdraught—See *Sink*.

Downwind—When the wind is coming from behind you (the opposite of *into wind)*. Although, once airborne, a *tailwind* speeds your progress, landing downwind is (unless there is no alternative) a mistake—hair-raising, too fast and you are likely to run out of runway before stopping.

Downwind leg—Second leg of the circuit, flown parallel to—but in the reciprocal direction of—the take-off runway. See *Circuit*.

Drift—Unless there is no wind at all, a plane is always subject to wind drift. Accordingly, to fly from A to B, it is necessary to 'aim off'. You work out how much to aim off by entering the wind's estimated strength and direction on the *flight calculator*, turning the dial to your heading and getting a reading which sounds precise and factual but is frequently no more accurate than reading your tea leaves.

Dual-ignition—Also known as 'twin-spark'. The general practice since the Second World War of equipping aero engines with a double electrical system, right down to two sparking plugs on top of each cylinder; the idea being that if one system fails there is always a back-up. The Thruster—needless to say—was single ignition.

Elevators—The large, twin, hinged, horizontal flaps on the tail-plane which move (together) either down or up, by moving the stick forward or back, to alter the plane's attitude and make it descend or ascend.

Engine Icing—See *Icing*.

Fin—Fixed, vertical part of the tail-plane, to which the *rudder* is attached. Has the same role in the air as the keel of a boat in water.

Final or **Final leg**—See *Circuit*. Always referred to as 'finals' for some reason.

Fixed-wing microlight—Like the Thruster. The alternative type of microlight to a *flexwing*. It has a conventional wing, fixed immovably to the fuselage of the aircraft, with control in three-axes—vertical, horizontal and lateral—as opposed to having a wing like a hang-glider.

Flaps—Hinged surfaces on the *trailing edge* of the wings, applied in unison to allow planes to fly more slowly during take-off and landing (all that grinding and whirring from the wings of your passenger jet shortly before you come into land). Sometimes confused with *ailerons*, because they look similar and appear on much the same part of the aircraft. No flaps necessary on the Thruster because it already takes-off and lands so slowly.

Flaring or **Flaring Out**—As you come into land, the act of 'rounding out' from a descending 'nose down' attitude to fly level along the runway in preparation for landing. No connection with Tom Cruise or afterburners.

Flexwing—Most people's idea of a microlight: a hang-glider with a tricycle pod suspended (but not rigidly attached) beneath. Where *fixed-wing microlights* have the standard three-axis (*yaw*, *pitch* and *roll*) control system, operated by a *stick* and *rudder*, flexwings are manoeuvred in the air by shifting the weight of the tricycle pod relative to the wing via a control bar. Accordingly, all fixed-wing pilots are agreed: flexwings are grossly inferior. Also known as *weight-shifts* or *trikes*.

Flight calculator—Gadget resembling a circular slide rule which, with ruler and protractor, is still supposed to be a primary instrument of navigation. If you know how to use it, lets you read off all kinds of useful information. *Global positioning systems* (GPSs) have made the flight calculator seem as obsolete as—well, the slide rule.

Flight log—Blank printed form, filled out in preparation for a cross country journey, with details, for each leg, of distance, heading (corrected for magnetic variation, deviation and wind drift), fuel consumption, obvious landmarks or hazards or high ground, controlled air space; timed way-points, etc. Sounds time-consuming? 'If you've time to spare, go by air'.

Flight plan—Details of a planned flight officially lodged with air traffic control before departure. Advisable if crossing mountains, sparsely populated terrain or water (where you might require Air-Sea rescue) under two-stroke power. Mandatory if crossing international borders.

General aviation—Non-commercial or non-military aviation. In short, private flying: Cessnas and choppers.

Global Positioning System (GPS)—Fancy satellite navigation gizmo that allows pilots to throw away traditional navigation aids like compass, ruler, protractor, chinagraph, flight calculator—and even maps. Updating every second, preposterously accurate, a GPS tells you not just where you are, but how far you are from your destination in seconds, how fast you are moving, how to correct your course, warns of controlled airspace . . . in fact does everything but make the tea. Sneered at by the purists, drooled over by the gizmophiles, banned by most flying competitions, GPSs are the navigator's panacea. Until the batteries go flat or they cut out en route, in which case you're stuffed.

Go around—Pilot's lore says that it is better to open the throttle and 'go around' for another try than to persist with a landing that is going awry.

Greaser—Landing so smooth that it is impossible to tell when the wheels touch the ground. Seldom occurs with spectators present. Seldom occurs, full stop.

Ground signals—See *Signals Area*.

Ground speed—See *Air Speed*.

Hangar rash—Small grazes or abrasions to the sailcloth of the wings and tail-plane caused by the parts of one aeroplane rubbing up against another in a crowded hangar.

Headwind—When the wind is blowing against your course. If the wind is from anywhere apart from behind you or a direct side-wind, then there will be a headwind component which will slow you down. See also *Tailwind*.

Height—A technical definition in flying. Refers to distance in feet above the ground beneath you, as opposed to 'altitude' which refers to the distance in feet above mean sea level.

Hill lift—See *Soaring*.

Hobb's meter—Records hours the engine is running.

Holding off—The action, as you come in to land, of holding the plane off the ground as long as possible while, simultaneously, reducing the power so that she cannot fly. Birds, landing on bird-tables, 'hold off' beautifully.

Icing—Two kinds. Engine icing occurs in damp or humid weather when moisture in the air, cooled by being rapidly sucked into the carburettors, condenses and freezes, blocking the carburettor and strangling the engine (and giving the pilot palpitations). More sophisticated machines than microlights have a device called a 'carb heat' for blowing hot air into the carburettors to prevent this occurring. Airframe icing, when ice builds up on the wings and airframe of the aircraft, seldom affects Thrusters.

Into wind—All aircraft, even 747s, take-off and land as nearly as possible into wind, (ie. into the direction from which the wind is blowing). A ten-knot wind, obviously, gives an immediate ten-knot speed advantage on take-off, and allows you, on landing, a slower *ground speed* and shorter stopping distance.

Joystick—The word seems to have been coined around 1910. 'Control column' was being complained about as 'the new official term' in 1927.

Knot—One nautical mile per hour: unit of measurement of speed adopted by the flying fraternity. For reason, See *Nautical mile*.

Landing fees—Fee payable for visiting an airfield: anything between nothing and a free cup of tea (or a voluntary contribution in an honesty box) to a hefty, receipted £25 or more at airfields with pretensions (and over £1,000 for a 747). Major regional or international British airports tend not to allow microlights near them. As fees are charged per landing, bouncy arrivals prompt waggish remarks about the sum payable.

Leading edge—Front, blunt edge of the wing.

Left-hand seat—Driving seat on aircraft with side-by-side seating. The rules of the air decree that when overtaking another plane you do so on the right. Therefore, for maximum safety and visibility, the pilot sits on the left.

Leg—Section of a journey. Even by microlight, you cannot travel directly as the crow flies. To avoid controlled airspace, built-up areas, live firing ranges, nature reserves, or to minimise time over unlandable country, longer journeys tend to be divided into a number of straight 'legs' for easy flight planning.

Levelling off—After climbing or descending, the action of returning to straight and level flight at normal cruise speed and power setting.

Lift—Magical force that makes a wing fly and gets hundreds of tons of Jumbo Jet off the deck, or 'the component of the aerodynamic force on an aircraft acting upwards at right angles to the relative air-flow', according to how you see these things. See also *Thermals*.

Microlight—'A one or two seat aeroplane whose maximum total weight authorised at take-off shall not exceed 390 kg... , nor shall the fuel capacity exceed 50 litres.' This, at least, was the definition during the timespan of the events described in this book, but in 2000, in line with EU regulations, the maximum weight limit was increased to 450 kg, attracting many sleek, sophisticated new designs to the market.

Mods—Modifications.

Mogas—See *Avgas*.

Nautical mile—One nautical mile equals one minute of longitude measured along the equator (or of latitude anywhere) and is, therefore, as for seafarers, the appropriate unit for terrestrial navigation—with the added advantage of being meaningless to riff-raff landlubbers. 1.15 statute miles.

Night flying—Not allowed in microlights.

Overshoot—Where, on landing, it looks as if you may run out of runway, the only option is to open the throttle and *go around* for another try.

Ozee suit—Amazingly uncool (stylistically and, if worn on the ground, literally) lightweight, windproof, thermally-insulated, one-piece, zip-up flying overall. Indispensable, though, for high or winter flying.

Panhandle—The 'cylinder' of airspace around military airbases has two extra stubs sticking out at either end of the main runway: the 'panhandles'.

Peri-track—Perimeter track. Most ex-wartime airfields have a concrete or tarmac taxi-way round the edge to link the runways.

Permit or **Permit to Fly.** Annual certificate of mechanical soundness for certain kinds of flying machine (especially microlights, homebuilt and vintage aircraft). Issued by approved inspectors for the CAA; the aerial equivalent of an MOT and the microlighting equivalent of the *Certificate of Airworthiness.*

Phonetic alphabet—Alpha, Bravo, Charlie, Delta, etc; used to aid clear and unmistakable recognition of letters in radio transmissions. (The international language of radio and flying is English.)

Pilot-in-Command—Captain. Every flight with 'two-up' has to have a designated person in charge, who can be blamed when things go pear-shaped. Normally (unless instructing) he or she will occupy (if side-by-side seating) the left-hand seat, or (if tandem seating) the rear seat. This may sound obvious, but on long flights, where flying activities are often shared, it can get confusing.

Pitch—Movement up and down in the air: along with *yaw* and *roll*, one of the crucial planes of movement in the air, made possible by the *elevators*, or pushing the stick forward or back. On propellers, specifically, pitch refers to the angle of bite of the blades (many propeller aircraft can vary the pitch of their propeller blades, but this level of sophistication is yet to become generally available to microlights).

Pitot tube—Intake for the *air speed indicator.*

Poles'n'pedals—Stick'n'rudder. (As opposed to the control bar arrangement on flexwing microlights or the 'yokes' favoured by most modern private aircraft manufacturers.)

Pooleys (sic) **Flight Guide**—The best known of the various flight guides, and for forty years the private pilot's bible; updated annually, this aviator's almanack gives details of all Britain's principal airfields and their runways, from 4 kilometers at Heathrow to unmarked grass strips, plus masses and masses of technical information.

Prevailing wind—Default wind, which (with local variations) in Britain blows from the south-west. Most airfields, accordingly, have one runway orientated in a NE/SW direction.

Private Pilot's Licence (PPL)—Microlights are flown on a 'Group D' private pilot's licence; essentially similar to a 'Group A' licence (normal planes) though requires only 25 rather than 40 hours minimum flying time.

Prop wash—Churned up air left behind by a spinning propeller. If you execute a perfect 360° medium turn you can feel the buffet as you come back into your own prop wash.

Purple airspace—Airspace temporarily reserved for royal flights, for which warnings are issued to flying clubs.

Quadrantal and semi-circular rules—Collision-avoidance navigation rules, to keep planes flying on opposing compass headings at different heights. Of little relevance to low and slow pilots like us, as they apply only above 3,000 feet.

Recency requirements—Holders of Private Pilot's Licences for microlights have to complete a minimum of five hours flying per year to keep their licences. Fortunately the system is operated on trust (you fill the hours into your log book: your instructor checks and stamps it) so need not prove unduly inconvenient.

Reduction gear—Gear between propeller and engine to stop the propeller spinning as fast as the engine (because two-stroke engines rev so highly, without this the propeller tips might exceed the speed of sound, making a hideous noise and providing further grounds for people to hate microlighters). Apparently, as much thrust can be obtained from larger propellers, turning more slowly.

Roll—With *pitch* and *yaw*, one of the three key flight planes of movement in the air. Banking in turns—movement in the rolling plane—is made possible by *ailerons*. Right stick; roll right. Left stick; roll left.

Rotor effect—Churning effect that ground obstacles like trees and buildings or rough ground can have on air blowing over them near the surface, producing random and treacherous turbulence just when you least need it: on take-off or landing.

Rounding out—See *Flaring*.

Rudder—As on boats, for steering, except that in flying, the rudder must be combined with *bank* or the aircraft will 'skid' round in an absurdly wide and inefficient arc. Although the early pioneers soon agreed that the most natural way for elevators and ailerons to be operated was by a stick moving back and forth, and from side to side, there was disagreement about which way the foot-operated rudder pedals should work. Should depressing the left-foot turn you right (as on a kid's cart or bicycle handlebars) or left? In the end the (arguably) less natural second option was settled on, to be adapted by all three-axis aircraft from the Thruster to the 747. Flexwings do the opposite.

Side-slip—Way of losing height rapidly, without increasing speed, by *crossing the controls*.

Signals area—Area in front of '*C*' or *Control*, where ground signals indicating information like which runway is in use are displayed, so as to be visible from the air.

Slip indicator—Ball suspended in liquid in a curved glass tube, like an upside-down spirit level. If *rudder* and *ailerons* are correctly combined in a turn, and there is no 'slipping' or 'skidding', the ball remains central. If not, it shoots off to the right or left.

Sink—Rock and woodland and dark areas of the landscape (like ploughed fields) absorb heat from the sun and release it into the air above them, offering bumps of 'lift'. Similarly, the air over water or lighter-coloured land is often cooler and provides 'sink'.

Soaring—Along the edge of hills, air is often forced up into rising currents and these may be used, as gliders and buzzards do, for soaring.

Spin—With the stall, the most potentially lethal manoeuvre in flying, whereby an aircraft is stalled and can be in any number of unusual attitudes requiring positive recovery techniques. (Just so you know: opposite rudder—to the direction of the spin—and stick forward.)

Stabilisers—See *Tailplane.*

Stall—Refers not to the engine (though that might stall); but to the air-flow over the wing. If the air-flow becomes insufficient because, say, you are going too slowly, then the wing ceases to act as a wing. Accidental stalling is the supreme, unpardonable sin of flying—and if done at low level, usually the last thing you do.

Static vent—Measures static air pressure for the *altimeter*. This is then compared to the dynamic (moving) air pressure in the *Pitot tube* to give a reading for the air speed.

Stick—See *Control Column.*

Tail-dragger—An aeroplane whose fuselage tilts back to rest on a little tail-wheel or tail-skid, like the Tiger Moth, Lancaster bomber, Spitfire or, indeed, Thruster. A currency of aviation snobbery—perpetuated by tail-dragger flyers—maintains that of propeller-driven aircraft, only tail draggers are the Real Thing. ('Real pilots fly tail-draggers: real tail-draggers fly the pilots.) Tail-draggers tend to look prettier and be dogs to land.

Tail-plane—*Fin*, *rudder* and *stabilisers*: as it sounds, the bit (on a typical single-engined plane) at the opposite end of the fuselage to the propeller.

Tailwind—Opposite of *headwind* when the wind is from behind you.

Thermal—Column of warm, rising air, frequently culminating in a *cumulus* cloud.

Three-axis controls—Standard control system for conventionally laid-out fixed-wing aircraft, about three-axes (vertical, horizontal and lateral) by means of *elevators*, *rudder* and *ailerons*. See *Control column*, *Fixed-wing microlight*.

Three-pointer—Text-book landing for a tail-dragger aircraft, where the plane stalls at the exact moment that all three wheels touch the ground. Takes considerable skill. See *Greaser* and *Wheeler.*

Throttle—Accelerator; well sort of. Chiefly used at two settings: full power for climbing; and around two-thirds power for cruising. Operated, in the Thruster, by a lever to the left of the pilot (who keeps his left hand on the throttle, and his right on the stick throughout the flight).

Trailing edge—Rear (sharp) edge of the wing, to which the *ailerons* are attached.

Transceiver—Two-way radio transmitter/receiver.

Trike—See *Flexwing*.

Turbulence—Results from churned-up air, which may be for several reasons: wake turbulence; mixing warm and cold air; a sudden change in wind speed or direction; or (at low level) rotor effect where wind has passed over rough ground. Not, as the early pioneers believed, due to 'holes in the air'.

Twin-spark—See *Dual ignition*.

Two-stroke **engine**—The kind on the Thruster, where the four actions of internal combustion—sucking in the fuel and air, compressing the mixture, firing, and expelling the exhaust gases, are combined into two strokes of the piston. Two-stroke engines rev highly and produce a lot of power for their weight. Every seriously reliable, smooth, silent, sexy piston engine ever built has been a four-stroke.

Two-stroke **mixture**—On a two-stroke engine, rather than adding lubricating oil to a separate sump, you mix it into the fuel. In the Thruster's case the ratio is 50:1 of *mogas* or *avgas* to two-stroke motorcycle oil.

Ultralight—Everywhere in the world except the UK, 'microlights' are called 'ultralights'. The term could not be used here because the Popular Flying Association already had an 'ultralight' category for their homebuilt aircraft. 'Microlight' was settled on, permitting the fledgling BMAA—then the British *Minimum* Aircraft Association, and already attracting comments along the lines of 'minimum standards', 'minimum competence', 'minimum life expectancy'—to switch its name to the less readily adaptable British *Microlight* Aircraft Association.

Visibility—See *Clouds, Visual Flight Rules*.

Visual Flight Rules (VFR)—Because microlights are not equipped with fancy gyro-mounted 'blind flying' instruments, we are only supposed to fly where we can see: clear of cloud, in sight of the ground, with visibility of at least three kilometers below 3,000 feet (five kilometers in controlled airspace). *VFR* is the first acronym you learn in flying. Also the reason we cannot fly at night.

Wake turbulence—Churned up air caused by spiral vortices from the trailing edge tips of the wings of aircraft. Off large airliners, wake turbulence is a hazard anything up to five minutes or more after they have passed.

Way-points—Easily identifiable features on the map (railway lines, lakes, rivers, castles, masts) marked at intervals before setting out on a cross-country flight to provide quick and easy confirmation of your course.

Weightshift—See *Flexwing*.

Wheeler or **Wheelie**—'Two point' or 'wheel' landing where the front two wheels touch down, and the tail-skid (or wheel) drops down later. A reference normally used sneeringly. See *Three-pointer*.

Wind—Air moving from a high pressure area to a lower pressure area; friend or enemy according to direction. Given on forecasts as the compass direction *from* which the wind blows (a westerly blows from the west), plus speed in knots, eg. 110°/15. See *Headwind* and *Tailwind*.

Yaw—Steering. Horizontal directional movement in flight, effected by means of the *rudder*. *Pitch, roll* and *yaw* are the three planes of flight movement. Dramatically more effective when combined with *bank*.

Thruster TST (1989)—Vital Statistics

AIRFRAME:

Wing Span: 9.6 metres (31'6")
Length: 5.5 metres (18')
Height: 2.0 metres (6'6")
Empty weight: 150 kgs (331 lbs)
Max take-off weight: 358 kgs (788 lbs)

ENGINE:

Rotax 503, two-cylinder, two-stroke, twin-carburettor, single-ignition, pull-start.
Capacity: 500cc
Maximum power: 58 hp at 6,300 rpm
Cooling: Air-cooled by propeller slipstream

INSTRUMENTS:

Tachometer (rev counter), engine cylinder head temperature, altimeter, slip indicator, compass, air speed indicator, Hobbs meter.

PERFORMANCE:

Cruise speed   (90 % power): 55 knots (63 mph)
                 (70 % power): 45 knots (52 mph)
Stall speed at max take-off weight: 35 knots (40 mph)
Never exceed speed (VNE): 80 knots (92 mph)
Take-off run to clear 15 metres (50'): 110 metres (120 yards)
Rate of climb: 150 metres (500 feet) per minute
Rate of descent: 230 metres (750 feet) per minute
Minimum landing roll distance: 100 metres (109 yards)
Fuel capacity: 40 litres (9 gallons)
Fuel consumption (solo): 15 litres (three-quarters of a jerry can) per hour
Fuel consumption (two passengers of 12-15 stone): 22+ litres per hour
Safe endurance at max weight: 1.5 hours
Crosswind capability: 15 knots

Thanks

To Roddy and Robbie (and Dave and Will), of course. To Ron and Phyl B, and especially Ness, for twenty years of friendship, generosity and innumerable kindnesses, and without whom none of this would have happened. To my agent Stephanie Cabot, and Eugenie Furniss. To Arabella Pike and Mike Fishwick for buying the proposal—to Arabella, especially, for her friendship, support, patience, guidance, skill and indefatigable energy in working to rescue me—and therefore you—from some gruesome passages. To Katie Collins and Merryn Somerset Webb for loyally reading and re-reading numerous drafts. To Mac Smith, a founding father of British microlighting, and Patrick Caruth, 767 captain, for casting their experienced eyes over the text without so much as a raised eyebrow or sarcastic remark. To Mike Town for what little meteorology I know. To Ged Edmondson for translation work. To Gerry Moira, whose patient and generous patronage nearly didn't run out. To the irrepressible Molly Godet, for being such an entertaining and glamorous office companion. To John Daniel, for explaining all kinds of things I didn't know I hadn't understood. To Jan and Edie for looking after me through the thick and thin of their own traumas. To Angus Grahame, for his flying references and, as a fellow flyer, heart-warming ignorance. To Gerry Fox, Charles Dupplin, Kasia Robinski, John Micklethwait, Owen Inskip and other loyal and supportive friends *in absentia* who I have let down, messed about or otherwise generally maddened. To Toby Young for his attempts to get me to Hollywood. To George and Libby Birkbeck, who know exactly why. To Chris Ellis, for help and information. To Mark and Bin Johnston, the Crawley family (especially Anne and Bex), Pev and Hils, Ben and Silvy, Eck and Lucy and the many other generous people and pilots who have, over the years, cancelled engagements at short notice in order to drive us to petrol stations, feed us, accommodate us, calm us, help us, bale us out of crises and mop up after our disasters.

And to Vez the Viking for everything else.